FLOOD TIDE IN CHINA

FLOOD TIDE IN CHINA

BY

C. P. FITZGERALD

Professor in Far Eastern History in
the Australian National University
Canberra

LONDON
THE CRESSET PRESS
MCMLVIII

Copyright © by C. P. Fitzgerald, 1958
First Published 1958
by the Cresset Press, 11 Fitzroy Square
London W1

Printed in Great Britain by the Shenval Press Ltd
London, Hertford and Harlow

PREFACE

'WE INVITE your criticism', every organization in China today unfailingly makes this claim, and expects that it will be met. This book is therefore a response to such an invitation. In 1956 the author was asked to organize a party of Australian writers, artists, academic and professional men and women to form a cultural delegation which was invited by the Chinese People's Association for Cultural Relations with Foreign Countries to make a short tour in China. To our hosts on that occasion I tender our thanks for providing an opportunity to revisit China and assess the great changes which six years of the People's Republic have brought about. Criticism, to be of value, must be both sincere and objective; while the impressions formed by ardent supporters or implacable opponents have their value, a more detached standpoint is appropriate for a historian. This book is consequently an attempt to make an objective appraisal of the achievements of the present regime in China, of the response which the Chinese people are themselves making to that regime, and of the future trend of thought and action.

Revolution is a long and continuing process; like the effect of a stone cast into a still pond of water, it is easier to mark the moment of the initial disturbance than to determine when at last the final ripples have died away. No one can yet say that the Chinese Revolution has reached its final phase; the Communist Party itself looks forward to that perhaps distant day when the Party will 'wither away' and the Classless Society come into being. In the meantime it is possible to record the development of the process in intermediate stages, and if predictions prove as mistaken as they generally do, they at least provide for future historians evidence of what was thought to be likely at the time they were written, and so become part of the source material of history. In so far as this book incorporates the results of first hand observation by one to whom the

vii

former China was also familiar it may provide some facts upon the present situation which will be useful to contemporaries.

My thanks are due to the Department of Geography in the School of Pacific Studies, Australian National University, for the preparation of the endpaper map, and to Mrs N. Moy, for the preparation of the manuscript.

C. P. FITZGERALD

Australian National University
Canberra, 1958

CONTENTS

ix

CONTENTS

CHAPTER ONE

PEKING

'THERE ARE ONLY two cities in the world: Paris and Peking.'
The speaker was an old French resident of Peking, and it was
natural that he should give pride of place to Paris; what was
significant was his perception, ten years ago, of the affinity
between the two historic capitals of France and China, seemingly denied by the then declined and fallen status of Peking.
Until the Communists captured the city, in the last months of
1948, Peking had for more than twenty years lost its position as
capital of China, had even lost its ancient name, and was officially known as Peiping. It was fast acquiring the derelict
appearance of an abandoned capital, even though it remained
the most important educational centre in China. Yet in a
symbolical sense it continued to be the only city in China, the
focus of the efforts and aspirations of the Chinese people during
the last six centuries of their long history, the most harmonious
and complete realization, the distilled essence, of the Chinese
civilization.

In this lay its affinity with Paris; for these are perhaps the
only two existing cities in which nations have chosen to concentrate their national life to an intense degree, often, it may be,
to the detriment of the rest of the country. Peking, like Paris,
was the political capital, the greatest centre of population, the
main centre of education, the studio of the arts, the seat of
luxury and refinement. Like Paris, it was a beautiful city,
consciously planned to fulfil the role of an imperial capital;
no haphazard growth, but built to a grand design to serve as a
stage and setting for the glory and magnificence of the
Emperors. These qualities outlived the Empire which created
them and have survived to attract to Peking the regime which
has revived, in a new and strange form, the power, though not
the luxury, of the fallen Empire. Peking is once more the capital

I

of China; a new China, and a new Peking, doubled in size, twice as populous, her ancient parks and wide imperial streets throbbing with the earnest, vibrant activity of the People' Republic.

For Peking—this was its charm—appealed equally to all men: to the Western traveller, businessman or scholar, to the Chinese royalist and to his revolutionary successor. These differing characters will see the charm of Peking in diverse forms, but essentially the cause is the same; all are in the presence of a most powerful manifestation of an ancient and culturally harmonious civilization which acts upon them as an inspiration and a release. The European resident is taken out of his own world, but not truly incorporated in this strange and fascinating alternative. He cannot become a Chinese; he can never, however long he lives in China, however well he speaks the language, lose his Western identity and acquire a Chinese character. For the Chinese are not only, or indeed mainly, a people and a nation, but members of a civilization which arose independently of that of Western Asia and Europe, long continued in virtual isolation, and developed traits, which although often truly admirable, are fundamentally unlike the characteristics of our own.

The Western foreigner in Peking is thus suspended between two worlds; pulled away from the conventions and practices of his own culture, but unable to merge into the equally powerful, and more rigid, conventions of the Chinese world. He floats, pleasantly disembodied in a cultural sense, above the surface of Chinese life, admiring, studying, sometimes understanding, but never entering into that forceful current. Thus Peking appeals to the frivolous and the sedate alike, the pleasure seeker who relaxes in a society which cares nothing for his oddities and barely observes his existence, and the serious scholar who meditates upon the fortunes of dynasties and the phases of art. For some it was *Peking Picnic*, for others *Twilight in the Forbidden City**: for all it held a nostalgia which no other place could evoke.

* Ann Bridge, *Peking Picnic*. Penguin Books Ltd. 1938.
Sir Reginald Johnston, *Twilight in the Forbidden City*. Gollancz. London. 1934.

The Chinese saw Peking in a different light. They were in the strong swirl of their national life, and Peking was the centre and vortex of that movement. The official seeking influence and office, the student from the far provinces who came to the great city of learning, the ambitious politician, the artist, the clever craftsman, the skilled professional man, all came to Peking because those who hoped to escape from the provincial rut must start their careers in the capital, at the point where wealth accumulated and power radiated over all China. Peking was no dream city of palaces and carefree freedom for the Chinese resident. Few ever saw the inside of a palace, very few were free from care, thousands lived in poverty and hardship, but all were conscious of the pride and power of the city; acquired, or hoped to acquire, that disdainful assurance, that polished but ineffable superiority which marked the 'Lao Ching Yu'—'The Old Fish of the Capital'—and so impressed the provincials if one should chance to stray among them.

But Peking, of course, 'is not China'. It was not typical of the country as a whole, but far more magnificent, more cultured, more sophisticated; less practical, less hard-headed, wasteful, decadent. Such criticisms were often made, and hold much truth, yet are irrelevant. The course of Chinese history for some two thousand years had been set, fluctuatingly at first, then more and more steadily towards centralization, unity and concentration of power in the capital. Peking is the last of a long series in which this form of polity grew and matured. In the T'ang period Ch'angan acquired much of the same quality, but had yet a rival in the twin capital of Loyang. It was the foundation of Peking as capital, and its continuance in this status under three successive imperial dynasties for more than six centuries, that has given the city the unique place which it occupies in the life of China. No other city ever retained the prize for so long in unbroken continuity.

It has often seemed strange to foreign observers that a place situated on what was almost the frontier of China, remote from the main centres of population and commerce, should have been chosen as capital and maintained in that character by dynasties so different as the alien Mongols, the native, southern, Ming, and the foreign Manchus. Peking is only forty miles from the Great Wall of China, the traditional frontier between the pastoral Mongols and the agricultural Chinese. It stands, some ten miles from the mountain chain, in a flat plain which offers no natural defence to the city. South-eastward the land is low and often flooded by the complex river system which flows into the gulf of Chihli, barely eighty miles from Peking. The city is several hundred miles north of the Yangtze, hemmed in on the west by rugged mountains, and lies at the north-western tip of the North China plain, an area which though fertile if irrigated, is very subject to devastating droughts.

Yet these unfavourable aspects of the site conceal strategic values of the highest importance to any government ruling in China. It is true that Peking is only forty miles from the Great Wall, but that wall runs along the mountain chain which divides China from the Mongolian steppe, the home of the enemy for so many centuries, and Peking at the foot of the range controls the exits of the two main passes by which any invader must enter China. Lying, anciently, on the higher and drier rim of the flood plain, Peking also, by its situation at the foot of the mountains, controlled the route by which invaders from Manchuria must pass if they were to make more than a mere local frontier raid into China. Thus any ruler who had as his main duty the defence of the great plains against the horse-men of the steppes must concentrate his forces at this nodal point, whence, holding the passes, he could strike out in three directions against the potential invaders. For centuries before Peking became the capital of China it was a local royal capital, and later the seat of the main military command in the north of China.

Modern development has served to underline these ancient facts and give them new significance. The main railway system of North China centres on Peking, following the ancient strategic routes. Now that Manchuria and Inner Mongolia are no longer the lands of the national enemy, but the rising in-dustrial regions of the New China, the importance of Peking, which controls their communications with the rest of the country, is immeasurably enhanced. Very real practical considerations of political control and economic development as well as the prestige and aura of the ancient capital determined the choice of Peking as the capital of the People's Republic, after twenty years of Nationalist neglect.

For the Nationalist Party, like the early republicans, feared Peking. It was too imperial, too dominated by the past, too northern—and the North had never been enthusiastic for the republic or its Nationalist successors. So the early republicans wished to make Nanking the capital and the Nationalist Party actually did so. Nanking seemed to have all the advantages which Peking in the modern age lacked. It was on the Yangtze, with excellent communications north and south. It was within two hundred miles of Shanghai, the great industrial city and chief port of China. It was in the heart of the most fertile agricultural region, free from drought, and rarely devastated by flood. It was of course hundreds of miles from the northern frontier, but the Great Wall was no longer a frontier, and Peking's strategic qualities in that respect seemed out-dated.

But Nanking has been an unlucky city, especially as capital of China. Its first age of glory was the period of 273 years when China was divided between Tartar conquerors ruling the north and Chinese dynasties which had taken refuge south of the Yangtze. From AD 316 to AD 589 Nanking was the capital of the Chinese half of China, but never of the whole country. When unity was restored by Chinese dynasties the capital was removed to the north. It was not until the expulsion of the Mongols in AD 1368 that the first Ming made Nanking, for the first time, capital of all China. His son and successor, after a civil war, moved the capital to Peking which he built in 1403 in the form that it now stands. Ming Hung Wu reigned in Nanking for only thirty-five years.

More than 500 years later the Nationalist Party brought the capital back to Nanking, in 1928. Nine years later they were driven from it by the Japanese invader and, after a brief restoration of three years from 1946 to 1948, Nanking once more ceased to be the capital when the People's Republic was established in Peking.

The Nationalists in their dislike and fear of imperial Peking had failed to see that its ancient strategic importance had been renewed and transformed by the industrial development of Manchuria, while the Japanese domination of that region actually underlined the old strategic reasons for making Peking the capital. They also failed to see that the apparent advantages of Nanking were very unreal to a weak power such as China was in the first decades of the twentieth century. Without a navy to protect it, Nanking's situation on a huge navigable river was extremely exposed to alien attack. The proximity of Shanghai, a great commercial city then mainly under foreign rule and military occupation, was anything but beneficial either to the security or the morality of the government and its servants. The remoteness of Nanking from the frontier meant that a weak government, threatened by internal enemies, kept its major military forces at this centre, far from the frontiers, and thus unable to defend them. All these disadvantages were brought to light first by the Japanese invasion, and secondly by the civil war which ended in the Communist victory.

When Peking fell into the hands of the Communists at the end of January 1949, everyone in the city knew at once that it would soon once more be the capital. No official announcement was made, the Kuomintang name of 'Peiping' was still officially used, but the people of Peking were assured of their future, and nothing reconciled them more fully to the new regime than the knowledge that it would make Peking its seat of government. Few, perhaps, foresaw how far-reaching this change of fortune would be, or dreamed of the transformation which their city was to undergo in the next six years. Nor were the reasons for the choice clearly understood. Many thought that the Communists had chosen Peking simply because the Kuomintang had rejected it. Others were very surprised that this regime which denounced 'imperialism' with such vigour should establish itself in a city built by and for imperial luxury and display.

6

The people of Peking were not accustomed to thinking of their city as having either industrial or commercial importance, and the significance of the expulsion of the Japanese from Manchuria was as yet little appreciated. Manchuria, the North East, as the Chinese call it (for 'Manchuria' is but a foreign coinage), had for nearly twenty years been a foreign state, a Japanese puppet, and for many years before the actual separation it had been so dominated by Japan that the Chinese felt it to be a lost province.

Yet it has subsequently become quite clear that in the minds of the rulers of the Communist Party the importance of Peking lay certainly as much in its situation in relation to Manchuria and Inner Mongolia as in its famous past and potent tradition. But, unlike the Kuomintang, they were not afraid of that tradition. Anti-imperialist though they certainly are, they looked upon the ancient splendours of the Court as a national inheritance, to be bequeathed to the People, and to be preserved and restored. Thus by a strange turn of fortune imperial Peking has become People's Peking, and continues to enjoy its unique significance and play its role with still enhanced prestige.

As the capital of the emperors, old Peking was built to an ancient pattern, evolved, perhaps, in the dawn of history and subsequently embodied with ever increasing magnificence in Ch'angan, Loyang, K'aifeng and Peking. The city must be a rectangle, though not necessarily a perfect square. The outer walls enclosed within them two further cities: the Imperial, reserved for the residence of officials and for public buildings, and the Palace itself, a moated and walled fortress so aligned that the great south gate of the city was in a direct line north to south with the southern gates of the Palace, the centre of the Throne Hall, and the great raised Throne itself. Immediately behind the palace enclosure rises a large and high artificial hill, built from the soil dug from moats and lakes, which acts as a screen to keep away the evil influences emanating from the north. The only palace buildings on the further, northern side of this hill are, significantly enough, the stately hall in which the encoffined body of an Emperor awaited final entombment.

7 B

Peking was, in fact, a gigantic exercise in the ancient Chinese quasi-science of geomancy, the theory of which postulated favourable or malign influences arising from the trend of the land, the confluence of streams, the situation of hills, forests, lakes and the four directions. This theory also regulated the height of walls and towers—which must never exceed ninety Chinese feet, because devils fly at the hundred foot level—the disposition of buildings, which should always face south, but should have the doorway screened by a detached wall, as devils, being notoriously a lower form of life and stupid, cannot turn corners. Many other prescriptions of geomancy were incorporated in the design of roofs, the placing of pagodas and temples.

Since geomancy paid great attention to the four directions, and gave pride of place and good fortune to the south, it necessarily taught the Chinese a great deal of the real science of geometry and proportion. Its object was to place human constructions in harmonious relation with the natural features of the landscape, and if the reasons for doing so were originally superstitious the requirement imposed a strict discipline upon the Chinese architect who acquired an almost infallible skill in proportion, the use of space, and balanced design. All these qualities were exemplified to the highest degree in the great palace halls of the Forbidden City in Peking, whose flawless proportion and superb grace eliminate all sense of the ponderous from buildings which are in fact on a massive and immense scale.

The purpose of an imperial city was to enshrine the palace, which indeed occupied a very large part of the whole walled enclosure, but the rest of the city in which the people dwelt was not allowed to develop in any haphazard manner. Wide straight streets ran from north to south and east to west, streets far wider than the traffic of the age required, a fact which has fortunately saved Peking from the sad necessity of demolishing many ancient buildings to accommodate the traffic of modern times. The purpose of this design was probably not so much a geomantic requirement as a measure of military precaution.

8

The wide streets giving unhindered access to all parts of the city enabled troops to move swiftly to any point threatened by riot or rebellion. The convenience of the public was certainly not the major consideration, for in imperial Peking the inhabitants of the western and eastern halves of the city were unable to pass directly from one side to the other except by skirting the palace enclosure to the north of the artificial hill called popularly Coal Hill, or passing through the narrow passage between the great south gate of the city, nicknamed 'Ch'ien Men' or 'Front Gate', and the most southerly of the outer gates of the immense fore-courts of the palace. The ordinary citizen had thus a choice of detours, each two to three miles out of the direct line, when passing from the eastern to the western side of the city. These two communicating streets in the south of the city were respectively known, and still are named 'East and West Peoples Communicating Streets', the eastern one subsequently acquiring the foreign nickname of Legation Street, since it was in this street that the foreign legations were located, and which after the Boxer Rebellion became the heart of the walled off, foreign controlled Legation Quarter.

The grand design of ancient Peking survived intact until the end of the Empire, almost the only important change to occur in six centuries being the addition of a further large walled rectangle to the south embracing what had originally been an extra-mural suburb, in which were also situated, to east and west of the main axis road, the Altar of Heaven and the Altar of Agriculture, two shrines of the most ancient imperial cult, which were always from the remotest times placed outside the capital in these respective positions. The area thus enclosed developed into the busiest commercial quarter of the city, and after the Manchu conquest, when for a time the native Chinese were expelled from the original city, became known as the 'Chinese City'—a term which, however, is not commonly current among the Chinese inhabitants of Peking.

When the Communists captured Peking in the early days of 1949, the city was still wholly enclosed within its walls. Open country began immediately outside the gates, which were always shut at night. The enclosure was very large—more than fourteen miles around—and contained nearly two million people, but Peking was still a walled city in the ancient meaning of the term. In the final days of the Nationalist rule in the middle of the twentieth century, this city was actually defended from its walls by a modern army, and the Communist attackers were only prevented by a timely surrender from the necessity of blowing a breach in the walls in the approved manner of ancient warfare.

The city which the new regime thus acquired and soon made once more the capital of China had also changed very little inside the walls. The strict prohibition against even crossing the Palace forecourts to reach the eastern or western sides had long been relaxed, although traffic still passed across through gates which could be closed at will. In the south-eastern quarter, favoured by foreign residents for the proximity to their legations, some undignified and unflattering examples of Western architecture had defaced the harmony of the ancient streets. The Protocol imposed on China at the end of the Boxer Rebellion in 1901 had created, round the Legation Quarter, a 'glacis'—a bare and dusty wilderness of broken tiles, overlooked by the loopholed but comparatively puny wall which Western military science at the beginning of the century deemed necessary for the defence of the Legation Quarter. Most of the main streets had been surfaced with tarmac, but the innumerable small and twisting lanes between them, known in Peking by the Manchu name of Hutung, remained dirty and dusty in the long dry winter, deep in sticky black mud during the wet months of summer. Piped water reached only a comparatively few wealthy houses, sanitation was still mainly effected by the wheelbarrow men who daily passed out through the gates with their unsavoury loads to fertilize the surrounding farm lands.

It is alleged in Peking folklore that this duty was imposed on men from Shantung province. The great architect of Peking, Liu Po-wen, who disliked Shantung, gave no privilege to men of that province when the city was founded whereas people from other parts were induced to settle there by grant of some right or monopoly. The men of Shantung protested, and were assigned this necessary duty which no others coveted.

Peking in 1949 was thus archaic, an amazing survival for so great a city, an almost unmodernized metropolis, living, apart from a superficial veneer of Western innovations, as it had always lived, and as its predecessors Ch'angan and Loyang had lived a thousand years before. It appeared strange indeed that the new men who now ruled should choose this place for their capital when their creed and their aspirations all pointed to some bustling centre of modern industry as the most appropriate centre for the new China, in which the industrial worker was to be exalted and the efforts of the whole nation turned to mechanization and mass production.

But such centres were rare in China: Mukden, which the Japanese had largely modernized; Shanghai, which was the creation and the mirror of Western commerce—or as the Communists would say, of Western imperialism; Harbin, which the Russians had built in Tsarist days in what had been a wilderness. All of these, it seems, had associations which the new rulers disliked, or were situated in regions too remote for convenience. If the Communists found Peking archaic, neglected, almost derelict after eight years of Japanese occupation and four more of civil war, they had no intention of settling their government in an archaic city, even when cleaned and repaired. Peking was to be preserved, yes, but also transformed, and at breathtaking speed.

Peking is still in 1958 a walled city, but the walls are now pierced by many new openings, streets have been projected through these gaps, gates doubled in width, and far beyond in what was open country the New Peking, equal in area to the Old, stretches out into the plain. So far from being contained within the old rectangle Peking today is a double city, the old city within, and the new, which surrounds it on all sides and expands with every passing month. The returning former resident, astounded by this immense development, feels as if he had not been away for a mere six years but for a century or more; he sees a transformation such as Napoleon accomplished when he turned the walls of Paris into boulevards and laid out the wide and spacious avenues of the modern city. He sees, indeed, much more than this, for the New Peking is not merely an expansion in area but a change in character. To the east, selected because the prevailing wind is westerly, the industrial quarter smokes into the clear North China sky; factories where there were farms, textile mills more modern, so Western observers state, than any to be found in the advanced countries of Europe. Peking six years ago had no factory; her industries were ancient handicrafts.

Westward, where the two universities of Yenching and Tsinghua stand some eight miles from the city walls, there is now a continuous settlement devoted to institutions of learning and science, hospitals, schools, government offices, exhibition buildings, technical institutes, laboratories, experimental stations, all the apparatus and buildings needed for modern science and technology. Apart from the small and ill-equipped laboratories of the universities, nothing of this existed in Old Peking, nor indeed in China. The same expansion is visible to the north and to the south of the old city, colleges, residential quarters for the new workers of these proliferating institutions. All are built permanently in brick and tile. Ferro-concrete is too expensive, for China needs her steel and cement for her factories; the flimsy prefabricated hut—temporary, but all too lasting, which is the architectural curse of the twentieth century, is hardly seen in China. Labour is cheap and inexhaustible, materials are made at hand from the clay of the North China plain.

On the architectural merits or demerits of this vast programme of construction, opinions among the Chinese themselves differ sharply. The architects rightly point out that they have a task far beyond the powers of supervision of the most active man. They can but plan, or approve the plans made by recent graduates. These young men find themselves entrusted with the work of building a large institute or hospital as their first task on leaving the university. No wonder that an architect friend who studied in England under Professor Abercrombie should exclaim, half in amazement, half in embarrassment, 'Do you know, I have built more in the last two years than Abercrombie built in all his life!'

The criticism of the architects in the Press (and it is often most outspoken) is not, however, directed at the extent of their constructions or the haste of the programme, but at the styles employed. There have been a number of buildings erected in what is called the Palace style, in which the coloured glazed tiles used on the Forbidden City and temples have been employed, with a Chinese curving roof, to crown a three- or four-storey modern building of brick, otherwise Western in design. The effect can be pleasing, but does not harmonize well with neighbouring buildings in which Western design has been used. The criticism most often made, that this style is too expensive and wastes the People's money, may be true, but a more enduring standard of judgement would rather suggest that the Palace style, so superbly preserved in the Forbidden City itself, should only be employed for buildings of comparable significance which stand in surroundings with which this style can harmonize. Many buildings of the new universities and institutes, such as the Institute of National Minorities, have adopted a more workable compromise, using the curving Chinese roof executed in the ordinary grey tiles commonly employed on Peking houses. This manner can be graceful and still distinctive. Others have the straight pitched roof of Western architecture, without any Chinese curve or character, yet, since the Chinese architect has not lost his gift for proportion and the roof was the most important feature of the old Chinese style, these buildings are often more graceful and satisfying than their more ambitious neighbours.

So much of New Peking is still in course of construction, the unfinished, the barely begun, and the completed jostling each other in the same street, that it is hardly possible to say yet what the final effect of this competition of the styles will be in the finished city. It seems improbable that it will achieve the harmony and grace of the Old Peking, but likely that it will escape the tasteless vulgarity and planless ugliness of the former foreign Concessions in Shanghai. One striking feature of the New Peking is the total absence of what in the West is known as Modern Architecture. The glass walls, multistoried buildings, and other devices now widespread throughout the world are never seen in New Peking, or indeed in China. Whether there exists some ideological prejudice against these styles, or whether the reason for their rejection is economic, or shortage of materials, it is certainly not due to ignorance of the modern trend in the West, since the chief architects of New Peking are all men trained in Europe or America and familiar with modern developments.

Another aspect of New Peking which marks the radical change in the structure of society is the almost complete absence in these new quarters of the individual family house. The residential constructions are all large blocks of flats, not ill-designed, and often quite pleasing to the eye, standing in courts and groups back from the main roads. These flats are assigned to the workers—both by brain and hand—who will be, or already are, employed in the multitude of new institutes and offices which are rising all over the western suburb. They represent a type of accommodation which, although familiar to a tiny handful of the more wealthy citizens of Shanghai, was otherwise almost entirely alien to the Chinese tradition of domestic architecture. It was so, also, because the implications of the flat were themselves entirely alien to the Chinese family system. It was still, well within living memory, the aspiration of most Chinese of wealth to gather their family under one capacious roof, or rather establish them in a series of inter-communicating courtyards, several generations and collateral relatives dwelling together in one of those huge spreading houses which are so typical of Old Peking.

Economic factors, the distresses of a turbulent age, wars and invasions, had already greatly eroded this ancient system. The great houses were being split up, so that parts could be rented to strangers; yet it was still, up to 1949, common enough to find capacious dwellings in which parents and children, some uncles and aunts, cousins and connections lived together, each group occupying a separate courtyard or part of one, but sharing kitchens and reception rooms. By building blocks of flats which barely suffice to house a single family in each apartment the government would appear to be deliberately striking at the old system, by the relatively painless method of providing accommodation which can hardly be adapted to its uses.

It is of course true that, as the population of Peking has increased by one and a half millions in the last six years, the most part of those new citizens are immigrants from other parts of China, and above all from Shanghai. Such newcomers are also young adult workers, with small families, and if technical, scientific or professional men, were very likely more accustomed to the life of flats in the former foreign Concessions of Shanghai. They would be less at home in an Old Peking house, are very eager to occupy the flats, and have usually no older relatives, or very few, a widowed mother or retired father, to accompany them to their new homes. It would be instructive if a social survey of the New Peking could be made revealing how many of the inhabitants of the apartment blocks are not, in fact, Peking residents, but newcomers from the South. It may well be that New Peking is not only new in structure, but also in population.

This social change is not entirely a consequence of the revolution; even in imperial Peking it was often said that you could never find a family which claimed to be true natives of city. The Chinese custom of maintaining, as a fiction perhaps, the claim of the family to belong to its province and city of origin, long after it had migrated elsewhere, gave a rather false impression to the uninitiated inquirer. Men would say they were Cantonese, when in fact the family, following some eminent member many years before, had established itself in Peking for several generations. The practice of recruiting officials from all parts of the Empire and stationing them always in provinces other than their own had led to widespread migration among the educated classes who were also intermarried with other families similarly displaced.

Thus the new character of the Peking population is really an acceleration, due to the restoration of the city as capital and its rapid expansion, of an old process which was also characteristic, at a lesser tempo, of the old imperial Peking. Peking is, moreover, a great solvent of provincial characteristics. Its dialect, which is said to be in part influenced by traces of Manchu pronunciation and speech, has become the standard spoken Chinese, at least in the educated form of that speech. Formerly, this was known as 'Kuan Hua', 'Official Speech', or by foreigners as Mandarin. Under the Republic this was thought to be too reminiscent of the Empire and was renamed 'Kuo Yu', or 'National Speech'. This term seeming to smack too much of the Kuomintang, the new regime has altered it to 'P'u T'ung Hua', or 'Standard Speech', but when asked to define what this meant, the Prime Minister, Chou En-lai, expressed it as the 'educated speech of Peking'. No better definition of the old Mandarin could be made.

Since the regime actively encourages the use of this dialect, and discourages the employment of the provincial dialects, the newcomers to Peking struggle to express themselves in Standard Speech—often with indifferent success—and their children, educated in the local schools and mixing with the older inhabitants, will soon acquire the Peking intonation. Within a few years the new inhabitants, still, perhaps, remembering their southern origin and calling themselves Cantonese or men of Shanghai, will be speaking a tongue indistinguishable from that of the long established Peking people, a process which has continued for several centuries past.

Yet, when on a Sunday or other holiday, the crowds resort to the Palaces and their great gardens, now all public, there is evident a great change in the appearance of the population. Peking was formerly very conservative, and especially in dress. The long gown, split down the sides, a garment of Manchu origin, was worn by a great proportion of the men and women of all social classes. Unlike remoter parts of China where this dress signified wealth or education, and had originally indicated official or scholarly status, in Peking it was worn by all but the poorest labouring class. No doubt once a mark of social aspirations, it had become almost the standard attire of the Peking people. It was worn, moreover, in the correct manner, less affected by modern innovations than in other cities. The ankles of the long trousers were secured by short white bands, the head covered with the small round cap, features which had largely disappeared elsewhere.

Today it has all but vanished. A few, a very few, old men can still be seen dressed like their forefathers, but the mass of the population no matter what their position, wear the plain blue coat and trousers which, formerly the garb of the working man, are now honoured for that reason and have become the universal attire of China. The causes of this change are not all political. China in 1949 was desperately short of all commodities and cloth was no exception. The State decided that the urgent need was to clothe the population in the quickest possible time, since many millions had little but rags. The textile mills produced one standard material, nothing else was available for purchase. The need for every man and woman to work, often in factories or offices, made elegant attire unpractical as well as unfashionable, and the use of the old dress came to symbolize reactionary opinions. The director of an institute of higher learning, a university professor, a high party official, a boiler-maker or a textile mill-hand all now wear the same dress, indistinguishable, plain and rather shapeless, the outward sign that all alike are workers.

Women suffered, or accepted, the same revolution. The elegant long gown has vanished, so have make-up, coiffure and fine materials. Women adopted, perhaps in partly conscious imitation of the heroine of the revolutionary opera the 'White Haired Girl', the simple peasant girl style which was traditional in the countryside: long trousers, a three-quarter length coat buttoning up in front, long pigtails, a fringe of hair across the forehead. It may be added that, in many cases, some subtle refinement of this peasant dress can be perceived discreetly evident. The trousers are sometimes of better cloth than peasants could ever afford; beneath the workaday coat can be seen one of gayer colours, to be exhibited when the day is done, the hair ribbons are elegant, the clothes well cut. As life gets easier and the shops carry a greater variety of materials, these signs of feminine taste become more frequent.

Quite recently, in the early part of 1956, the government began to encourage diversity of dress and more interesting styles for women. The Press carried illustrations of new designs for frocks, some modelled on the European, or rather on the Russian pattern, others based on the old Chinese long gown, which itself began to appear again as evening dress on very formal occasions. It was reiterated that the simple blue coat and trousers were not to be regarded as a badge of rectitude, but more as working clothes, imposed in part by the necessity of the revolutionary age. No such change as yet affects the dress of the men. At most they will wear, on formal occasions, the better cut version of their working dress which is the Party uniform, and is itself adapted from the style first introduced by Dr. Sun Yat-sen in the early days of the Revolution. The long gown, once the costume of men under the Empire, and then never worn by women, if it survives at all, is to be the formal costume of women in the future.

It must be presumed that many historically-minded Chinese are aware that this is an ironic sartorial revolution, for the peasant dress which women of quality and education now affect is really only the simple form of the formal dress which their own great-grandmothers wore in the nineteenth century, the difference in men's and women's attire being marked by the fact that only men wore the gown. The fashion for women to wear this dress came in with the Republic, when it was regarded as a more modern compromise, half-way towards the Western frock or skirt. It had come, however, to stand for the luxury and the vice of the wealthy classes of Shanghai, the home of 'bourgeois imperialism', and was condemned as unpractical, frivolous, even licentious.

Many of these foibles of the revolutionary society are attributed to the prejudices of the 'Old Comrades from Yenan', the hard core of the Communist Party which endured for twenty years the rigours of the guerrilla campaigns. In those bitter days elegance could only be a hindrance. Men and women lived like peasants, merging with the country population, sharing the simple poverty of their rural supporters. When the day of Liberation—the term always used for the victory of the Communist Party—at last arrived, the Old Comrades were on guard against the luxury and 'bourgeois' manners of the city folk who had not shared these experiences. The Puritan streak which is so evident in Chinese society today comes at least in part from this source, as well as from a genuine revulsion against the decadence of the old society, and the austerities which the present national effort of reconstruction demands.

One of the minor but striking changes in Peking today is the total disappearance of dogs. This, too, is a consequence of the peculiarities of the Old Comrades from Yenan. These former guerrilla warriors were accustomed to move on their military operations by night, to avoid the air reconnaisance of their enemies. In old China every village was inhabited by a swarm of mangy, ownerless dogs, who beset every traveller who approached, whether by day or night, with shrill barking and weakly pressed attacks. The Old Comrades found this tiresome and too revealing of their movements. So did the Japanese invaders who pursued them. Both sides combined to exterminate the dogs, and these unfortunate creatures came to be regarded as little better than a canine Fifth Column. Peking had its legions of dogs, hardly better kept than those of the countryside. The Old Comrades viewed them with unappeased rancour. Their death was decreed, and every dog, lest some should escape and breed up a new race, had to be brought to the police stations where they were humanely destroyed. Only a tiny handful of Legation dogs, sharing the diplomatic privileges of their masters, now survive in all Peking. By many, even of the most converted, this massacre was regarded as, at least, outmoded.

If the city has thus become both more proletarian in the appearance of its inhabitants and far cleaner than of old, as a result of the massacre of the dogs and the famous slaughter of the flies—an elimination which is virtually complete, and to the old inhabitant nearly incredible—Peking has also seen its old imperial glories refreshed and renovated. The Forbidden City, in need of extensive repair and formerly in a state of dilapidation, has had many thousands of pounds spent upon the most thorough restoration, carried out with careful attention to historic decor and design, and is now undoubtedly in more perfect repair than it has been for several centuries. Under the rule of the Emperors themselves, especially in the later years of the dynasty, the caprice or the superstition of the monarch or his women might leave some large series of courts shut up, decaying and shunned, because some person of importance had died there of an infectious disease. Money devoted to repair of those parts of the Palace actually in use was embezzled by the eunuchs charged with the work. More conscientious Emperors sometimes really felt ashamed to spend large sums upon restoring their palaces when drought or famine prevailed in the land. Others found more frivolous uses for such money as they obtained.

But today the Palace, the imperial temples and gardens, are all the property of the People, a fact of which they are constantly reminded by notices displayed in prominent parts of the grounds. As the heirs of the age of feudal subservience they can now enjoy the pleasures and the beauty which they themselves, or rather their ancestors, provided by their money and toil for the magnificence of their ruler. Consequently this inheritance must be preserved for future generations to enjoy, to the greater glory of the Chinese People.

Whatever the mixture of motives the nation has accepted the imperial past as its inheritance and is ready to spend much money in preserving and restoring its monuments. Outside Peking, to the north at the foot of the mountain range along which runs the Wall, are the tombs of the Ming Emperors, thirteen in all, which had survived, in a state of decay which was still not beyond repair, for nearly 500 years. The fact that a fallen dynasty's imperial tombs had not been destroyed by their successors was regarded in China as a unique fortune, and Peking lore attributed the peaceful abdication of the Manchus in 1912, and the physical survival of the imperial family, to the forbearance that their ancestors had shown in refraining from destroying the Tombs of the Ming. Nevertheless the Ming Tombs, magnificent examples of Chinese imperial architecture in its greatest age, continued neglected and decaying. Although the early republicans claimed to have 'restored the Ming' (by which they meant expelled the Manchu dynasty) they did nothing to repair the Ming Tombs.

It has been left, strangely enough, to a Communist government, ruling in the name of the People and under the slogans of anti-imperialism to spend a great sum on a most complete and beautifully executed restoration of the tomb of Ming Yung Lo, the founder of Peking, and a wholehearted autocrat. Nor is it intended to stop there; as money can be found the other Ming Tombs, many of which were still more decayed, will also be restored as far as this is still possible.

Peking today thus presents two faces: the creation of a new, modern, industrial and administrative city, equipped with all the institutions of learning and science which an advanced society requires, and the careful, meticulous restoration and preservation of the capital of imperial China; on the one hand a vast effort to overcome the inertia and backwardness of the recent past, on the other a conscious tribute of admiration and respect to a more ancient past which has been accepted as contributing to the future glory of the reborn China. Neither process is yet complete; the new city is but half built, perhaps less, for the plans for expansion are immense; very much work still also remains to be done before the monuments of the past are wholly rescued from neglect and decay. Yet, judging by the speed with which the programme already undertaken has been accomplished in the past six years there is no doubt that, with gathering momentum, all will be swiftly achieved.

Peking in imperial days was the supreme expression in material terms of the aims and achievements of the old Chinese society. Today it is intended as the pilot city for the new

Chinese society, which, already several years ago, Mao Tse-tung announced as the aim of his movement. In 1940, when the Japanese invasion was at its height and the prospects of China whether Communist or Nationalist were never darker, Mao wrote a book which he called *New Democracy*. In this he stated very clearly the purposes which he hoped to accomplish when, and if, he was in a position to direct the destiny of China.

'The problem is quite plain; we wish to eradicate the old Chinese culture; it is inseparable from the old Chinese government and the old Chinese economic system. We intend to establish a new kind of Chinese national culture and this equally cannot be separated from the new kind of Chinese government and the new kind of Chinese economy.'*

After six years of power one may see in Peking the first fruits of this policy, the emerging pattern of the new kind of government, the new economy and the new culture. Clearly this pattern is most quickly appreciated in the national capital, the show place of the New China, to which scores of visiting delegations from inside China and from abroad are annually invited. Nowhere else can the changes be more vividly observed, for nowhere else was the quintessence of ancient China so perfectly preserved. It may be thought that the Communist regime has done more for Peking than any other city or region, just as the imperial regime concentrated the wealth and artistic skill of the nation to its service at the capital. But the parallel is inexact; Old Peking represented not only the power but also the limitations of the imperial system. The city was embellished, enriched and refined precisely because, in ages when communications were bad and the authority of the central government, though universally acknowledged, decreasingly effective at a distance from the Court, it was not really possible to employ great resources and engage in vast schemes of development except under the immediate eye of the Emperor, and under the supervision of officials whose mistakes or peculations he could thus easily detect.

* Selected Works of Mao Tse-tung. Vol. 3. p. 107, *New Democracy*. Lawrence & Wishart Ltd. London. 1954.

New Peking is the seat of the most powerful government China has ever possessed. It has an organization, the Communist Party, which reaches to every province and penetrates every village. Centralized control is absolute, the orders from Peking are made known by modern means of communication, and unhesitatingly obeyed. Officials, educators, party workers, museum directors, scientists from all parts of China are constantly summoned to Peking to learn the wishes of the government, to confer with their colleagues, and return to their posts to carry out the policy which Peking has determined. Provincial autonomy has virtually no meaning in China today; the accent is all on centralization—Democratic Centralization it is called, but the practical effects, if not the theory behind them, are often very similar indeed to the autocracy of earlier ages, or rather what that form of government would have aspired to be if it had had the means.

Peking is therefore more than ever the Capital, the centre of power and culture—the mirror of the Chinese world, but with a different role to play from that of the Old Peking of the Empire. It must not only reflect the glory of the rulers, and radiate their power throughout China, but also serve as the model which all China must aspire to copy and take as its inspiration. Speech must be the Standard Chinese which is the language of Peking. Architecture, whether ornamental in the Palace style, or practical as in New Peking, follows the same lead, dress conforms to the new fashions of the capital, education is controlled and curricula laid down in Peking.

Peking, moreover, must be not only the capital which all China admires and imitates, but a great exhibition of the achievements of the new regime to be shown to foreign visitors for their enlightenment and instruction. Asia, above all Asia, must see Peking and understand what can be done to an ancient city and an outworn economy by the application of Marxist principles under the leadership of the Communist Party. The point is constantly emphasized; it is not just the effort of the Chinese people revived and refreshed, but the guidance of the Party, the employment of correct methods and

23   C

the right ideology which has brought about this transformation. Like Ozymandias, Peking would say to Asia, 'Look on my works, ye mighty, and (if you are Capitalists) despair.'

On a May evening in 1956, a Western newcomer to Peking took his first walk through the city, down the broad Ch'angan street which leads to and past the T'ien An Men, the great south gate of the Forbidden City. Turning to gaze down the long street aswarm with workers returning home at the end of the day, he exclaimed, 'But this is a metropolis, like London or Paris.' The same thought, inspired by a different aspect of the great city, had moved the old French resident to make a similar comparison; each observer, in his time, had penetratingly uncovered the essential quality of the Old and the New Peking.

CHAPTER TWO

SCHOLARS

THE GREAT BRITISH scholar and translator of the Chinese classics, James Legge, made an unfortunate choice of an English term to render a Confucian expression: he translated the Chinese words *Chün Tzu* as 'Superior Man', and thus left upon the Western mind the persistent impression that the Sage of ancient China was a prig. But *Chün Tzu* means literally the 'Son of a Lord'; it was an expression having almost exactly the same force as the German 'Junker'—young Lord—had in the Middle Ages, meaning a member of the landed aristocracy, not necessarily the title-holder. Confucius used it to mean a member of the feudal aristocracy to whom his writings were addressed, because in his age no other literate class existed. He gave the term, which could as well, or better, be translated as 'gentleman' (in the eighteenth-century sense) the meaning of the man of cultivation, education and social responsibility who should be occupied in the service of his prince or in the study of philosophy. As such he contrasts the 'little man', the non-aristocratic, and still more the aristocrat who has failed to live up to his duties and thus betrayed his class and his master.

The teachings of Confucius became under the early Empire, in the Han period, the orthodox doctrine of the Chinese world. By that age the feudal system of China had passed away and the ruling class were no longer really *Chün Tzu*, sons of lords, but scholar gentry, at first the members and clients of powerful clans, in later times, from the T'ang period (seventh to ninth centuries AD) members of more widespread landed gentry. Through all these changes the ruling class continued to identify themselves with the Confucian *Chün Tzu* and to take the duties of the ancient aristocracy as their model. Since the new passport to membership of this class was not birth but learning, and the possession of land was only an economic means to achieve education, in itself conferring no political privilege, the name of scholar came in ordinary parlance to attach itself to this whole class, whether in or out of official employment. No one who was not well educated, even if very rich, could claim to be a *Chün Tzu*, or a scholar; a man who had the learning, even if poor, was so regarded and so honoured.

There thus arose in China a social class, long powerful and always returning to the ascendant, which differed very profoundly from the aristocracies of birth dominant in the West, or the country gentry who gradually succeeded to their power. In China, education, long, arduous training in a difficult literature, was the mark of the gentleman; his career should be the civil service, he expected to leave his country home at an early age, take the great public examination, pass into the civil service and spend the active years of his life on duty in provinces always other than his own, or in the Capital, returning home only in old age or in periods of compulsory mourning for his parents. The management of the country estate, usually of very modest size, was left to the less intelligent members of the family, who had failed, or who could never hope to pass the civil service examination.

The scholars who succeeded became what the West has called, from a Portuguese word, the Mandarins; those who remained on the land are those whom the present regime has stigmatized as 'landlords' and has dispossessed. But the scholars, in a very great proportion, are of landlord origin, country gentry by birth, scholars and officials by education. In a population which for some five centuries already exceeded one hundred millions, and in later ages rose to four or five times that number, the scholars formed only a tiny percentage, yet still a large number, but as the only educated class they were never too numerous to find employment. The Empire was vast, it was administered by a large civil service, inefficient by modern standards, yet by many centuries the forerunner of the public services of all modern states.

The scholars and their civil service were also indispensable to any dynasty, Chinese or foreign, which hoped to continue on the Throne. The Chinese disliked and disapproved of soldiers and still more of military men in power. The founders of dynasties were usually soldiers of fortune risen in times of rebellion and tumult. Fearing that their own example was all too easy to follow they no sooner consolidated their power than they reduced their forces, depressed the power of the generals, and turned to the scholars to reconstruct the civil service and administer the Empire in the time-honoured way.

Thus the many changes of dynasty did not constitute social revolutions. There was some redistribution of land to the followers of the new regime, a timely easing of the pressure which had lain at the root of the troubles by which the last dynasty had been dethroned, but the scholar class as a whole came out unscathed, returned to office and soon to the further accumulation of land, thus building up the same pressure till another revolution, perhaps three centuries later, brought about the fall of the dynasty and the rise of a successor. There was a fatal symbiosis between Court and gentry. The Court could not govern without the scholars, nor the scholars find a career without a strong central government; but they sought their reward in wealth which was invested in land; the peasants were progressively depressed and impoverished until rebellion broke out, the military had to be called in to defend the dynasty, and one or other general, either a rebel, an ex-rebel or an imperial officer, dethroned the feeble dynasty and set up his own.

The generation of scholar gentry which experienced this convulsion no doubt suffered in it. Peasant armies burnt and looted in the countryside, the imperial armies behaved no better—for the soldiers were peasants too, and often the officers came from the same class. But when the new dynasty was assured of the Throne, the ship of state came back to an even keel, and the scholars were once more enlisted as the crew. Land might be redistributed, but private property as an institution was never abolished, the scholar officials soon started to rebuild the family fortunes, nothing really changed except the name of the dynasty in power.

For a complex of reasons, which it is the province of modern historians of China to investigate, there never arose a powerful urban middle class which could afford an alternative to the continuing ever-restored power of the scholar gentry, based on land ownership and education. Merchants, often wealthy, and certainly literate, existed in the great cities, particularly along the southern seaboard and the Yangtze river; they were excluded from political power and ranked below farmers in the social scale. They might, in the last dynasty, and no doubt in other ages of decline, purchase official rank which removed them from some of the more drastic penalties of the law and served to protect their property, but they did not receive office. In so far as they purchased land they became scholar gentry and merged in that class, the more willingly as it had the social prestige which commerce lacked. Moreover, the merchant class, which had no land, was more liable to suffer the total loss of wealth in a period of disorder when cities were sacked and burned by rebels. The vast extent of China remained strictly agricultural, smaller cities served merely as market towns and administrative centres, small merchants were shopkeepers serving a mainly rural population.

This ancient social system continued with no significant change almost until the fall of the Manchu Dynasty in 1912. The one new factor which bulked large in the eyes of foreigners was the intrusion of the West, the establishment of Treaty Ports in which foreign merchants lived under their own laws, and in which, too, Chinese merchants, dwelling in the foreign Concessions, soon grew richer and more influential than ever before. But there were very few large Treaty Ports with Concessions: Shanghai, Tientsin, Hankow; and by far the greatest of these was Shanghai, where the Concessions occupied five-sixths of the urban area, wholly overshadowing what had been a very insignificant Chinese city. Shanghai, which had a population of over four millions by the turn of the century, was a foreign city planted on Chinese soil, administered by foreigners, but inhabited by Chinese. Yet there was only one Shanghai, only one city where the Chinese merchant urban class really grew wealthy and enjoyed security for its riches, in the foreign

Concessions. The rest of China remained as before under the control of the civil service and the scholar gentry.

The fall of the Manchu dynasty and the establishment of the Republic did not produce the rapid modernization and social change which the revolutionaries expected, and the foreigners half feared. The period between 1912 and 1928 resembled the type of tumultuous interregnum which usually followed the collapse of a long established dynasty. Generals fought for power, at first openly, or secretly, expecting to restore the Throne and establish a new dynasty, later when this hope gradually faded, simply for power which meant wealth. The rise of the Nationalist Party, a new phenomenon in China, and the establishment of the capital at Nanking in 1928, seemed at first to be about to afford a new solution for the old problem, a new type of state to replace the monarchy and end the anarchy.

The Nationalist Party or Kuomintang was formed in the image of the Russian Communist Party, organized with the aid of Russian Soviet advisers as a result of the agreement of 1923 made between Dr. Sun Yat-sen and the Russian envoy, Joffe. It did not, of course, accept the Communist programme, but endeavoured to create a new kind of government based upon the power of the Party. '*I Tang chih kuo*'—'Use the Party to govern the State'—was its motto and its aim. The Nationalists had turned away from the democratic ideals of the early republicans, disgusted by the hopeless failure of these theories when applied to the Chinese political scene. Democracy had to wait until the people had passed through a period of tutelage, under the rule of the Nationalist Party.

The theory and practice of a Party State, in which a political party assumes the sovereign power and makes every organ of government its instrument, has had several recent applications in different parts of the world, but, except among the Communist powers, it has had no lasting success. The reason would appear to be that these attempts to use a Communist system of government without applying a Communist programme, which includes first and foremost a social revolution, are no more likely to succeed than the converse attempt, so haltingly undertaken, and so doubtful of fulfilment, of applying demo-cratic processes to a society under a Communist regime. The Party State system takes as its point of departure the fact that social classes have been levelled and that from that now uniform social population it can pick and train the Party *élite*.

In Nationalist China, as in the other imitators of the Soviet system, this was not true; the revolution of 1911 had only dethroned the dynasty, the years of confusion had only raised up the officer class, the gulf between rich and poor remained, the other gulf between educated and illiterate was still un-bridged. The Chinese social order had not been over-thrown or replaced, it had merely decayed. Consequently the new Party State was founded on the same social order as the last years of the Empire, but with the further deterioration that in the succeeding years of disorder the power of the military officer class had greatly increased, and that of the scholar gentry proportionately declined. This symptom of disorder in a post-dynastic period of confusion was not abnormal in China, but it had hitherto been merely a temporary phase ending in a new dynasty and a new opportunity for the restored civil service.

The Nationalist Party was in theory to be recruited from all classes, from men and women who believed in the restoration of the Chinese nation and its power. Its guiding principle was nationalism, its social programme faltering and obscure. In practice this meant that the Party came to be dominated by two groups, both newcomers to power in China: the military officer class, led by the Head of the Party, Chiang Kai-shek, and the Shanghai merchant bankers, led by his relations by marriage, the Soong family. Neither of these groups possessed the tradition of government and service which the scholar gentry, though often failing, still cherished and sometimes applied.

The military group understood nothing but political power and command. Social and economic problems were beyond the scope of their education and did not arouse their interest. The banker group understood nothing but how to acquire wealth, operate the financial manipulations of the exchange, establish monopolies, rig the market. They were not very much interested in power, except as a means of gathering money. They left political power to the generals. They were wholly uninterested in the social problem of the land and the peasants, since as urban merchants from Shanghai, they had no understanding of these problems and no experience of the life of the countryside.

The Party membership tended more and more to fall into line with this division of authority at the top. Military men brought in their relatives and subordinates, who followed the army as a career; the bankers brought in their clients, who imitated their masters and sought office to gain wealth. Neither the scholar gentry nor the peasants had a significant role to play in the Kuomintang. If the new Party State was to be the solution for China, then for the first time a regime had come to power which did not rely upon the scholars, nor upon their aid in reconstructing the civil service. It was also a regime which made no attempt to grapple with the problems of the countryside, nor even to engage in the minor land redistribution which every preceding dynasty had judged wise and necessary when it came to power.

In the years between the fall of the Empire and the fall of the Nationalist regime, from 1912 to 1949, a whole generation of the scholar gentry found no real opening in the service of the state. Some few careers, the new foreign service being the most conspicuous, became their preserve. For the rest they turned in large numbers to their old alternative occupation, teaching. The one advantage which the Republic conferred upon this large class was the establishment of the new universities, which multiplied under the early Republic, and soon became the strongholds of the sons and grandsons of the official families of the Empire. The rolls of the professors and staff members of the great universities read like the old civil service list, filled with the names which had been famous in the imperial service. The scholars had lost control of the State but they had gained a new vantage ground to perpetuate their learning and their tradition in the minds of the coming generation.

This new concentration of the best and most intelligent members of the scholar gentry in the teaching professions was characteristic of China, but underlines one of the main differences between the European and the Chinese culture. The Western aristocracies, though adorned with some famous names in the world of learning, have never, as a whole, been the intellectual leaders of the nation. For several centuries after they had obtained political and economic power over the land they remained illiterate, leaving learning to Churchmen. In China there was no Church; from the earliest period of which reliable records remain the aristocracy, later the gentry, were also the literate class, and sought to distinguish themselves in the academy rather than on the hunting or battlefields.

Consequently, the Chinese gentry did not look upon their ancestral lands, often held for a longer period by one family than the proudest nobles of Europe could claim, as their normal dwelling or a fitting scene for their careers. These ancient estates are very rarely furnished with a noble mansion; no castles dot the landscape, even the equivalent of the more simple manor house is hardly to be identified. The Chinese landowning family preferred to dwell in the neighbouring city; on the land there was a modest house, furnished sparsely enough, inhabited by relatives actually in charge of the day to day management of the farms—or the bailiff charged with the collection of rent from tenants. In certain provinces where security had for long been exceptionally good, a better mansion was built on the family lands (Ssuchuan is a case in point) but these were the exceptions. Today, when the former chief landlord's home is the centre of the collective farm, the visitor, penetrating what would have been a very private establishment, is struck by the bleakness, the sparse poor furniture, and the general discomfort and lack of adornment in the houses of what are now described as the former oppressors of the people.

Not that the rich landlord families were strangers to luxury and refinement, but these amenities were found in their city homes, in the capital or the great cities of the provinces, nourished by the toil of the tenants on a distant estate, which the members of the family very rarely even visited. The one building of elegance and style which was to be found on the country estate was the Ancestral Temple, the original head-quarters of the clan or sub-clan, in which the genealogies were recorded, the ancestral tablets displayed, and where, perhaps once a year or on some special occasion, the head of the family would perform the ancient rites of ancestor worship.

Thus, in speaking of the scholar gentry as 'landlords' or as 'country gentlemen' it must be understood that their way of life and their careers were wholly unlike the country gentry of the European nations. Country pursuits were scorned as boorish, the army was the last career a member of this class would adopt; physical exercise was regarded as a mark of peasant manners; the scholar cultivated, and often acquired, a permanent stoop, so characteristic that this poise is used in the Peking Opera as the distinguishing mark of characters who play the role of scholar gentry. The connection with the land was reduced to two functions, an economic aspect, which enabled the gentry families to spend years in unrewarded study before they could pass into the civil service, and a spiritual connection typified by the ancestral temple and the almost fictional claim that the family 'came from' such and such a county and village, which was officially classed as the birthplace of its members.

Thus families of high official standing, who had for genera-tions made their homes in Peking, and followed their careers throughout China, still claimed to be natives of some distant province, county and village, a place which most of them had never so much as seen. Moreover, though the scholar gentry were in this restricted sense a landed gentry, they did not for the most part possess great estates. There were very few really large land holdings, no enormous tracts of territory such as were typical of the aristocratic estates of eastern Europe; the average family estate was small, but usually consisted of the best and most fertile land available. Most of this was let out to tenant farmers.

33

Great officials acquired huge wealth during a long career, but if they survived to leave it to their descendants, the large number of these, the widespread obligations of the Chinese family system, quickly eroded the greatest fortunes. If a family were deprived of office for some crime or misdemeanour, the loss of wealth was very rapid; the land alone could not sustain so large a group in luxury, official service was an economic necessity as well as a cherished tradition. The scholars were drawn into the service of the Throne by their needs as much as by their hopes. Disgrace and dismissal were indeed virtually equivalent to bankruptcy, but if forced to return to the ancestral estate, the one endeavour of the disgraced official was to use the influence of his friends, relatives and patrons to recover his post, or at least some post, however distant, however arduous.

In order to assess rightly the effect upon this class of the two revolutions which China has undergone in the lifetime of the present generation these facts must be stressed. For it is obvious that as their previous experience was wholly different from that of the landed aristocracy of Europe, they may be expected to have reacted to the sweeping changes of revolution in a manner unlike the dispossessed ruling class of eastern Europe. The overthrow of the monarchy and the military dominance which followed under the Republic, the Party State of the Kuomintang, were all in their several ways deleterious to the standing of the scholar gentry; deleterious, but not disastrous. They retained their lands, but they could hardly live on them or by them. The countryside became more unsafe than ever; bandit gangs, often as large as small military formations, and as well armed (for they were composed of mutinous soldiery), swept through the provinces, burning, extorting, kidnapping and carrying off the women. From these evils the gentry families escaped to the strong cities, where they had always preferred to dwell. They left bailiffs—expressively known to the peasants as 'dog legs'—to collect what rents they could.

The connection with the land became ever more tenuous,

and since under these conditions the revenue constantly diminished, the scholars were more than previously dependent on other forms of livelihood. The fall of the Empire and the subsequent confusion disorganized, almost destroyed, the old civil service. The examination system was abolished,* the old learning no longer acted as the key to an official career; for that, influence with some militarist was needed, and such favours were of short duration. The military overlords came and went within a few years, their followers went out with them. Influence and Party membership were essential to an official career under the Kuomintang, but this Party had its own type of follower and few scholar gentry were among them. But if the old learning in the narrow sense in which it was pursued to pass the great examinations had gone out, the new learning, Western and Chinese, was in high favour. Schools and universities multiplied, students were numerous and ever-increasing, and only the literate class, the scholars, could meet the need for staff and teachers.

They now followed a new pattern of education. All who could, after completing their studies in a Chinese university, went abroad to acquire the Western learning, to 'drink foreign ink' as the expression went. They returned with the certainty or the strong expectation of a good teaching post, which in the period prior to the Japanese invasion afforded a very reasonable living. Thus the scholars became, if possible, more urban than before the revolution. They no longer travelled the length of China from one provincial post to another. They no longer sojourned for years as magistrates of a small rural city. They lived in Peking, Shanghai, Canton and many other cities where schools and universities, often three or four in each great city, provided them with their new careers. The family income from the ancestral estate became less important, especially to those whose abilities gained them superior academic posts.

Many generations of intellectual pursuits, the stiff mental discipline of a difficult literature and a complex script, had

* Actually in 1905, in the last years of the Empire.

developed among this class a very high average of intelligence. The Chinese scholars are, with the Indian Brahmins, perhaps the most consistently intelligent group of people living in the world today. Such a class cannot easily be overthrown by adverse circumstances; but having skilfully survived the catastrophe of the end of the Empire and the chaos which followed, they were before long to undergo a more searching test, the social revolution which struck at their old economic base on the land and at the same time denied to them their ancient place of privilege in society.

In other parts of the world perhaps the most sincere and steadfast opponents of the Communist system are found in the ranks of the landed gentry. From this class the 'White Officers' who vainly opposed the Bolsheviks derived. Their descendants, in exile, remain wholly unreconciled. In the homelands they have been virtually eliminated. They lived on the land, without it they are lost. Deprived of this resource and of the military career which went with it, they sink swiftly into poverty. But the most striking characteristic of present-day China is precisely the absence of this phenomenon. In the People's Republic the scholar gentry are neither exiles nor paupers, they are academics, professional men, administrators, technical experts, scientists.

This fact has been largely unobserved because it is, in one way, well concealed. No one now claims to be a *Chün Tzu*, a gentleman. All are workers, and dress as such. But anyone who walks among the holiday crowds in China on a Sunday (for this is the day of rest in Communist China) or visits a university, a scientific institute, hospital or even a government office, will very soon hear the accents of the educated speech of China, unmistakable as educated English, and he will hear very little other speech. Dressed as workmen, and working very long hours, poorly paid in money terms, but not in want, the former scholars are still at the heart of the Chinese world, their abilities at the service of the new regime, professing the new orthodoxy, and to all appearances accepted, satisfied and secure. So surprising a consequence of the Communist revolution must be explained, if it is possible, and confirmed by clear and plentiful evidence.

The explanation does not lie in one cause, but in many factors. Firstly, the Communist regime, like every previous government of China must employ the educated class if it is to administer a vast country more thoroughly than ever before and at the same time push forward, at breakneck speed, a huge programme of industrial development and technical advance. Owing to the perhaps fortunate fact that the scholar gentry of China were deprived, during the Republic and Nationalist periods, of their old careers as civil servants and forced to turn to education, which in turn made them the only class learned in the new science of the West, they are now indispensable to the new regime. A great programme of popular education has been put under way; in one or two generations literacy will not be the monopoly of a small class, education will be available to the masses, and many able men of peasant origin will rise to the highest academic and professional posts. But even one generation is a long time.

In that interim the existing educated class, who are overwhelmingly of what is now called 'landlord origin', that is, former scholar gentry, have their chance to adjust, to win a place for themselves and a future for their children; a place very different and a future quite unlike that of their forefathers, but yet a place in the centre of the Chinese social system. They are, manifestly, as a whole, seizing this chance and embracing this future. The new dynasty has come to power and the scholars flock to serve it.

That is only a partial explanation, needing much qualification. If the needs of the regime, without which no opening could exist, are one evident cause of the present relatively favourable situation of this class, their own experiences and traditions are another, less obvious cause. The events of the past thirty years had greatly weakened and in many cases virtually destroyed the connection between the educated *élite* of the scholar gentry and the land. They had become an urban class, once well to do, but very nearly ruined by the Japanese

invasion and the economic chaos which followed it. The un-
controlled inflation of the post-war years of Nationalist rule,
the rise in prices, the impoverishment of a long war fought in
the heart of the country, the devastation of cities, the corruption of the government, partly itself a consequence of these evils,
had brought to the city-dwelling Chinese, the scholars among
them, the same misery which the warlords had inflicted on the
countryside in the early years of the Republic. Their wealth
was gone, their lands largely devastated, in some cases already
under Communist rule. They had only their now pitifully
inadequate salaries, paid late, devalued by the fantastic inflation.
As defenders of the Capitalist system they had been left with
singularly little to preserve.

Nor in fact, did many of them wish to preserve values which
had not been central to their former way of life. They were,
as a class, hereditary officials, not by virtue of birth, but by
education and intellect. Other professions had opened to them
when official service was closed, but these, too, were won by
education and brains, rewarded by annual salaries, largely
independent of accumulated capital or landed estate. Provided
these professions continued to flourish and no ideological or
class origin barrier was erected to exclude them, the scholars
were willing to serve and work at the only occupations for
which they were trained and which they alone could maintain.

The most important single difference between the Communist system as it operates in Russia and as it has been applied
to China is unquestionably the virtual absence in China of the
class war and the creation of an outcast class, such as the former
nobility of Russia in the earlier years of the Bolshevik regime.
The Chinese Communists of course profess the full doctrine of
Lenin, there is much talk in the propaganda of class enemies,
capitalists and landlords, which would lead an outside observer
to expect that the full rigour of revolutionary class warfare had
been applied to these opponents of the People. But on closer
examination it is found that all this is very largely theory.

The capitalists, if they remained in China, have been made

into partners in their own concerns with the state. Usually they act as general managers. Their incomes and profits are much reduced, but they are physically safe, they are styled 'National Bourgeoisie' and as such have a sanctioned role in society and are represented in the government by the small coalition party called the National Revolutionary Kuomintang. The landlords, if they were the active managers and residents on the estates, saw their land taken from them and divided, but they themselves received the same share as the other villagers, provided they were prepared to work it. Those whom the villagers accused of crimes and abuses were subjected to the celebrated mass trials, and in many cases suffered death. This class, that part of the scholar gentry which, being less intelligent than their cousins, remained to work the family lands, is the only class which suffered persecutions or penalties in any way comparable to the revolutionary violence of the Russian Bolshevik period. Estimates of those who suffered in the various campaigns against counter-reaction vary enormously, and the subject will be further discussed.

That some class or group, obnoxious to a large number of the population, should suffer in a social revolution is to be expected, though deplored. That certain members of this class, or a whole large section of it, should be accepted, employed, even honoured in spite of their unconcealed landlord-gentry origin, is the factor in the Chinese revolution which is new and different from the Russian model. This is clearly recognized and expressed openly in China. 'We can learn from Russia's mistakes.' 'We do not have to copy Russia in every respect; Chinese conditions are different.' Finally, and to the speakers conclusively, 'There is nothing in Marxist-Leninism against this policy.' These remarks are made to the foreign inquirer, not once, but very many times.

The scope and some examples of the application of this new policy of accepting all who submit and conform remain astonishing to the Western visitor. The Emperor Kuang Hsü, who died in 1908, had a younger brother Prince Tsai T'ao, who in the last days of the Empire was for a short time Chief of the General Staff Council and one of the most influential members of the Government.

The Empire fell; Tsai T'ao, an able man, made the best of the changed circumstances of the imperial family. He engaged in horse breeding, and was presently, under the Republic, given the directorship of the national stud. Unlike most Manchu princes, he had a business head, and leased his country palace to the university of Yenching, a Christian institution, his property having a common boundary with that of the university. For many years this part of the campus was always known as Tsai T'ao's garden. Inquiring, at Yenching, about the present status of this property (as Yenching has been now amalgamated with the National University of Peking) the answer came, 'Why, it still belongs to Tsai T'ao, of course.' 'And what does the former Prince do now?' 'He is, you know, the younger brother of the Emperor Kuang Hsü, and stands well with the government. He is still Director of the National Stud, and a People's Deputy for the Manchu Minority.' It is difficult to believe that a Romanoff Grand Duke, brother to the late Tsar, could live in Russia today—even if he desired to do so—and still harder to imagine that he could hold a public office and sit as a member of the body that is the equivalent to the national parliament.

Such an example from the top of the old social system may seem surprising, but perhaps exceptional; it can be paralleled by many who were never princes, but were quite certainly the sons of great officials of the Empire, landlords all, men who naturally by their abilities would have risen to the highest posts in the imperial service had the dynasty survived. They had turned instead, during the Republic, to letters and science; they include the most eminent names in those fields in China, and they are now at the head of the new institutes, universities and research organizations which the People's Republic has so proliferated.

Among them are men and women who occupied high posts under the Republic, who are Christians, who were educated in America, whose background and training was in the old

Chinese culture (which Mao Tse-tung claims must be destroyed) and whose later education was Western, scientific and international. Yet these people have accepted the new government and the new economic system. They have no lands, no capital, only their salaries and allowances. They are influential and frequently consulted by the members of the government. Some of them are probably members of the Communist Party.

Class origin has been discarded as a qualification for this membership, nor is it held against non-members who are willing to serve the state. It would be possible, though unnecessary, to list many names, often widely known in academic and scientific circles throughout the world, and many hundreds of others, less well known outside China, who have made this choice and found acceptance. No secret is made of their family origin or of their descent from eminent statesmen of the nineteenth century. The fact is often mentioned. It is clear that absolutely no prejudice is entertained against one whose father was a famous imperial statesman, or whose grandfather was one of the pillars of the declining Manchu dynasty.

It is thus a fact that the new regime has been accepted by, and has received, the more intelligent and above all the academic, professional and scientific members of the class of landlords—scholar gentry—which is officially reprobated as the former oppressors of the people, 'feudal remnants' and other hard names. But if the Communists have received these people, it is on their terms, not such as the same class would have made with an old incoming dynasty. They have not restored the ancient system of government, they cannot once more accumulate wealth and lands, they do not live in privileged luxury. A Communist official of Canton city, himself, by his speech, a man of this same origin, put it clearly enough. When asked how it was that many members of the former educated, landlord class were now eminent Party men, and why it was necessary to maintain a form of coalition government in which one Party, the Democratic League, had the role of representing in the government this class of intellectuals; he replied that members of that class could only become Communist Party members when they had 'wholly renounced the standpoint, outlook and habits of mind of their class of origin'. Not by any means all, or even most of the intellectuals now in government service have achieved this metamorphosis.

It is not, perhaps, expected of them; instead they must have first submitted to a course of re-education—or brainwashing—a prolonged study of Marxist-Leninism, attendance at many hundreds of study meetings, sojourn for some months in a rural village so that they may understand how the people live, and what wrongs were done to them in former times. Finally, they must publish a confession, a full and detailed document showing the errors of their former ideas and ways, the faults of their education and upbringing, the mistakes which resulted from these, their full and complete realization of what is now required of them. If this document is regarded as not fully sincere, or as incomplete, it must be amended, after further study, and a new version published. In some cases this process was repeated several times. The comparison will be odious to some, but the Instruction which a heretic receives before being admitted to the Catholic Church has many points of similarity, the main difference being the public character of the proceedings in China.

The economic and political factors which made this solution less difficult for the Chinese intelligentsia than it might be for the same class in other countries have been glanced at, but it is clear that these would not in themselves suffice to cause so large and widespread a conversion unless some other, psychological cause were at work. That cause lies in the sense of shame which the Chinese of this class felt for the fallen condition of their country, the contempt in which it was held in the world —a fact which their foreign education made them better able to appreciate than their stay-at-home relatives. They were the near descendants of the rulers of a great Empire, which, less than a century ago, still held itself to be the centre of civilization, the fount of all the arts and refinements. They grew up in a country undergoing the most senseless and futile type of revolution, one which put power into the hands of ignorant and corrupt men or brutal ex-bandit militarists. All their lives they had seen things go from bad to worse, China falling further and further behind in the international race, her rights invaded, her territory annexed, almost without resistance, often bartered away by venal traitors. They were utterly disgusted, deeply mortified by the failure of the nation which their forefathers had made the greatest power in Asia, which even the early Western travellers had respected and admired.

No change was really for the better. The Kuomintang betrayed the hopes which many had set upon it in the early days of its triumph. They were not at first attracted to the Communist Party. In its early guerrilla period it made ruthless war upon the country landlords, who were their cousins. But intellectual Marxism began, at a very early date, to invade the universities and colour the literature of the time. The example of Russia was potent and seemed far less repulsive to the Chinese than to the nations of western Europe. They saw that Russia had raised herself from defeat and ruin under the Communists. An ancient, decadent absolutism, like their own, had been transformed into a powerful industrial state. The authoritarian character of the Soviet system troubled them less, since their own experience for centuries had been to live under and work for an absolute monarchy whose power was limited more by its inefficiency than by its lack of pretensions. As the official class they had always run the risk of suffering the violent penalties of imperial disfavour, and such eventualities were an accepted part of their tradition. The Empire might have been weak, but it was never so weak that it could not at will decapitate and destroy its own servants.

So gradually, even before the Japanese invasion, the younger men began to turn to Communism, to examine this new doctrine, to discover what it aimed to do, why it claimed to be the one sure solution. After the Communist movement established itself in Yenan, following the Long March from south China, its policy changed from one of violence towards the landlords to an appeal to all patriotic elements to resist the

43

manifest designs of Japan. This appeal aroused a great response among the younger intellectuals and students. Many hundreds left their universities or homes to go to Yenan and enrol in the Communist university which had been set up there to attract them. The number of those of scholar gentry origin who were now received by the Communists was certainly very large, and exercised a perceptible influence on those, who, however disgusted with the vacillation and corruption of the Kuomintang, were not prepared for a drastic renunciation of their old way of life.

The Japanese invasion, which proved the Kuomintang incapable of defending the country, and threatened to extinguish its independence, proved a turning point. China had no real friends. The Western Powers, themselves not yet at war, were afraid to antagonize powerful Japan. They still hoped against hope to save their trading interests in the Treaty Ports. Those who had believed in Western Democracy and hoped for aid from its homelands were disconcerted and discouraged. The Communists explained why these things must be so, declared that the only hope for China was in national and popular resistance, and organized that resistance, very effectively, behind the Japanese lines. When the Western Powers were forced into the Pacific War by the attacks made upon them by Japan, they at once suffered a series of catastrophic defeats. Their aid proved, for a time, useless. The old illusion of their invincibility was shaken. Meantime the Kuomintang decayed. So far from rising to the test of war and invasion by shedding some of its evil ways and basing itself upon the nation's will to resist, it withdrew to the inaccessible western provinces, where it became more subject to corruption and nepotism than it had been in Nanking.

When the war ended, as a result of victories won by the Western Allies, China's condition was more pitiful than ever. The country was now deeply divided between the Communist-held rural areas in the north, former Japanese occupied territory, and the south and west which the Kuomintang reoccupied. Civil war seemed imminent, and all feared that such a war might finally ruin the country. The government exhibited in this dangerous crisis wilful obstinacy, gross corruption, brutal repression. Feeling that the obvious drift of the intelligentsia towards the Communists represented a true '*trahison des clercs*', it treated the universities with scant respect, persecuted well-known scholars, made secret arrests among students, planted its spies and informers in every academic institution.

All attempts to mediate failing, the civil war broke out, but contrary to the fears of most Chinese, was neither long nor very devastating; for from the first the victory of the Communist side was apparent. The Kuomintang armies would not fight. Huge surrenders of whole divisions, even of armies, revealed the fact that the people, as represented by the conscript soldiers, had no more loyalty and hope in the Kuomintang than the scholars. The Communists won the war by default, because their opponents would not resist. The attitude of the Chinese intellectuals to this event was simple. 'It cannot be worse than before, it may be better, it is at least something that has not been tried before. Let us see what they do.' They were soon to see, but also to find that this attitude of passive acceptance and sideline onlooking was not acceptable to the new masters of the Chinese world.

It has been very generally assumed in the West, more particularly in America, where objective consideration of the facts about Communist China is inhibited by official disapproval and an absence of first-hand evidence, that the apparatus of re-education, or brainwashing, confession and self-accusation which it is admitted by all has been applied to the Chinese educated class, forms only one, open, aspect of a secret and pervading terror which has broken their spirit and brought them to abject submission. Evidence from the purges of Soviet Russia, and more recently from Kruschev's famous speech of 14 February 1956 are brought forward to support this theory. The question of whether this hypothesis is true, or inadequate to explain all the facts, is very important, since it touches upon the central question which must be asked concerning the Communist regime: how it maintains its power.

The first piece of evidence which an observer can offer is the attitude of mind which he perceived to prevail among old friends, known for many years, who belong to the group who are suspected of having been subjected to this form of terrorization. It would be at least improbable that such people should all, unsuspected for years, have the talents of consummate actors. It is reasonable to think that their behaviour reflects the real state of their minds, whether nervous and anxious, calm and collected, or what you will. On the basis of this evidence it must be said that tokens of broken spirit, abject submission, fear and anxiety were not encountered. Nor on the other hand, did these people show no changed attitude from their former demeanour. One cannot mix for more than a very short time with the Chinese intellectuals and professional men of the present day without detecting obvious signs of a very new, a wholly changed approach to life and its problems.

The Chinese intellectual used to cultivate an apparent dilettantism, an easy charm, a polished sophistication, manners which often really concealed wounded pride, bitter frustration and an angry consciousness of the futility of wasted talents and opportunities denied. These mannerisms have gone; the courtesy and the charm, surely innate, remain, but now there is a sense of determination, an earnestness of purpose, an admitted absorption in the work on hand which is new and uncharacteristic of the past. With this goes, very often, an attitude which can only be described as a sense of sin, or more accurately, remorse; the remorse of the rich: or rather of those who once were rich. This takes the form of a frank avowal of all that was neglected by this class in the old society. The absence of care for the poor, either on a national or on a charitable basis, the indifference to public health, the toleration of exploitation and organized vice, the assumption, as one of them put it, 'that the people were of a different species to us'.

These attitudes, or some of them, are not uncommon in Western society among men of goodwill or strong religious views. But they are quite new, on any class-wide scale, in

China. Nor can it be in doubt that to a great extent they are the fruits of the process of re-education, the phrases which may well have been found in a published confession are heard in conversation. Yet this is not the whole explanation. The phrase which is more used than any other by a man or woman who seeks to explain to an old foreign friend why they now work for the regime, accept it, and acclaim it, is, 'It was when I saw what they (the Communists) were doing for the people, that I realized it was wrong to hold off, that I must work for them, too.'

The claim that the Communists have done things of merit for the people will be examined in later chapters, the point is that many thousands believe this to be true, and the belief has acted upon them with great power. All the foreign remedies, democracy, a Republic, a Party State based on the existing society, foreign education, all regarded as panaceas in their day, had failed. But no one had done anything for the People of China. They remained, as under the Empire, indeed worse off, poor, neglected, unhealthy, exploited and despised. The Communists claimed that this was the clue to all the failures, this neglect of the vital forces of the nation vitiated all reforms. They also claimed that the educated class, the landlords and gentry, the erstwhile governors of China for so many centuries, were primarily responsible for this neglect. They should pay the penalty for their selfishness and indifference.

Still, they needed this class; China must use all her talents; re-educated, brainwashed, brought to an understanding of where the fault lay, what must be done to remedy it, what sacrifices were required, what efforts demanded, the class of the scholars, purged of their less desirable members, deprived of their old economic foundation, but still equipped with their brains and their skills, could be redeemed and employed. They would soon cease to be a special class, education and selection would bring up the talented poor to their level, would permeate the new ruling group, would take a long step towards the Communist goal, the classless society.

The present condition of the Chinese scholar class is thus an intermediate one. It will not endure, but it will merge into something still forming, it will slowly be changed into an integral part of the new society which Mao Tse-tung predicted, and which the regime he presides over strives so tirelessly to achieve. But, 'we can learn from Russia's mistakes'. China could not afford a vast purge of the educated and the skilled; the explanation of the changed character of the scholar class, as of its present relatively favourable situation, is the fruit of the lesson learned from the errors of the Bolsheviks. There are better ways of transforming a society than by wholesale liquidation and massacre: more certain and lasting success can be attained by converting opponents than by persecuting them to death. Persuasion and Propaganda, the techniques of the modern age, are the chosen instruments of Chinese Communist government. Force is kept in reserve.

CHAPTER THREE

PERSUASION AND PROPAGANDA

'EDUCATION THROUGH PERSUASION is the principal method of dealing with class contradictions and the class struggle.'*

The word propaganda has acquired, in our age, an evil connotation, meaning to the average man lies disseminated by his own or some other government with the intention of misleading the public and concealing some unpleasant truth. It is almost with a shock that the modern, if he did not know it, learns that the word came into use in the Catholic Church to mean propagating the faith of Christ; in other words, the attempt to convince unbelievers of truths in which the propagandists themselves most earnestly believe: the exact opposite of the present colloquial use of the word. If the efforts of the Chinese government to convince their former opponents of the value of their doctrines and bring them to belief in the Communist interpretation of history and economics are described as 'propaganda', many will suppose that this implies that the Communists themselves do not believe these things, but are merely seeking to deceive their compatriots for selfish ends.

Without in any way prejudging the question of whether or no these Marxist ideas have a value for China, it would be quite certainly mistaken to suppose that the Chinese Communist Party does not wholeheartedly believe in them, and that its members are not ready to spend time, infinite trouble, and great patience in expounding these beliefs to those whom they hope to convert. To the very great surprise of the Chinese people themselves, and also of the foreign observers, the first, the dominant, and the incessant technique of Communist rule

* Speech made at third session of the first National People's Congress, Peking, June 1956, by Li Wei-han, Director of the Department of United Front Work, Central Committee of the Chinese Communist Party, Vice-Chairman of the Standing Committee, National People's Congress.

turned out to be not violence, but talk; talk, talk, unending talks. '*K'ai Hui*', to hold, or attend, a meeting, became the duty of every citizen, very often the burdensome duty, the inescapable obligation to talk and be talked to, occupied time he wished to devote to his business, his pleasure, or merely to sleep. At first relieved to find no revolutionary violence in evidence, the Chinese citizens of the early Communist period became almost restive under the contrary obligation, not to obey unthinkingly, but to explain themselves, to listen to reasons, to study doctrines. Communist rule seemed to be an unending viva voce examination.

Six years later this system has crystallized into a vast apparatus of Persuasion. Since the persuaders are no doubt convinced believers in what they say, and sincerely hope to convert the nation to these ideas, this system is not propaganda in the modern false sense, but much nearer to the original meaning of the word. It very soon becomes clear that the system of confessions and re-education applied to the scholar class is only one small, but important facet of the chief instrument of government which the new regime has adopted as the mainstay of its authority, or as it would be put in China, of the dictatorship of the People. This fact will seem strange to those who assume that every Communist regime must be a close copy of the Russian model, and that every population under Communist rule must share the sentiments which undoubtedly animate the peoples of, say, Hungary and other eastern European nations.

Moral suasion, precept and exhortation had always had a value in Chinese statecraft, both in practice and theory. Whatever the reality, Chinese political theory had always decried the use of force, had upheld the belief that the good and virtuous ruler did not need soldiers to defend him, that barbarians and other enemies were more surely overcome by the display of virtue than by force of arms. Very few, if any of the Chinese Emperors, wholly relied on this utopian expectation, but since the startling failure of the early centralizing Ch'in dynasty (255–206 BC) which had relied solely on force and derided the value of persuasion, no Chinese dynasty had omitted the duty of inculcating the Confucian virtues by education and by precept.

It was a very old and strong conviction among all Chinese that the use of force is an admission of failure; a doctrine central to Confucian teaching. The Communist Party was not introducing a wholly new idea of government by persuasion, or what would formerly have been called by the power of virtue, but it was introducing a new technique for applying an ancient policy. There can be no doubt that the Chinese people, who had always been exhorted and preached at by their rulers, find this form of leadership much more familiar and less distasteful than nations which have for some centuries, at least, lived under a democratic system which permits and encourages the contests of opposed opinions.

Thus the importance now attached to Persuasion and Propaganda in China is characteristic of the country, but not necessarily of eastern Europe, where the oldest political tradition is that of Byzantine autocracy. Not only had the Chinese a different political background to the Russians and Slavs, but the circumstances in which the Chinese Communist Party came to power differed entirely from the history of either Russia or her satellites. These varying traditions, the ancient Chinese belief in the power of virtue, the modern story of the Chinese Communist Party, have together produced an atmosphere sharply different from that prevailing in the other Communist countries.

Unlike their eastern European colleagues the Chinese Communists did not acquire power by following in the wake of the advancing flood of the Russian Red Army, nor, like their Russian predecessors, did they seize the government of all China in one swift revolutionary coup. They fought, alone, a long and doubtful struggle which endured for twenty years. At no time, until after final victory was achieved, did they receive even the assistance of supplies and war material from Russia. At best the Russian occupation of Manchuria at the surrender of Japan enabled the Chinese Communist army to seize and use the great dumps of war material which the Japanese had to abandon in the Manchurian countryside. These were without question a significant factor in the victory of the People's Liberation Army, as it was called, but they were not the main factor, nor comparable in any way with the support which Russia gave to the Communist Parties of the eastern European countries.

Decisive victory was obtained by military skill, profiting by the errors of the Kuomintang, and also by the defection in battle of large Nationalist units, who no longer had any stomach for the Kuomintang.* These events created a climate of opinion unlike that of the eastern European countries, and one in which the Communist Party had a different task to undertake. They were the military victors, who had ended, at long last, the endemic civil war, and brought peace and unity to the distracted nation. But they were not content to be just another regime founded on force and the passing goodwill of a war-weary nation. They were also missionaries who saw as their real task the much more difficult feat of converting an individualist people to sincere belief in the collective principle.

This was not possible by the simple use of force. Power can be used to destroy more easily than to create; the great cultural revolutions of history were often initiated by forceful means, but have always been consolidated by the conquest of the minds rather than the bodies of mankind. Open, armed hostility whether by Kuomintang 'remnants' or dispossessed landlords could be, and was, subject to military or police repression. But such methods have been confined to a comparatively small sector of the nation and do not represent the foundations of policy.

Very widely differing estimates of the number of those slain or imprisoned for counter-revolutionary activity have been made, both by outside observers who are partisans of the Nationalists, and observers within China who are either favour-

* O. Edmund Clubb, *Chiang Kai-shek's Waterloo: The Battle of Hwai-Hai*. The Pacific Historical Review. Vol. XXV, No. 4. November 1956. University of California Press. Berkeley 4.

able to the People's Republic or objective in their approach. No certainty is possible, but the most careful and thorough investigation carried out by foreign observers on the spot, whose official position and political standpoint excludes the possibility of Communist sympathies, suggests that 50,000 may be the real approximate total of those put to death throughout China for 'treasonable acts'.

The number is itself great, but the percentage of a population which exceeds 560 millions is very small. It is not a fraction which would bulk large in the experience of the average Chinese citizen and family, even if in certain groups it was more hardly felt. Whatever the real figures, which may never be accurately known, the fact of importance in assessing the reactions of the Chinese people to their new government is that they have no consciousness of having lived through a 'terror'. They are, on the other hand, very conscious of having undergone a process of reformation, and of 'Liberation'.

Liberation, the word always used for the victory of the Communists both in the sense of the actual event (before Liberation, after Liberation, etc.) and of the transformation of the country since 1949, is of course one of the main slogans of the system of Persuasion and Propaganda. Another slogan, 'the War of Resistance', is always used to mean the war against Japan, this conflict is never referred to as a national war against Japan. The purpose of these terms is to instil a point of view until it becomes an axiom, an innate belief, something which is accepted without question or cavil. 'Liberation', because old China must be exhibited as a system of double exploitation, that of the landlords internally, of the foreign imperialists externally. 'War of Resistance', because the Japanese people must not be held responsible for the sins of their rulers, the 'imperialists', who were 'resisted by the People of China'. The Japanese, like other peoples, are depicted as suffering from the exploitation of their rulers and capitalists until for them, too, the day of their Liberation dawns.

But there can be no doubt that if the 'War of Resistance' is still felt by thousands and thousands to have been none the less very much a war against that part of the Japanese people who acted as brutal and cruel masters, Liberation is by a far greater number accepted as an accurate description of the facts. On this field the Communists had an easy run; no one can be found in China who has a word of sympathy or regret for the regime of Chiang Kai-shek. The courteous restraint, with which Chinese friends will discuss other countries, and other aspects of the international scene, breaks down when the Kuomintang and its record are mentioned. Then real bitterness, unassuaged hate and anger come to the surface. It must also be recorded that the bitterness still felt and shown towards the United States, at least among ordinary individual people, springs almost entirely from the close association which the government of the United States still maintains with the Nationalist regime in Formosa.

The first and easiest victory of Persuasion and Propaganda has been to convince the Chinese people, who needed very little encouragement, that the evils of the old society and the backwardness of China were mainly the result of Nationalist neglect and misrule—a verdict which history will no doubt qualify in many ways, but which for this generation has become Truth. The second purpose, directed more particularly towards the educated class, can be described in the terminology of older Chinese moral teaching as 'to arouse a sense of shame'. Shame and remorse for the treatment of the poor by the former rich, a constant enlargement of the theme of the selfishness, viciousness and anti-social character of the old system. The corollary is that these vices produced national debility, led to the encroachments of the foreigner, the Japanese invasion, every other modern calamity, and that from this catastrophe the Communist Party saved the nation by its leadership, and by the response among 'progressive elements' which this leadership evoked.

The progressive elements are the classes which, in part or wholly, co-operated with the Communists and accepted their regime. They are represented, politically, by the smaller parties forming the coalition government which rules China.

The only two of these smaller parties which are of any significance are the Democratic League, and the National Revolutionary Kuomintang. The Democratic League arose in the war and pre-war years as a party of the liberal element in Chinese society, in practice of the academic and professional men, the scholar gentry who had taken up those pursuits, and aimed to introduce genuine democratic government modelled on the European or American models. It never gained the support of military power, and thus was left defenceless against the Kuomintang, which wanted no such development, and distrusted the class who supported the Democratic League. It was at first covertly persecuted, and finally openly suppressed by Chiang Kai-shek (July 1947) at the time when he reopened the civil war against the Communists. Surviving members and leaders of the Democratic League then joined the Communists, were admitted as a party to the coalition government, and now have the role of representing the academic and intellectual classes in the regime.

The National Revolutionary Kuomintang has a stranger history. It is at first sight surprising enough to find that any Party in coalition with the Communist government can bear a name which includes the term 'Kuomintang'. The Party, however, stems from the old Kuangsi group, Kuomintang generals from that southern province who had for several decades maintained an attitude of dissidence to Chiang Kai-shek, partly based on provincial jealousies, and partly the comparative neglect of the south after the Nanking government was established, and some real objections to the later policy followed by that government.

That its founders were not, originally, men of goodwill towards the Communists is very clearly illustrated by one incident in the life of the founder and leader of this Party, General Li Chi-shen, often known to foreigners in the south of China by the Cantonese pronunciation of his name, Li Chai-sum. There has recently been completed in Canton a fine memorial tomb and park in honour of the 'Martyrs of the Canton Commune of 1928'. The buildings are elegant, the

E

gardens well planned. Visitors are told that many thousands of the Communists who perished in that ill-fated rising are now buried here, their bones retrieved, after 'Liberation', from the common execution ground, where they had lain for more than twenty years.

The Canton Commune was indeed a sanguinary uprising, in which not only the revolutionaries suffered very heavy losses. Memory stirring, the guide was asked, 'But which Kuomintang general was responsible for the massacre?' 'Oh,' came the reply, 'Li Chi-shen of course; you know that he is now a Deputy Prime Minister and Leader of the National Revolutionary Kuomintang?' When it was pointed out that this consummation of a political career, begun under such ill-omened auspices, was without a parallel in Russia, the replies, 'We can learn from Russian mistakes', and 'He has subsequently changed his attitude; any Chinese who sincerely repents of his past conduct towards the People and now serves them is acceptable', were made. Repentance and remorse; sincere conversion, redemption through work for the People; even Chiang Kaishek himself, so one was assured, could return to China in peace, and perhaps to some office, if he really manifested these signs of grace.

If there is thus no one too eminent to be redeemed through Persuasion, however difficult, however long the task, there is equally no one too obscure, or too humble to be ignored and neglected by the indefatigible Persuaders. The divorce laws of new China, recast to liberate women from the bondage of 'feudal subservience', at first were mainly directly to that end, the freeing of concubines from unwelcome marriages, the parting of incompatibles, the establishment in real practice of equality of the sexes. More recently, injustice corrected, the attitude has changed. Marriage is not lightly to be broken up; the efforts of the Courts are now turned towards reconciliation and adjustment, divorce is growing more difficult.

The Supreme Court of Peking was reviewing a case between man and wife, in which the wife, a girl of twenty-four, wished to divorce her husband, aged nineteen. They came of peasant stock, but both were now workers in the city. They had been married, before Liberation, by their parents' arrangement, under the old laws. The lower Court had already rejected the wife's petition. She had appealed, and the case had now come before the higher Court, from which there lies no further appeal. It was argued very informally. No counsel were present, only a bench of three judges, one being a woman. The parties sat on two chairs before the bench, addressed them at will, were questioned, made answers, with little sense of awe or embarrassment.

The wife argued that the marriage, of which there were no children, had never been a reality; no sense of affection remained, they were incompatible—he was clearly a weakling, she a strong, determined character. From the first it was evident that the Court was concerned to preserve the marriage. True, the husband was reminded that he could not retain his wife, as she claimed was the case, merely because her earnings swelled the family budget. Women had freedom now. But the wife was even more stringently urged to reflect, to reconsider, to seek for some evidences of continuing affection, to make a further effort to make the marriage a success. She constantly and vehemently denied that any such possibility remained. Finally the Court refused her a divorce. They must try again, they would be helped by their Work Committee, by their Street Committee, by the Court itself.

Asked what form this help could take, seeing that, even as the Court was rising, the wife continued to interrupt and detain them with her reiterated pleas, the answer came that all these committees, her relatives, her work comrades, the judges themselves, whenever they had the time, would continue to exhort and persuade her to accept her status and continue the marriage. Yes; even the judges of the Supreme Court of Peking would make time or find time to undertake this thankless, and seemingly hopeless task. No effort would be spared.

Adultery is a criminal offence in China today; they might live apart, if they could find lodgings, but without a divorce they could not part finally. When asked what would happen if, despite this flood of exhortation, the wife remained firm in her opinions, it was rather reluctantly admitted that then, no doubt, the case, in several months' time, would be once more considered. Young women who were themselves ardent enthusiasts for the regime, gave their opinion that the girl would finally, if she persevered, get her freedom. Even to Persuasion and Propaganda there is a limit.

Water will wash away the hardest rock, persuasion and exhortation might ultimately shake the resolution of a strong-minded girl, but for the most of the people of China there are no such personal reasons for resisting the persistent erosion of the system of persuasion. There are, in fact, good reasons for accepting the ideas and exhortations which the regime un-remittingly puts forward. The campaign to clean up the filth of cities and villages, to enforce hygiene, to eliminate flies and rats, carried on with a vast apparatus of publicity, met with a wholehearted response. China is now a clean country, by any standard. Many virulent endemic diseases have been stamped out, others greatly reduced. Everyone appreciates the improvement which these campaigns have brought, everyone knows that so striking a change could only have been accomplished by the co-operation of millions, and that this was won by persuasion, publicity and constant exhortation.

No adverse views, no doubts, no contrary opinions can be published; criticism of 'why' is not possible; of how the work is being done, it is welcomed and publicized. Criticism is another essential part of the system. Men must not merely obey, they must obey intelligently, of their free will, understanding the reasons for their actions, working towards an end which is comprehensible and desirable. So they must be persuaded that these ends are such, that the means employed are correct, and if they doubt the latter point they are free to say so, are indeed at weekly meetings encouraged to speak out so that all may hear the criticism and those in charge defend their actions, or amend them. 'We invite your criticisms'; every institution makes this claim, and keeps a book in which such criticisms can be recorded.

Public opinion, silent on the great issues which are not contested in the national Press, may be voiced on the methods employed through the innumerable meetings and study groups which every citizen attends, and also aired in the correspondence columns of the newspapers. Policy, laid down by the Government, under the guidance of the Communist Party, is decided at a level where no hint of contrary opinions voiced or alternatives suggested is revealed to the nation. Execution of the policy is open to the criticism of any citizen of goodwill who makes his point at a meeting or by a letter. Whether there comes a point where criticism of methods begins to imply dissatisfaction with aims remains obscure.

In Western and non-Communist societies the modern medium of advertisement has gained a significant place in the economy and the life of the nation. People see, every day, urgent commands to buy this or that article, the press carries many pages of advertising, and the great expense which manufacturers incur in these campaigns has been shown to be well worth the money. Without advertisement the sales of even the most useful and popular articles fall away. Although everyone knows that the claims are exaggerated, that some other brand is just as good, that all are sold at the same price, nevertheless advertisement still determines whether demand shall be brisk or flagging.

In China there is no commercial advertising; instead there is compelling, pervasive and universal advertisement of the policies of the government; their current demands from the people in the way of national effort, or emphasis upon some aspect of policy which at the time it is desired to stress. Press, broadcasting, hoardings, public speeches, party canvassing, meetings and study groups all sing the same tune, all gear into the universal system of persuasion no matter how important or how relatively trivial the subject may be. 'We must liberate Tai Wan' (Formosa)—the implications of which slogan are certainly vast—and 'kill rats, flies and sparrows', 'keep your streets clean', 'Promote Advanced Worker movement', 'Onward to the Higher Stage of Co-operative Farming'.

The citizen, constantly subjected to this barrage of admonition, on matters so diverse, and never hearing or seeing any contrary opinion, must sooner or later yield his judgement and accept the ideas so proffered. Some are obviously sensible and wise. Others obscure in their bearing on his life, or again of the greatest significance to his occupation, but all come to him with compelling force, ceaselessly, everywhere, vouched for, it seems to him, by the manifest fact that many of these policies have produced great and beneficial transformations, so why should he doubt that the others are just as likely to do so when translated into action. He is not in the position of the Western citizen, reading advertisements for two kinds of soap or motor-cars. He cannot choose another policy, nor discriminate between those offered to him. The Western citizen buys his favourite brand of soap because, the manufacturers have found out, he has constantly been told to do so. The Chinese support the policies of their government for the same reason.

The purposes to which the system of persuasion have been put are not wholly concerned with campaigns to enforce some part of government policy. These objectives are pursued by the more obvious means of advertisement, slogan, press article and radio talks. There is also the aspect of what can only be called Moral Reformation, or indeed, Puritanism, Communist Puritanism, which has just as surely been engendered by the more subtle working of the persuasion mechanism. China is represented as a nation recovering from an almost mortal sickness. The doctors, the Communist Party, not only warn the patient that he must take care of his health, abstain from indulgence and high living, but they also warn him that one major cause of his sickness was not only the wrong regimen he followed, but his moral weakness and open vices.

Prostitution, free love, adultery, unnatural vice, these are no longer merely sins, they are crimes, punishable with terms of imprisonment. Here is one great paradox of the New China. The vices against which generations of Christian missionaries strove, with slight success, have at one stroke been abolished, suppressed, or at least driven into the deepest concealment, by a government which openly and firmly rejects the Christian and every other deist theology. The virtues which the Christian missionaries instilled, laboriously, into a handful of their small flock—austerity of living, temperance, clean language, a sense of sin, moral purity—these things have now become, to an amazing degree, common attitudes among millions of men and women.

China was famous, among those foreigners who could understand the language, for the truly phenomenal obscenity of its oaths, the frequency and indifference to mixed company with which such language was used, the strange fact that 'turtle's egg', the worst term of abuse in the language, was the only one which could have been printed in a Western book. And this was only because the subtlety of its indecency was not communicable without a lengthy commentary. All this has disappeared. Such terms are never heard, either on the lips of carters and muleteers, from which they were hardly ever absent, or in street disputes, at which the crowds used to gather to appreciate the competition in abuse. Once only, in a month of travel, was the commonest, and perhaps the least offensive of such expressions heard from any angry, jostled passenger. Those present reacted as if they had seen a snake. Startled looks, followed by visible embarrassment; shocked train attendants hastened forward to admonish.

This Roundhead attitude to swearing, so astonishingly changed from the old habitual indifference, is but a surface manifestation of what must truly be the most profound effect yet produced by Persuasion and Propaganda. Austerity of living, dull and shapeless clothes, are accepted not merely as hardships of the revolutionary era, but as good in themselves. It needed a new turn to the propaganda, put forward as usual through every medium, to induce women to adopt more graceful styles and gayer colours. Guests may be entertained, officially, with all the delicacies of the superb Chinese cuisine, an art which fortunately still flourishes. But it may be doubted very much whether this sort of food is ever seen when guests are not present. On those railway dining cars, off the main routes, where foreign delegations rarely travel, the food was plainer, coarser, less appetizing than was ever found in a wayside inn of one of the poorer provinces of China. Then there were always delicacies for those who could pay for them, now such food is kept for guests and for places which guests may frequent.

Constant emphasis of past vices, which if sometimes true, is certainly greatly overdrawn, has induced in the younger generation an almost fanatical horror of the society of pre-Communist China. Driving down one of the streets of the former International Settlement in Shanghai, the young girl of twenty who was interpreting, remarked to a visitor, 'In the old days you could not enter this street; there were nothing but prostitutes, pimps, and gangsters.' The visitor asked, pointing out that she could not have been more than fourteen at the time of Liberation, and was certainly well brought up in an erstwhile 'bourgeois family', how she had known what Kiangsi Road was like in the bad old days. The question seemed to surprise her, she thought a minute, and then replied, 'But, of course, we have read all about it in our study group.'

It would seem that history, at least social history, is being taught in a manner quite the reverse of that, almost equally distorted, on which the nineteenth- and early twentieth-century Western child was brought up. Instead of the Christmas Card picture of Merry England, the jolly innkeeper, the benevolent squire and the simple, healthy, devoted yokels, the Chinese child now shrinks in horror from (or perhaps revels in) a nightmare China of slave girls beaten by cruel masters, prostitutes imprisoned in garrets till they died of diseases, gangsters kidnapping innocent girls, poor men driven to suicide by grasping landlords. All of which was, on occasion, certainly true.

The young may grow up as genuine puritan fanatics; for those who remember old China, both republican and even imperial, the men of forty, and their still living fathers, this aspect of the new regime must involve difficult adjustments. It is normal for older men to deplore the follies and vices of their youth, but rarer for them to feel really ashamed of those gay days. Many thousands who now see what is said and printed about wicked imperialist foreign-controlled Shanghai, must know that much is false and the rest exaggerated. Yet no evidence of this widespread knowledge is found in conversation. The Moral Reformation is accepted with fervent enthusiasm by the young, with pride and satisfaction by the older generation.

Western observers recently in China have frequently remarked upon the new puritanism, and the striking change in the condition and outlook of Chinese women. It is assumed that the 'asexual' quality now so evident in these women who work at occupations hitherto reserved for men is something entirely new, a product of the Communist regime. To Europeans it is not only the disappearance of prostitution and vice that appears astonishing and almost incredible, it is also, even more, the obvious lack of interest in love and sex, the serious character of the young people of China, their evident preoccupation with their work rather than with members of the opposite sex. This seems to Westerners unnatural, forced, untrue to the real character of the people.

This assumption needs careful examination. The West has formed for itself a picture of Asia which owes a great deal to the Arabian Nights on the romantic side, to the experience of seaports and their inhabitants on the material, practical side. The picture so formed is of peoples naturally licentious, without the restraint of Christian morals, uninhibited sexually and devoted to luxury and debauchery. The rich and powerful Asian, be he Indian rajah or Chinese mandarin, was represented, as Macauley put it, spending his time 'chewing *bhang* and fondling concubines', smoking opium being substituted in the Chinese case for the first accomplishment. The facility with which Western residents acquired their own local concubines was not taken as any reflection on the morality of Europeans so much as a confirmation of the traditional picture of Asia.

But the real Asia is, has always been, austere. It is, in Asian eyes, the Europeans, right back to the ancient Greeks, who have always been free, licentious, sex centred. Art reveals the facts; the Chinese never represented the human figure nude, except in works of undisguised pornography. Nor could they readily believe that Western art was not in fact very thinly disguised pornography. The very rich might indeed take undue advantage of a marriage system which recognized polygamy, but the Chinese and other Asians may be pardoned for thinking, as they did, and probably still do, that such a system, with all its abuses, was preferable to the unregulated amours of their Western counterparts, who paid such scant attention to the bonds of matrimony.

Old-fashioned Chinese were scandalized at the light and, to them, licentious clothing of Western women; they assumed that the free social intercourse of the sexes masked, or even proclaimed, an equally free and unrestrained sexual licence. A great part of the Western literature they read seemed to confirm this idea. The decorous and sophisticated portrayal of feminine charm and intrigue on the Chinese stage was contrasted with the flaunting of sexual attractions in the European 'leg show'. The debauchery which the Westerner believed to be the secret entertainment of the Asian rich was apparently the everyday fare of the average European. It might be true that the degenerate heirs of the Moguls had indeed, within the privacy of their harems, neglected their duties in favour of 'chewing *bhang* and fondling concubines'; it seemed to the Chinese people that the members of the Western nations whom they saw every day on the verandahs of the large hotels and clubs were similarly and publicly engaged, drinking whisky rather than chewing betel nut.

Consequently the untravelled Chinese would have been astounded to learn that the peoples of these profligate nations regarded his own as licentious and immoral; his travelled cousin was indignant and scandalized at the extraordinary ignorance and prejudice of the Western peoples, and also experienced great difficulty in deciding how far the freedom of Western manners did in fact connote a far less rigorous morality than that of his own society.

In such seaport cities as Shanghai, or such colonies as Hong Kong, Western manners invaded China with Western commerce. A certain element in the Chinese people responded to these influences which were held to be modern as well as Western, and therefore desirable. But to the vast mass of the people they remained alien, repellent and incomprehensible. It must therefore be considered as possible that the new puritanism, the asexual character of Chinese social life today, is not so much new and characteristic of the Communist regime as a re-emergence of Chinese values which, although always held by the majority of the Chinese people, have been overlaid by the temporary dominance of Western fashions. In Chinese society love was never the determinant factor in marriage, for marriages were arranged by parents; bride and groom met for the first time at the altar. Consequently the whole European tradition on this wide field of social life was outside Chinese experience.

The Chinese erotic tale more often than not begins at the point where the European love story stops—at marriage. Only in the last and perhaps the greatest of the Chinese classical novels, *The Dream in the Red Chamber*, are the problems of the arranged marriage, frustrated affection, and the emotional stresses of young men and women treated from a point of view which the Western reader will find sympathetic. In the other famous novels of the Ming and later periods these situations are resolved in a manner which to the European would seem unreal: by the happy and tolerant association of two or more heroines in the household of the hero, one as wife, another as concubine; or by a more realistic but unromantic portrayal of the hero as a collector of women for whom he feels lust, but never love.

In actual practice the overwhelming majority of the Chinese people were monogamous, for the simple economic reason that a poor man cannot support more than one wife and a restricted number of children. He did not choose this partner, nor did she have any say in her destiny. She remained for years the drudge and servant of her mother-in-law, whose authority over her was far greater than that of her husband. For such a family the conception of romantic love had no meaning, nor did the excesses of the wealthy have for them as much force as an example as the extravagances of the Hollywood divorce courts have for the sober Western working class.

It is therefore the values of the Chinese people, not those of the westernized Chinese of Shanghai nor those of the decadent Court which have now come to the surface and have been given the blessing of the new regime. To these values the regime has added a new freedom for women. Women, as before, will spend most of their lives at work rather than in the boudoir, they are taught and encouraged to become model workers rather than attractive women, but they are freed from the bondage of the mother-in-law and the arranged marriage. They may still work, but now they work for themselves and for wages.

It has therefore been comparatively easy for the system of Persuasion to turn this resurgence of the popular morality to its own purpose. The sexual licence found in small sectors of Chinese society and conspicuous only in large urban centres can now be isolated and condemned. These practices, now so reprobated, are attributed, without qualification, to one class, the rich. It would not appear that the system of propaganda on this theme intends to stick too closely to objective inquiry or scientific, sociological fact. All peasants pure, all landlords vicious, all bourgeois girls wanton, all workers' daughters chaste, these are the key words to the propaganda on the sexual morality of the former capitalist and lordland dominated society of China. The purpose is clear, to depress the pride of the converted scholar gentry and urban bourgeois, to instil that sense of shame for the old society which will lead people born of the stigmatized class to 'renounce wholly the standpoint, outlook and habits of mind of their class of origin', and so fit themselves for Communist society and, perhaps, even for Party membership.

One great aim of the system of Persuasion is thus to make all men and women accept the same ideas, at least on all the main subjects of politics, economics, morality and philosophy. On scholarship and on points of scientific knowledge they may differ and dispute, are indeed encouraged to do so, that truth may be discovered. But in the great wide matters with which Persuasion deals, Truth has already been made known, by Marx, Lenin, Stalin and Mao Tse-tung. It must now be proclaimed, driven home, accepted, until it enters into the texture of men's minds from earliest infancy, for this is how the great changes of culture were effected in the past; but slowly, over several generations, even centuries.

There is no need to waste all that time now. The possibilities of mass media of instruction and communication are vast and new discoveries constantly add to their efficacy. In China television is not yet in general use, but Persuasion will not leave such an instrument idle for long. In one generation, or perhaps two at most—it hardly seems possible that it can take so long judging by what has been achieved in six years—the guidance of the Communist Party and the system of Persuasion will have effected in China a cultural change more profound than any she has experienced, even at the end of the true feudal, classical age and the rise of the central Empire in the third century BC.

This change can be likened to the transformation of pagan society in the late Roman Empire into the Christian society of the early Middle Ages—a process which, aided by extensive barbarian intrusions and political collapse, still required all of five centuries. An age of faith then gradually succeeded to an age of disillusion, of doubt and sophisticated philosophy. The new believers were widely sundered both by time and language from the very last of the former men of open mind. Truth, Christian Truth, came to prevail, but it was a slow process, and it was assisted by a growing illiteracy which helped to obliterate the memory of the past.

Only the earlier of the Christian Fathers of the Church really had personal experience of a pagan world. The later ones were already born into a new, Christian or dominantly Christian society. But the whole generation of the present Communist Party of China, and a very large proportion of all the citizens of China, were educated, or brought up, and grew to manhood before ever the Communist Party came to power and instituted the system of Persuasion. The Fathers of the Communist Party came themselves, for the most part, precisely from that section of society which they most condemn. They know what they are talking about, they have first-hand experience of the society they wish to destroy, they can direct the system of Persuasion, the whole vast apparatus of publicity, like the jet of a hose, in concentrated force upon that aspect of society which most needs their attention. The instrument is highly efficient, it is wielded by experts.

But, of course, all the younger generation are alike subject to this treatment, all alike are having their class origin effaced, their morals reformed, their politics explained to them; a similar picture of the modern world forms in every younger mind. Soon a new generation of men and women will appear, differing still in their capacities, their natural bent, their temperaments and characters, but moulded by Persuasion as the Western proletariat is moulded by the cinema and popular Press (but far more thoroughly and consistently). From them the *élite* can be drawn, the Party members, who have indeed not merely renounced, but who never will have known or understood the standpoint and outlook of the class of their parents' origin.

In due course such new men must succeed to the highest posts; they will have the direction of the system of Persuasion, the supreme instrument of Chinese Communist government, the culture-making machine. No one can foresee how they will use it, for they will not, thirty or forty years hence, have any personal knowledge of the old society, they will themselves have been brought up on the beliefs about it which Persuasion now instils; what corrective to an increasingly distorted picture not only of the past, but of contemporary non-Communist society can be introduced is hard to see. Persuasion undoubtedly runs a grave risk of persuading the persuaders; it is also a very difficult machine to stop, or to relax.

The Chinese people have responded with an immense surge

of enthusiasm and faith to the calls upon their endurance, their courage, their energy and their strength of character which the regime has made by means of Persuasion and Propaganda. The tempo is tense, the effort unremitting. No people can work as the Chinese now work year after year; Liberation has been followed by Reconstruction, visible and amazing progress has been made, men are buoyed up with a real sense of achievement. The next generation will enjoy the fruit of so much work and thought; to what ends and aims will Persuasion direct their efforts? Can Persuasion teach men to take it easy, or must it always be geared to a sense of crisis and urgency, campaign after campaign, plan after plan? The present rulers of China need not consider these problems. They will all be dead before they become urgent. The next generation of leadership, the children of Persuasion today, will have the really difficult task of directing the rays of Persuasion from inside the prism of Persuasion itself.

In an age of sharp ideological conflict, such as our own, the objective treatment of the beliefs and practices of the 'other side', whichever it may be, is very hard and often extremely unpopular. In the ages of Faith one may search the Christian and the Moslem writers in vain to discover any evidence at all that the opposite party was admitted to have any virtues, or to have any part of Truth. Later, when the divisions among the Christians themselves became more ferocious than the antagonism of either faction towards the Moslems, Protestant and Catholic divines, writers of popular religious books, sermonizers, have filled vast libraries with polemics, very little indeed of which contains a tolerant thought.

This is a chastening reflection, either when reading the popular Press in the West, or when doing the same in Communist China. In each case the argument is identical:

(a) The Communists (or the Capitalists) are not sincere; they are using their power to beguile the People. They do not believe all that rubbish which they put in their newspapers, they know it is all propaganda lies.

(b) The doctrines of the Communists (or the Capitalists) are manifestly false; they have been disproved philosophically, and by economics. It is amazing that intelligent men should ignore these facts, it can only be explained by self-interest. Truth must prevail, the Communist (or the Capitalist) system is tottering to its fall.

(c) These people (Communists or Capitalists) are actuated only by selfish motives, they are utterly insincere, can never be trusted to keep any engagement. It is really useless to deal with them. War may not be absolutely inevitable, but it will only be avoided in the long run by the probable prior collapse of the (Communist or Capitalist) system.

Put back into the contemporary idiom these sentiments can be matched in the age of Moselm-Christian conflict, and in words much more familiar in the period of the Wars of Religion and their aftermath. What did in fact happen was no final crusade or anti-crusade to eliminate the Crescent or stamp down the Cross. Military stalemate, the trading instincts of the Italian merchant city states, a sense, maybe, that the Crusades and the Jehad were out of fashion, belonged to grandfather's time, all this led to a slow subsidence of the passionate hatreds of the Age of Faith. By the Renaissance the fire was almost quenched. The first generation of European Orientalists, men of learning interested in Islam for its own sake, though not Moslems, followed soon after. But in his day the Emperor Frederick II with his Moslem wives and followers, his easy tolerance and his knowledge of the East was not only Stupor Mundi, but the great near-Renegade—or, as we would now say, Fellow Traveller.

An almost identical historical sequence attended the quarrel of Catholic and Protestant, though this still lingers with some of its pristine prejudice in certain parts of the world. When massacre and the stake failed to eliminate whichever party was weakest in a particular country, war followed. But not that final, that complete wholehearted war to the end which the fanatics predicted. In actual fact the Thirty Years War saw the unseemly spectacle of Catholic powers fighting each other, and of Protestant princes in the pay of Catholic kings. Unseemly, in that age, but natural enough in any other. Strategic considerations of real significance dictated the covert opposition of France to Austrian ambitions, concealed in turn by a parade of religious fanaticism. Finally, the war having ended in the sensible, but theologically abominable, formula of *cujus regno ejus religio*—Let every kingdom have its own, or rather its sovereign's, religion—the Europeans turned away in utter disgust from the enthusiasms of their fathers and initiated the Age of Reason and Philosophy, the eighteenth century.

It is impossible for a historian to doubt that this sequence must one day succeed to the present age of fanaticism, which we call the Cold War. It is indeed quite probable that with the faster tempo of modern life the process will be accelerated. Already it is widely believed that the Great Final War to extirpate Communism or Capitalism will not eventuate. Curiously, few seem to give due weight to the fact, so reminiscent of the Thirty Years War, that in our own Second World War the Capitalists and Communists were as often allies as enemies, combining against a power which was equally dangerous, militarily rather than ideologically, to both.

Another change, a sure mark of the emerging historical sequence, already appears. The challenge is now not so much the clash of doctrines, but the fear of the political domination of the other side. Capitalist does not contrast himself with Communist on the Western side, as he did thirty years ago. He now talks of the 'Free World' contrasted with 'totalitarian powers'. On the Communist side, at least in China, where the revolution is young, the terms Capitalist and Imperialist are still much in vogue. On the other hand, it is the 'People' rather than the 'Communists' who are the 'we' group.

A student of history, viewing these characteristics of ages of faith and fanaticism as they slowly modify their violence, will quickly perceive that all the froth and fury is not nothing but meaningless verbiage. Beneath it, expressing itself thus crudely in its early stage, a new Belief has grown. Round this Belief a new form of society begins to crystallize, expelling the un-digestible parts of the old society with purges, heresy hunts, massacre and the stake. Historically what matters is not whether the Belief is false or true, philosophically sound, or logically full of flaws, but whether it is accepted by millions of men in a great community. If this comes about, whether they are deluded or enlightened, the new faith will move the mountains of old convention and long-established social structure. It is not what men believe that decides the movement of history, it is the fact that they believe.

Later they will begin to doubt; the philosophers will appear, historical criticism will re-examine the writings of the founding fathers. But it will hardly matter, for by then the landscape will be changed, the new society formed by the believers in the fires of fanaticism will have consolidated itself, and discovered, through wars most likely, its natural limit, the point at which belief stops and doubt or rival creeds dominate.

The old antagonists now meet in cautious friendship. Some things must be remembered, but not the things their forefathers would have never for a moment forgotten. The Christian European, entertaining a visiting Moslem guest, does not think of starting an argument about the Trinity, he reminds his wife that the guest must not be served with pork.

It is much too soon to expect Communists and non-Communists to meet on such terms as these. A capitalist host might remember that his Communist guest would never give the servants (if there are any) a tip—vile feudal custom degrading to the People. But it is still hard to avoid touching upon the great questions in dispute, even if, in China where courtesy has carried over through revolution, these subjects can still be treated with urbanity. It is at least possible to approach the phenomenon of the Chinese social revolution with history in mind, to detect the formation of Belief and the operation of this new dynamic force in a society which for several centuries has been without an active, formative religion.

Persuasion, the great instrument of cultural change, is busy forming the beliefs of the new Chinese society, beliefs no more, not visibly less, illogical than those of other ages of faith.

Already the force of these new beliefs is evident in the rapid transformation of society, the vast release of energy which is also at the same time driving forward a great programme of material development and industrial advance. Remembering the omnipresent instrument of change, the system of Persuasion, the achievements of this energy must now be considered and assessed.

CHAPTER FOUR

THE PROVINCES

THE EXPRESSION 'the Eighteen Provinces' used to be a synonym for all China. In fact there had been more than eighteen for several centuries, but the three into which the Manchu dynasty divided their homeland, Manchuria, were not then counted as part of China proper, being beyond the Great Wall. The Republic added three more, carving up what had been the territories of tributary princes in Inner Mongolia. The Communists have once more rearranged the map, again dividing the North East (the Chinese name, Tung Pei, for Manchuria) into three and restoring to the inhabitants parts of Chahar, Jehol and western Manchuria to be the Inner Mongolian Autonomous Area.*

This process of redivision and alteration has been several times repeated by new dynasties throughout Chinese history ever since, in the early seventh century, the T'ang Emperor T'ai Tsung first superseded the older, smaller units of Han and post-Han times with large areas called provinces. Some of the original divisions he made still exist, and his reform is still the basis of the division in North China. South China having grown much more populous was later sub-divided.

These great areas, the Chinese provinces, are mostly as large as a major European state, none are smaller than Belgium or Switzerland. All have a population exceeding several millions; that of Ssuchuan, the largest, was reckoned to be seventy million, but now is certainly much more. Western observers

* The People's Republic has also abolished the republican provinces of Si-kang (eastern Tibet) and Ning-hsia (western Inner Mongolia), incorporating these areas respectively in Ssuchuan and Kansu provinces (1955). This, combined with the restoration of the traditional three Manchurian provinces, and suppression of Jehol province, now divided between Hopei and Inner Mongolia, restores almost exactly the arrangement which existed under the Manchu dynasty. It would appear to be a silent acknowledgment of the superior character of the imperial pattern, which did acknowledge the rights of minority peoples to a special administration.

of China, with either the fragmentary political map of Europe in mind, or the federal system of the United States as background, concluded that one main cause of the troubles of the declining Empire and the Republic which followed it was the inordinate size of the provinces, and the consequent great authority which a governor or viceroy exercised in his vast domain. Some suggested that if the Chinese government wanted to keep control of the country they should split up the provinces into units comparable to French *départements*: American observers considered that the provinces could be retained, or perhaps slightly increased in number by some major divisions, and turned into federal states.

Arguing from the experience of the United States, they concluded that democracy required federalism in a very large country; centralized authority would always bring back autocratic government. Some attempt to adopt the federal principle, or at least to give the provinces self-government with democratic institutions, was made in the last years of the Manchu dynasty. It proved to be a great aid to the revolutionaries who sought to dethrone the dynasty, but was quickly swamped, after the Republic was set up, by the military power of the would-be usurper, Yüan Shih-k'ai.

The quasi-independence of the provinces, no longer seriously controlled by the feeble republican governments, was the first cause of the rise to power of the military governors, the 'warlords' of Western journalists, whose actual title of Tuchun, meant Military Inspector General of a Province. The Kuomintang gradually suppressed the independent warlords, brought the provinces back under regular government control, but made no attempt to introduce a federal system. The system of the Empire, modified to a slight degree by the apparatus of Kuomintang Party government, continued to prevail, the main difference being that unlike the Empire, the Military Governor, although subject to removal by Nanking, remained a very powerful figure, vastly overshadowing the Civil Governor, who in imperial days had been much the more important.

Under the People's Republic the provinces still exist, they have a form of provincial government, with bureaux of education, forestry, agriculture and other matters, but military authority has been organized on a new pattern, with area commands far exceeding one or even two or three provinces, arranged on strategic principles, disregarding provincial boundaries. There is no federalism, provinces as such have no constitutional rights, they are simply large units of local government. Asked, in Canton, the former home of provincial sentiment and local patriotism, what rights and powers, independent of Peking's direction, the government of the province possessed, a high official of that body reflected for a moment, then said that (as an example) the Canton government of Kuangtung Province could fix the price of theatre tickets at any figure below a maximum, and above a minimum laid down by Peking. Democratic Centralism is certainly no idle phrase in China today.

A degree of control is effectively exercised such as no Emperor could ever have hoped to impose. The instrument is the Party, with its branches reaching down to village level. Yet most of the characteristics which made Western political scientists doubtful of the viability of these great units (the provinces), or convinced them that their wide differences could only be reconciled by a federal system, remain. Dialects differ, especially, along the south-east coast, from Shanghai to the Viet-nam border. But these are very populous provinces, still with poor communications with the interior.

Topography and climate are widely different in North and South, East and West China. There are provinces of the great North China plain, and mountain provinces difficult of access and easily cut off. Crops and customs vary, even race, especially in the south-west, the provinces of Yunnan, Kueichou and Kuangsi, is intermingled with large numbers of non-Chinese peoples, now called National Minorities. Religion in the north-western province of Kansu, and much of neighbouring Shensi, is Islam which in other provinces is only the faith of small minorities. Buddhism remains very strong in parts of the lower Yangtze provinces, but is far gone in decay in the north. Railway building and road construction are being pushed forward very fast, but there are still provinces which have only just opened their first stretch of railway, where there is but one real main motor road in a country the size of Britain.

It might seem that the Communists are unnecessarily complicating a task in any case tremendous by insisting on this high degree of central control in a country so ill-equipped with communications and so marked off into diverse areas by nature. The importance of area and regional sentiment is very great in the United States, a country nearly the same size as China, but one covered with an immense network of railways and roads, criss-crossed with air lines, and inhabited by a people of the same culture and language, who have only occupied the major part of the land in the past century. Yet 'All China' centralism, unity, are keywords and dominant themes in the propaganda and publicity of the People's Republic.

Standard Speech, the language of Peking, editorials reprinted from the People's Daily, fresh from the Capital, constant calls to attend conferences, rallies, meetings, by these means the provincials are urged along the road of Democratic Centralism, while the theme 'All China'; All China this, that, and the other, sounds constantly in their ears. Medical Associations, Women's Federations, Workers' Unions, Young Pioneers, every type of organization is always 'All China, etc.'. The exclusive provincial guild, so characteristic of South China, and still so important among the Overseas Chinese, has gone. The All China Federation of Manufacturers, or Merchants, or Shipmasters, now takes its place. The Communists practise what they preach. No longer does the high official, or the general, select his staff and close colleagues exclusively from his own province, and even from the same part of it. These personnel are now chosen by merit, or promotion, but with an expressed anti-provincial bias. 'We try to avoid having my fellow provincials on my staff,' a general once explained to an observer surprised to find from what a variety of provinces the staff originated.

National unity is therefore to be pursued by every means,

but in contrast to this policy as applied to the Chinese provincials, the minority peoples, or as they are officially called, 'National Minorities', enjoy a separate, almost a favoured status, very different from the neglect, not to say contempt, which they suffered under the Empire and the Republic. The National Minorities are very large, numerous and famous peoples, such as the Inner Mongols, the Manchus and the Tibetans, and also small obscure tribal groups such as the widespread non-Chinese peoples of the south-west of China.* Some of these are large peoples, like the Miao and Chuang (really a branch of the Thai race) but time and political vicissitudes have fragmented what were once compact communities into scattered groups and sub-tribes, whose dialect of their own language has also often undergone marked changes.

The problem of these peoples is complicated by the fact that the areas which they inhabit are not so much divided merely into a patchwork of Chinese occupied and tribal regions, but that the divisions are, so to speak, vertical and not horizontal. The tribes, the minority peoples, occupy the highlands and mountain areas. The Chinese settlers centuries ago drove them from the cultivated rice valleys in which they settled and built their cities. A tribal group on some mountain may be only a few thousand strong, across the valley on some other high mountain will be another, and so no cohesive area can be formed in which people of the same·race can be given autonomy.

The solution adopted has been to constitute autonomous districts, and sub-districts. All groups which have separate languages and customs are classified in one or other of these divisions, depending on their strength. For some purposes such as communications, security and other large-scale functions of the provincial government they come under the rule of the province. For others, such as education, law, and custom they govern themselves. Every group, however small, has the right to a school in which teaching is carried on in the native language, Chinese being a second subject.

---

* The minority peoples number thirty-five million in all according to the *Handbook on People's China*. Foreign Language Press. Peking. 1957.

The Institute of National Minorities in Peking, an organization having something of the character of a university and also of a training and research institute, collects leading younger members of each community and gives them a three years course in which they learn not only Chinese and other subjects, but also are trained to return to administer their native sub-district, autonomous area or region. It is intended, if it is not yet actually in practice in all regions, that the administration should be entirely confided to members of the National Minority in their own region. The Institute of National Minorities also acts as a major anthropological research station, collecting the languages, songs, folklore and material artifacts of the National Minorities and studying their individual cultures.

The largest minority peoples, the Mongols and Tibetans, have, in theory at least, complete autonomy, controlling their own regional government, although this control does not extend to defence or foreign relations. How far this system works in practice, in, say, Tibet, where Chinese authority was only recently reimposed after an interval of more than forty years, since the fall of the Empire, is uncertain. In some cases the political authority is confided to members of the minority who are also Communist Party members. But this is certainly not invariably the case, notably in regions where there are, or were, no such Party members available.

National Minority status has also been conferred on two groups who have no real present local abode but are scattered in many parts of China, the Manchus and the Moslems.

The former ruling race, originating in northern Manchuria, was also settled under the Empire in military communities in all the major cities and provincial capitals of the Empire, above all in Peking. At the fall of the Empire, many of the provincial communities were massacred in the turmoil of the first Revolution. Others surrendered and survived.

Under the Republic, the Manchus, who had been forbidden by law to engage in either commerce or agriculture under the dynasty, being in theory either soldiers or civil officials, became very impoverished. While some retained their distinctive names and some peculiar customs, most merged in the Chinese masses around them. Exactly how far these assimilated Manchus have now been differentiated from their neighbours, with whom they had begun to intermarry, is not too clear. It may be that the status of Manchu National Minority is mainly confined to those families of former rank and standing who were known to be Manchus and maintained their tradition. Their representative in the People's Congress is, as mentioned before, the former imperial Prince Tsai T'ao, a younger brother of the late Emperor Kuang Hsü, now recognized as the head of the former imperial family and of the Manchu people.

The Moslems, a religion rather than a people, are classed as a National Minority none the less, presumably on the grounds that their remote ancesters were West Asian foreigners. They are found in every province of China, but most strongly in the north-west and in Yunnan, in the far south-west. There are more than 100,000 in Peking itself. Traditionally specialized in certain trades, butchering (which good Buddhists should never practice) the caravan and carrying trade, restaurant keeping, and oddly enough, the curio trade, the Chinese Moslems cling tenaciously to their religion in all essentials, but do not veil their women, and in other respects appear indistinguishable from the mass of the Chinese around them. In the north-west and in Yunnan a slightly West Asian cast of countenance reveals a higher proportion of the original stock. Among them are scholars of great distinction, many of whom, perhaps, are not always very active practitioners of the ancestral faith.

The policy of the People's Republic towards the National Minorities appears to be a major departure from the dominant theme of centralization and national unity. It is only apparently so; for its purpose is to secure a greater, more perfect unity by satisfying the idiosyncrasies of the minority groups and thus forestalling the rise among them of discontent, nationalism, and the appeal of foreign 'irredentist' propaganda. Some of these peoples, such as the Shans and Chuang of the south-west, Yunnan, Kueichou and Kuangsi, are Thai, and have close linguistic and cultural ties with the Shans of Burma and even with the Siamese. The Thai race is spread throughout these countries, and also much of Indo-China, but has, apart from Thailand itself, no political centre under Thai rule. Autonomy for the Chinese Shans and Thais—under the guidance of the Communist Party—prevents, it may be hoped, any movement towards a 'greater Thailand' taking root among them.

Equally the Mongols of Inner Mongolia are the kith and kin of the Outer Mongols, who are indeed under a Communist government, but not one subject to the control of Peking. Inner Mongolia is rapidly developing into a major industrial area contiguous to Peking itself and North China. Discontent among the Inner Mongols which might lead them to turn their eyes towards their Outer Mongol cousins, or to co-operate (as some of them did in the late war) with an invader would be a dangerous and unwelcome development. Autonomy, real enough here, is designed to appease it in advance. Since the Inner Mongols suffered much from the unscrupulous land grabbing and land settlement schemes of the Kuomintang and earlier Chinese regimes since the Empire fell, the Inner Mongols have some reason to welcome their new status and co-operate with the government in Peking which is developing their hitherto backward country.

Smaller groups, of which there are several scores, perhaps more than one hundred, have no such importance or affinity with outside peoples. They are usually backward, in some cases, such as the No Su, only just reaching the feudal stage of development. They were ruled until the advent of the Communists by local lords, themselves constantly at feud with their neighbours and oppressed by the Chinese provincial officials. Other groups are not far from the primitive, and in the case of the Wa of the Burma border, are still active headhunters. To absorb these peoples by force, drill them into being Young Pioneers and parrot-taught subjects (hardly citizens) of the People's Republic would be to create a number of indigestible, unassimilated and dumbly discontented underdogs who would disturb the pattern of Chinese society which the regime seeks to create and might become a focus of counter-revolutionary activity.

They are therefore given every freedom compatible with their cultural level, and trained to administer themselves in growing conformity with the system of the regime. So far from treating the former feudal lords as outcasts to be eliminated, it is these families themselves who are most subjected to the training of the Institute of National Minorities so that they can be transformed, still having the real prestige they enjoy among their people, into modern District Secretaries and Regional officials. Exchanging a life of order and some comfort for the dangerous blood feuds and primitive squalor of their bleak mountain castles, these pupils of the Institute, it is said, prove among its most successful and useful graduates.

At the same time a great campaign of the system of publicity is making the National Minorities and their cultures known to and appreciated by the Chinese, who formerly knew little of such peoples and had been brought up to despise them. The old opprobrious terms for the minority peoples are banned, their own real names brought into wide currency. Their music is publicly performed, their songs are heard on the radio, their drama adapted and translated for the Chinese stage. It is impossible to travel in China now without frequently encountering touring groups from these remote peoples, in their national costumes, being entertained, shown the historical monuments and the modern factories and other achievements of the People's Republic. In this way, not only is the horizon of the minority people enlarged to an 'All China' range, but the Chinese are taught to know, admire and respect peoples who used to have their names written with the dog radical as a sign of the contempt felt for them.

The policy of autonomy for the National Minorities, especially in cases such as the Yunnan Shans alarms and offends some of China's neighbours, notably the government of Thailand. It is feared that the autonomous Shan region is in fact

a training ground for breeding up Thai Communists who will
infiltrate Thailand and her neighbours, preparing the way for
a revolution partly based on Thai nationalism, with a Communist bias. The Chinese, naturally, deny any such intention;
they point out, quite truly, that the Communist government
of the People's Republic did not create the National Minorities,
nor even was it the first to give some of these groups a kind of
self government. It is a fact that the Yunnan Shan Autonomous
Area was under the Empire and Republic divided among a
number of Shan principalities, largely self governing under the
rule of Sawbwas often closely related to their colleagues on the
Burmese side of the frontier.

The Communists claim that all they have done is to
modernize this ancient administration, unite all the principalities in one area, deprive the princes of their arbitrary power
(which was certainly often cruelly abused) and bring these
Shans under the same system as is now operated throughout
South-West and West China. If, no doubt, they expect and
believe that the Yunnan Shans will come to appreciate and
admire the system under which they now live, and their
foreign cousins begin to hanker for it too, this is not the fault of
China, but of the 'reactionary tendencies' of her neighbours.
It is an argument which can not be proved or disproved; only
the development of the system and the future relations between
China and the countries of South-East Asia will in time disclose
the real trend.

A recent British observer who approached the Chinese Thai
area from the Burmese side gives evidence in support of the
Chinese claim.

'The surviving (Chinese) Shan states have been maintained under their Sawbwas, although there is evidence of
Chinese control, especially in economic affairs. The much
discussed Thai Autonomous Region appears to be little more
than a myth. Bangkok may buzz with accounts of a Free
Thai Government led by Pridi Phananomyong and of a
Free Thai Army 30,000 strong, but when this writer found
himself within a few dozen miles of the supposed capital of

the Autonomous Region he could obtain no confirmation of any of these stories, although there is a surprising amount of communication between Shans on both sides of the frontier.'*

In the modern period prior to the Communist regime, the pattern of Chinese urban life and wealth exhibited a very uneven and indeed, unnatural development. On the one hand was Peking, the former imperial capital, engrossing almost all that was of value and significance in the old Chinese culture; on the other the Treaty Ports, above all Shanghai, concentrating all the modern industry, commerce and technical development into a handful of cities partly under foreign rule. The great cities of the interior, however famous their names and glorious their histories, were astonishingly decayed and retarded. Little remained of the monuments of past prosperity and pride; massive city walls enclosed mean streets of dilapidated buildings. Modern industrial development was wholly absent, even modern conveniences such as sanitation, electricity and water supply were either non-existent or woefully defective. The spasmodic enthusiasm of some transitory governor had here and there adorned his capital with a factory, usually closed, a modern building incongruous, isolated and often already lapsing into neglect.

The interior was unsafe; capital shunned areas dominated by predatory military commanders. Foreign business and settlement was by law confined to the Treaty Ports. Some progress was made when, and where, the writ of the Nationalist government at Nanking was effective. But the invasion of the Japanese, the subsequent destruction and turmoil of war and civil war had largely arrested any such development. There had been virtually no change at all, except progressive decline and ruin in the smaller cities of the provinces. Many of the great interior cities, with large populations, were still linked to each other and the rest of China only by cart roads, mule paths or waterways; a motor road meant a rough earth surface over which, in dry

* 'Burma's North-east Borderland Problems.' Hugh Tinker, *Pacific Affairs*, Vol. XXIX, No. 4, December 1956, p. 343.

weather, a lorry could be driven with excruciating discomfort
to the passengers, grave risk of damage to any fragile cargo,
and rapid deterioration of the vehicle.

It was not surprising that under these circumstances commerce and capital had concentrated in the Treaty Ports where
there was some degree of security, a ready market, sea communications and an uninterrupted supply of raw materials.
The rise and growth of these cities was therefore very rapid,
matching the swift decline of the ancient centres of the interior.
Shanghai had been a small administrative centre of the third
rank in the mid-nineteenth century, when the site was selected
by the Western Powers as the best location for a Treaty Port
which should exploit the commerce and resources of the
Yangtze valley. In less than a century it became a great city
of four million inhabitants spreading far beyond and around the
original walled town and the first Concession areas.

Four-fifths of this city, divided into the French Concession
and the International Settlement, were under the control of the
foreign residents. After the troubles of the revolution of 1927,
which brought the Nationalists to power, the Settlement and
Concession areas of Shanghai were permanently garrisoned by
troops supplied by the major Treaty Powers, Britain, France,
U.S.A. and Japan. The Japanese used this vantage point to
launch attacks upon China, first in 1932, later and conclusively,
in 1937. When the present state of Shanghai is under consideration this history becomes important. The city as it still stands
is the city as built by the foreign residents and their Chinese co-
inhabitants within the boundaries of the Concession areas. This
self governing community, withdrawn from the control and
interference of the Chinese government, had developed a very
distinctive and peculiar character. Architecturally a haphazard
collection of modern Western buildings and partly Westernized Chinese dwellings, it had little systematic plan, no overall
unity of design.

The French Concession had become a favoured residential
area both for foreigners and the richer Chinese; the eastern
part of the International Settlement, in theory a part of the

Concession area reserved for foreign residence, was in fact the industrial region, exclusively inhabited by the Chinese working class; mean streets, crowded and unsavoury, were surrounded, just beyond the limits of the International Settlement, by the most appalling slums which have ever disfigured a city. The greater part of the original International Settlement, the centre of the city and its landward extensions, was the business and commercial zone, shading off inland into a middle class residential area. This region, intended for the residence of British and other Western citizens, was now overwhelmingly Chinese in population.

These Chinese inhabitants were for the most part not of local origin, but immigrants from all the coastal provinces; Cantonese, men from Ningpo in Chekiang, from north of the Yangtze river, who in their own uncouth speech styled themselves 'Kompo', 'Chiang Pei', 'North of the River Men'. Dialects were various, but dominated by the tongue known anciently as the language of Wu, the dialect of the lower Yangtze valley—a dialect difficult to the northern ear, incomprehensible to the Cantonese, having no wide currency in the rest of China, and therefore, to the foreign resident, hardly worth learning. The city lived under the divided rule of the French authorities of the Concession and the mainly British administration of the Settlement. Several systems of law were in force at the same time, each Treaty Power citizen being subject only to the laws of his own nation, while the Chinese inhabitants were for some purposes under Chinese law, for others under the jurisdiction of the authorities of the part of the city in which they lived.

In 1932, when the Japanese, using their garrison in the eastern part of the International Settlement as a spearhead, struck at the surrounding and contiguous Chinese governed quarter of Chapei, the Chinese resisted strongly, did not respect the border of the Settlement in this quarter, and carried the war almost to the water front. In 1937 the same sequence of events, this time prolonged not for weeks but for several months, caused immense devastation in this part of the city, and finally destroyed any pretension to immunity and international status which the

Settlement as a whole had enjoyed. Henceforward, until 1941, the eastern part of the Settlement was in fact a Japanese-occupied area, merging in the ever-expanding occupied area of eastern China.

When the Pacific War broke out with the attack upon Pearl Harbour, the Japanese at once occupied the whole of the International Settlement and French Concession, abolished their administrations, interned the Western residents, and ended, in one day, the Treaty Port Concession system which had flourished for just under a century. The old life of Shanghai stopped short on that day; it has never revived. During the course of the war the Western Treaty Powers gave up, by a new Treaty with China, the rights which they no longer enjoyed, and at the surrender of Japan the Nationalist government entered into full control of the whole city of Shanghai, Concession, Settlement, Chinese city and suburbs.

The four years of Nationalist rule were a period of chaotic inflation, open corruption, rapid deterioration and financial ruin for the vast majority of the Shanghai population. Hardly any development was possible, investment was folly, commerce a gamble. Racketeering and gang control reached fantastic proportions. It was more expensive to ship a crated motor-car across the Whangpoo, if by ill chance it had been unloaded on the Pootung side, opposite the city, than to send it back across the Pacific Ocean and have it reloaded in a ship which would berth, in due course, on the Shanghai side of this inconsiderable river. Shanghai, dirty, corrupt, gang ridden and forlorn awaited the end, the victory of the Communist Party, from which, as the centre and heart of capitalist China, it could expect no salvation.

The Communists, it must be supposed, approached Shanghai with an ambivalent attitude. On the one hand this was the city which to them typified all that was worst in the system they were bent on destroying; the stronghold of the former Western Imperialist Powers, the home of the bankers and monopolists who supplied the Kuomintang with its life blood and its leadership, the sink of iniquity and vice, the capital of corruption and racketeering. On the other hand, Shanghai was the largest industrial city in China, inhabited by the most numerous working class, the vast majority of the skilled artisans, the qualified professional men, the scientists and technicians. Twenty years previously, in 1927, it had been the heart of the revolutionary movement, the secret stronghold of the Party itself, before the decision to take to the hills and rouse the peasantry had transformed both the character and the prospects of the Communist Party of China. Communist China could not ignore Shanghai, could not accept Shanghai as she found it; the city was a challenge, the Party took up the gage.

The first impression received by the returning visitor to China today, who has known Shanghai in the days of its prosperity and of its decline, is one of stagnation. The city still stands, outwardly to all appearances as it stood in 1941. Hardly a new building can be found in the old Concession and Settlement areas, except the vast Soviet Exhibition Hall. The great banks and insurance companies' buildings are there, put to other uses, rather shabby. The former luxury shops of Nanking Road, once among the best in the world, sell soap or shirts, or are closed. Traffic in the old business centre is a thin trickle, incredibly diminished. The port is quiet, working to not more than a third of pre-war capacity, and even this is a very recent revival. The city is, however, clean; cleaner than at any previous period, including the heyday of foreign administration; clean, swept, empty, but ungarnished.

It is also decorous; the night clubs, bars, houses of ill fame, many, but not all, the restaurants, are closed. Not long after darkness the streets are empty and deserted. Presently the observer sees something which is new, or was not visible in the post-war period of confusion. The port may be quiet, but along the fringe of what was once the Settlement and in the eastern industrial area, hundreds of factory chimneys smoke into the sky; Shanghai is not a very active port, but it is still, and more than formerly, a great industrial city. Life has moved inland from the decaying centre of commerce and shipping and has taken vigorous root in an area which lay beyond the boundaries of the old foreign concessions where, across the barbed wire border, the workers who by day crossed into the Settlement to the factories on its edge, dwelt in miserable and revolting hovels.

In Shanghai today the authorities distinguish between the New Workers' Quarters, and the Old Workers' Quarters, terms which both express and disguise the main task which the People's Republic has set itself to achieve in this city now estimated to contain nearly six million people. The task is to rehouse about one million of these inhabitants who still live, or recently lived in the Old Workers' Quarters, that is, in slums of unimaginable squalor. A secondary task is to render those dwellings at least fit for human habitation until they can be replaced.

In the days of the foreign rule in Shanghai, the Concession and International Settlement authorities enforced a bare minimum of sanitation and construction standards in the areas under their control; the poorer parts of these zones, although by European standards low grade slums, were not deprived of all services. There was light, water, street drainage, and public conveniences. The factories which arose in the Settlement soon created a demand for labour which could not be supplied by the relatively well paid workers who could afford to live in the poor quarters of the Settlement. Just beyond it, in what had recently been open country or market gardens, a vast slum rapidly spread in which there were no services of any kind: neither piped water, nor light; no drainage of the filthy lanes nor sewerage, not even paved paths among the squalid huts of thin bamboo, mud and mats in which a million men, women and children dwelt. These conditions, already present more than thirty years ago, were greatly aggravated by the continual growth of the city, the great influx of population which the creation of an industrial centre in an already over-crowded agricultural area always brings about.

The boundaries of the International Settlement were not extended after the Republic was established, for Chinese nationalism greatly resented the existence of such enclaves in the national territory and sought to eliminate rather than to extend them. The authorities of the Chinese part of Shanghai were unable from lack of funds, administrative incompetence, political and military interference, to exercise any effective control over the development of this area. An immense festering scab of sub-human hovels surrounded the trim and orderly areas under foreign rule. As any further extension of the Settlement would have necessarily brought this region under foreign control, and landed the authorities of the Settlement with an insoluble problem, they soon gave up any desire to extend their boundaries.

The Communists therefore inherited in Shanghai, now wholly under their control, a social malady of daunting dimensions, which they could not ignore. They had come as the Liberators of the People, the Party which claimed to exalt the working class, to modernize China. The inhabitants of the 'Old Workers' Quarters' represented a very considerable fraction of that working class; their condition could be blamed upon the thoughtless capitalist exploitation of the fallen regime, the selfish indifference of the 'foreign imperialists', and did indeed represent the worst consequences, even if they were unintentional, of the old Treaty Port system. But this indictment would not improve their lot.

It is clear that it was early decided that every other aspect of Shanghai's decline and impoverishment must be subordinated to the task of eliminating this social disgrace. Two remedies have been applied, and the concentration on the work involved by so great an effort largely explains why the formerly prosperous parts of the city now seem shabby and unimproved. It was first necessary to give the inhabitants of the Old Workers' Quarters some earnest of the government's care and goodwill. Salvage work has been undertaken which in itself has undoubtedly enormously improved these neglected and condemned hovels. Electric light has been supplied, usually no more than one light to each hut. The lanes have been roughly paved with road metal; piped water, with communal taps in the streets, has removed the necessity to resort to stagnant filthy ponds for drinking and washing water. Sanitation, one public convenience to each lane, has been installed; there are clinics, schools and playgrounds constructed on the swamps and stanks which formerly covered large areas of unoccupied ground. All this is regarded as temporary expediency, to last five or six years until the whole of the area can be reclaimed, the hovels demolished, and 'New Workers' Quarters' built in their stead.

Fortunately for the town planners there was still, not far beyond the fringe of sub-standard slums, open country hitherto without roads or easy access. In this area the New Workers' Quarters, colloquially known as 'Long White Villages', have been built and are still building. The popular name comes from their design, long barrack-like two-storey structures in parallel lines, a broad road between them, with strips of grass and trees in front of each block. These blocks contain two-room flats, with a kitchen shared by every five families, a toilet and wash house on each floor, used by as many as ten or more families; schools, clinics, rows of shops in the lower storey of one block, a large meeting hall—that prime necessity of the new social system. Water, light, sewage, air and space, the first simple amenities of any dwelling are the only luxuries, but these were all unknown to the inhabitants before they came to their new Long White Village.

The Western visitor quickly realizes that this new accommodation represents at best the very minimum which he would expect to find in a temporary transit camp for refugees. The Chinese town planners are also well aware of this fact; the New Workers' Quarters are not expected to provide the final solution for the rehousing of the working class of Shanghai, but they will make it possible to house a million displaced slum dwellers in far better conditions than ever before until the rebuilding of the demolished slums make a further improvement feasible.

It was estimated in 1956 that approximately 400,000 people had then been moved to the New Workers' Quarters which now surround Shanghai; 600,000 still remained in the temporarily salvaged Old Workers' Quarters; at least six more years will be needed to complete the transfer. One of the major problems connected with this rehousing problem is the need to prevent the further inordinate growth of Shanghai, a city which the government already considers too big, and too badly planned to be extended. No new factories are being set up in Shanghai, and in some cases it has been possible to remove machinery from derelict installations to other places. While engaged on an immense task of transferring the working popula-tion from slums to new housing estates the government is also using the full power of the system of persuasion to induce wor-kers to migrate to the new centres of industry which it has established in other parts of the country. Government policy, for a number of reasons, seeks to reverse the trend which has governed the development of Chinese industry since its incep-tion, and develop, not the coastal cities, but the long neglected centres of the interior.

The first reason, freely admitted in conversation, is that the great cities of the coast are too exposed to enemy attack. Secondly, the pattern of development which the Treaty Port system had brought about is unnatural, does not accord with the real distribution of resources in the country, and conse-quently is uneconomic and inconvenient. It may well be that a further, subsidiary reason is the desire to break with the Treaty Port tradition, to make a clean sweep and start industrial centres in areas which never new the old order and in which the new pattern of socialist development can be inaugurated from the start. The fact that these new areas of industrial development are situated in the interior, far from the coast, and also closer to the seat of government in Peking, is mainly due to the presence of coal, iron ore and other mineral resources.

It was already well known, before the People's Republic was set up, that the mineral resources of China were to be found in the north-west, Manchuria (the north-east) and in the south-western mountain provinces. Except for Manchuria which Japan had developed, these regions were all remote, poorly served with modern communications, or wholly without them, and during the greater part of the history of the Republic beyond the effective control of the central government. Some development, greatly handicapped by the loss of all ports, was accomplished under the stress of war during the Japanese invasion, when the Nationalist government was forced to retire into these western provinces. The scientists and technical experts of the universities who then took refuge in the west, brought into this region for the first time men who were able to evaluate its resources and undertake the necessary surveys.

When the present regime began the intensive development of the north-western provinces they thus had solid research upon which to base their plans, a fact which in part accounts for the rapidity with which they have been carried out. Many of the new railways which have been pushed far into the north-west and western provinces during the last six years had been projected and surveyed years before, some indeed as long ago as the era of foreign railway building and loan finance which occurred in the last years of the dynasty. The existence and location of the coal beds and iron ore deposits had long been known; but political risks, military insecurity and lack of finance had prevented any serious attempt to profit by this knowledge. These facts are not stressed in the publicity and propaganda of the present regime, which, perhaps not unnaturally, prefers to give the impression that all the programme of modernization and development which is so swiftly transforming the interior stems entirely from the initiative and leadership of the government of the People's Republic.

The achievement is none the less impressive and vastly significant. For mile after mile railways have been relaid, double tracked and extended. Small cities which had never known a modern machine are now centres of some local manufacturing industry, the old walled town lost in the midst of new workers' suburbs, factories and mills. The expansion of Peking the capital, is matched by the transformation of such ancient cities as Loyang and Sian, decaying former capitals which, a few years ago, had little but administrative importance and the memory of past glories to distinguish them from the ruck of provincial cities.

The emphasis on industrial development, the key activity of the regime in the material sphere, has led to a great concentration of effort and resources in the areas where such development is most promising and immediately productive. The north-west, the provinces of Honan, Shansi, Suiyüan, Inner Mongolian Autonomous Area, and Kansu, where coal and iron are found, and where oil-fields show much promise, exhibit the most spectacular changes and progress. This region was one of the poorest and most backward parts of China, subsisting purely on agriculture in a climate which is very liable to periodic droughts. It is also now shown to be compensatingly rich in minerals, and the contrast already produced by the first wave of development is the more conspicuous.

Manchuria, the north-east, was on the contrary the most highly industrialized of any part of China. Japanese enterprise had opened the mines, built railways and roads, established heavy industry and manufactures. All this served no Chinese purpose in the days when Japan either dominated the region or had in practice, if not in form, annexed it outright. The influence and the output of-Japanese controlled Manchuria was very slight in China itself, since the economy of the region was wholly geared to the needs of the suzerain power. The Manchurian industries suffered from the Russian occupation at the end of the Second World War, being subjected to large-scale removal of plant and machinery; just how far-reaching this removal of 'war booty' was is now hard to gauge, since it is certain that some restitution has been made and much more rehabilitation with Russian assistance. Manchuria is once more the show piece of Chinese industry, and is now fully restored to its former pre-eminence; it serves as the workshop of all China and its production primes the pump of all Chinese industry and development. China has, in the long run, lost nothing and gained greatly from the intrusion of the Japanese in the decades before the war. Restored and expanded, the Manchurian industries are of the first importance for China and her government, but they were carried on from a flying start, and are not the best test of what the present regime can achieve, nor typical of the results already obtained in areas which had no such assistance, however involuntary, from foreign capital.

In the agricultural age which lasted so late in China the south, the Yangtze valley and all beyond it, were generally recognized as the richest and most prosperous half of the country. Less subject to drought, and also to flood in spite of the greater rainfall, the rice-growing provinces had a higher yield, a larger population, a more developed commerce, than the ancient home of the Chinese people in the provinces watered by the capricious and destructive Yellow River. This slow change in the relative importance and population of the north and south had been in progress for at least a thousand years, exercising a profound influence on the course of the country's history. For many centuries internal migration had been from north to south; only exceptionally, in the special case of such a city as Peking, the capital, had a northern centre attracted the men of South China. Foreign commerce and the era of the Treaty Port trade had accentuated the dominant trend. The best ports of China are along the south-eastern arc of her coastline; the great navigable rivers, her only ancient convenient means of communication, discharge at either end of the same arc.

The exports which had made China famous in the past, tea, silk and porcelain, came from the southern provinces. In more modern times when these had declined, other southern products came into demand. There was very little modern industry except in the Treaty Ports such as Shanghai and Hankow on the Yangtze, but the comparative wealth of the southern population and its active commerce made it by far the most important market for foreign imports. In spite of these advantages the southern provinces remained in many respects economically backward.

The difficulties of a terrain almost everywhere mountainous had retarded the building of railways and roads, which could be so easily and profitably constructed in the dry northern plains. The south had its rivers, on which were situated almost every city of commercial importance, and these could be reached by steamships, foreign-owned for the most part. There was much less incentive to invest in expensive land communications traversing mountain ranges, routes along which no great volume of trade had ever passed. The coastal provinces were cut off by nature from the hinterland, they had always intercommunicated by sea, and thus their trade was very easily developed by the foreign nations who had a monopoly of modern sea transport. The mineral wealth of the south is found mainly in the far south-western provinces, Yunnan and Kueichou, the most inaccessible in China, beyond the limits of river navigation, shut in by formidable mountain ranges which, until the building of the 'Burma Road' during the war with Japan, were only crossed by mule paths.

Since the sea is a precarious link for the present government of China, which is still at war with the Nationalists in Formosa and subject to a sporadic blockade from the navy of Chiang Kai-shek, it became an urgent need to provide alternative land communications between the coastal provinces themselves and between these provinces and those lying inland. When the People's Republic was established there was only one trunk line of railway connecting Canton with the Yangtze valley, one branch connecting this line with Shanghai, no railways at all linked Fukien either with the interior or with its neighbours, Chekiang to the north and Kuangtung to the south. The south-western provinces of Kueichou and Yunnan had equally no railways; the former French line from Hanoi to K'unming, the capital of Yunnan, had been destroyed during the war with Japan and never reopened. Ssuchuan, the great western province the size of Germany and as populous, depended entirely on the Yangtze for its communications, and had no railway in its boundaries.

By contrast with the north-west where industrial development and the expansion of existing communications has proceeded hand in hand, the effort of the government in the south had been mainly directed to railway construction. Four major lines have been projected, and in part already completed. The existing line to Canton from Wuhan (the three cities of Hankow, Wuch'ang and Hanyang on the Yangtze are collectively known by this name), now linked to the northern railway system by the completion of the great Yangtze bridge, has been extended through Kuangsi province to the border of Viet-nam, where it joins the former French line to Hanoi. It is thus now possible to travel by train without a change from Hanoi to Peking, Manchuria, and thence to Russia and Europe. A second main line to the south crosses the high Ch'ingling mountains between Shensi and Ssuchuan, connecting Sian and the northern lines with Chengtu and Chungking. This line will continue south through Kueichou to Yunnan, and also southeast to Canton.

The isolation of Fukien has been ended by the construction of a line from the neighbouring inland province of Kiangsi, thus giving through, though roundabout communication with Canton to the south and Shanghai to the north. It is planned to extend the Kiangsi-Fukien railway, which already links Fukien with the Yangtze region at Wuhan, southwards to the West River Valley and Canton. This, when completed, will provide a third trunk line from the Yangtze valley to the far south. The railway framework projected or already completed in the south will therefore provide these provinces with the essential bare minimum of main communications without which it would be premature to attempt the large-scale development of their mineral resources. It is also obvious that in the present state of international relations in the Far East the provision of land communications between North and South China well inland from the coast opposite Formosa is a strategic necessity which must be keenly felt.

There is thus still a marked difference in the rate of development between North and South China, particularly in the part of the latter region which lies to the south and south-west of the Yangtze valley itself. Furthermore, as will be seen later, although the Communist policy of Land Reform has been applied equally in north and south, the very different techniques of dry farming in the north and rice growing in the south, coupled with the wide difference in topography between the flat North China plain and the relatively narrow valleys and steep hillsides of the south have imposed important variations in the actual practice of the policy in the two regions.

Many of the greatest southern cities are on the coast, and were once Treaty Ports. The decline in overseas trade, possibly only a passing phenomenon, has none the less affected them all, and is revealed by the stagnation and inactivity of the port as clearly in Canton as in Shanghai. It would no doubt be even more conspicuous in Amoy, Swatow or Foochow, ports which are either partly or almost wholly paralysed by the Nationalist control of off-shore islands, Quemoy, Matsu and others which command their approaches. The decision of the regime to limit the growth of industry in such cities for strategic as well as for economic reasons has not yet been compensated, in the south, by the rapid development of industry in the inland cities where communications are still bad.

Along the Yangtze valley, far from hostile interference, this condition does not apply, and here, as at Wuhan, there is as much development and activity as in any new industrial centre in the north-west. But there is one exception, the former capital, Nanking. Nanking was a problem city for the new regime. After suffering the great calamity of the T'ai P'ing rebellion and its suppression in the fifties of the last century, the ancient southern capital of the Ming dynasty had declined and decayed inside the immense circuit of its massive walls. The Nationalist decision to make it capital of China in 1928 led to a swift revival, which though checked by the fresh catastrophe of the Japanese invasion and sack in 1937, was resumed even in the feverish inflation era of the brief post-war Nationalist restoration.

By 1949 Nanking had risen to nearly a million inhabitants, many thousands of whom were servants of the Nationalist government. While Shanghai wallowed in corruption and financial chaos, and Peking remained neglected and decaying, Nanking boomed. Much of the haphazard construction of those years was shoddy and flimsy, but the city had already, before the war, acquired a large number of substantial modern buildings in which the organs and ministries of the Nationalist government functioned for more than a decade. When the regime fell, and the capital was once more set up in Peking, all these became redundant, over-capacious for the smaller administration of the provincial government of the province of Kiangsu, and had to be put to other uses. In Nanking today, the returning visitor finds little or no change in the appearance of the city, except a marked decline in the population. No new building has taken place, the city is clean and well maintained, but has none the less a forlorn, forsaken, empty character, a hint of the ghost town.

If old Peking represented the concentrated product of the wealth and refinement of the former Empire, so Nanking embodied the most lasting and solid achievements of the far briefer period of Nationalist rule; in both eras, long or short, little was ever done for the provinces which was not the result of their own unco-ordinated efforts. Today the picture is already significantly changed. New Peking is indeed a monument to the energy and drive of the Communist regime, but it does not stand alone. The provinces, first the centres of new industry, secondly the remoter agricultural or undeveloped regions of the south and south-west, are receiving their full share of the ubiquitous attention which the most centralized and highly organized government China has ever possessed can bestow upon them. Whatever their future the provinces will never relapse into the seclusion and comparative neglect which bad communications and vast distances inevitably imposed in the pre-industrial age of Chinese history.

CHAPTER FIVE

PEASANTS AND THE LAND

'THE PEASANT IS the packhorse of civilization,' said Trotsky; but then Trotsky is no longer a name which it is proper to mention in Communist countries, and his opinions are condemned. It is certainly true, and the Chinese Communists would accept it as fact, that in China the peasant did carry the load on his broad back: land revenue was the main source of the imperial government's supply, rent was the economic foundation of the scholar gentry class, agriculture was called the 'fundamental occupation'. No Chinese writer or historian ever doubted that the peasant was the real essential worker, while the scholar, of course, was the equally essential, 'book perfumed' ruler. The peasant was honoured as the second rank of the social hierarchy; scholar, peasant, merchant and artisan, in that descending order. He was also, in practice, rack rented, overtaxed, underfed and oppressed.

Yet he was never servile, and oppression in the old order had its well defined limits. The imperial government had no great military strength, partly because the civil service, the chosen field of the scholar gentry, was jealous and afraid of military power, partly because the Chinese Empire was rarely aggressive, had few dangerous neighbours except the nomadic Tartars on the northern frontier, and therefore regarded war as a disagreeable necessity on that frontier, but otherwise as marking a failure of virtue in the imperial ruler. Rebellion by peasants who had reached the limit of endurance was not only always possible, but had a certain sanction in the writings of the classical authorities, notably Mencius. The aim of the government was always to appease such rebellions by punishing the oppressive officials responsible, only if this failed was military force invoked.

As poorly trained and archaically armed soldiery were no

match for peasants rendered desperate by famine, the great peasant rebellions of Chinese history achieved astonishing successes, but very rarely gained the final victory. Faced with the grim alternatives of peasant massacres or military authority, the scholar gentry chose the latter, which would for a generation or so deprive them of the supreme authority, but would lead in due course to the foundation of a new dynasty and their own return to power. The great rebellions therefore marked the closing stages of each dynasty's career, but did not achieve the final overthrow of the dynasty. Thus the Yellow Turbans AD 184 inaugurated the time of troubles which brought the Han dynasty to ruin, the rebellion of Huang T'sao in AD 875 marked the collapse of the T'ang, in 1644 Li Tzu-ch'eng dethroned the Ming, but failed to found a new dynasty, and the T'ai P'ing Heavenly King shook the Manchu dynasty, but was in the end defeated.

Many lesser revolts of the peasants throughout the course of Chinese history had driven home the lesson that oppression must not be carried too far, that however defenceless the individual farmer might be, the combination of thousands of such people was formidable, and could be fatal. In modern times the machine gun and the rifle, weapons which the peasants could not make, gave a new supremacy to the soldiers and those who employed them. The peasants appeared to be without any resource, deprived of their ancient means of protest; at this point the decision of Mao Tse-tung and Chu Teh, to take the revolution out of the cities where it had failed and base it upon rural discontent and peasant support, introduced a new and potent factor which in time transformed both the Communist Party of China and the future of the rural population.

The fundamental difference between the history of the Russian and the Chinese Communist Parties, and the revolutions they have directed, lies in their relations to the peasants. The Russian revolution was effected by the combination of a war-weary, defeated army and the urban working class. It was rapid; power was seized within a matter of days, and thereafter consolidated in civil war which lasted for only a few years. In

China the Communist Party after the break with the Nationalist regime in 1927, fought a guerrilla campaign for twenty-two years before achieving final victory. During this long struggle it had no city of any importance within its power, no direct contact with the Chinese industrial working class, was based wholly upon rural and mountainous regions, survived only through the support it received from the peasant population.

The Chinese Communist Party was none the less a Marxist Party, and it was not led by peasants. Mao Tse-tung was a member of a class which can be equated with the English yeoman farmer of an earlier age. He was educated, his father employed labour on the family estate, and would certainly not have considered himself to be a peasant. Chu Teh came from a wealthy landlord family; Chou En-lai was a scion of a scholar gentry family which had given the Empire several high officials. The industrial worker element in the Party remained small until after 'Liberation' and in the leadership insignificant. The army was wholly recruited from the peasants. With this composition and history it was certain that whatever difficulties and mistakes might be apparent in the Party's handling of the great cities, they had acquired an intimate and sure knowledge of the rural problem and had won the support and trust of the peasant masses.

The Party, moreover, knew very well that these millions of supporters had no understanding whatever of Marxist doctrine or political theory. The peasants had supported the Party because the People's Liberation Army, the Red Army, was their army, manned by their own kith and kin, and because it treated the people with justice and honesty, maintained an admirable discipline and protected them from their enemies whether Japanese invaders or Kuomintang troops. The peasants also wanted the land, title to their farms, abolition of rent, freedom from exactions from landlords and bailiffs. The Communist Party promised these things and performed them where it had power to do so. Communism for the peasants meant disciplined, well behaved soldiers, an honest administration, division of land, reduction or abolition of rent.

Very little of this programme has any specific relation to Marxism, and parts of it might be considered to be contrary to that teaching. Other forms of government have maintained well behaved armies, given clean administration, reformed land tenure in favour of the smallholder. But not in China; the Communist Party gained the support of the peasant millions by practising political virtues which were not peculiar to their beliefs, but had been neglected by their opponents, and by implementing a policy which the peasants desired, but which was, at least on the surface, opposed to the theory of Communism. The first stage of Land Reform, already enforced in the 'liberated areas'—the Communist territories controlled before the final collapse of the Kuomintang—was a simple redivision of the land, giving freehold title to the former tenants and landless labourers who now got their share of the landlords' property.

The implementation of this relatively easy policy took time, partly because it could not be applied to great areas of China until 1950, that is, after the expulsion of the Kuomintang from South China. It would then, no doubt, have been possible to pass legislation expropriating all landlords and providing for the redistribution of their property. But the Communist Party did not wish to proceed in this way; the belief in the value of persuasion, of an aroused political consciousness, caused them to prefer a more devious approach. Cadres, Party members, were sent to the newly liberated villages to instruct the people in what were now their rights, to arouse them to demand land reform as their due, to denounce their landlords and if these had been oppressive, to demand their public trial.

'*Tou cheng*', 'struggle', derived from the Chinese words for 'class struggle', became the term commonly used to denote this form of political activity in which the peasants were not to be the passive recipients of the government and Party's benefactions, but to be induced and encouraged to participate themselves in a struggle to gain their land. An unreal struggle, perhaps, since the government certainly had the power to expropriate, but one which served a dual purpose. Firstly the people were roused to an active political interest in a matter which closely concerned them. They went to meetings, attended lectures, listened to speeches, joined in the demonstrations, gave their voices in the mass trials at which accused landlords were either summarily condemned by the 'voice of the people', escaped with lesser penalties, or were set free.

Secondly the people, by means of this form of 'struggle', were themselves involved in the policy of the Party; they could not claim, if counter revolution had at some later date prevailed, that they had had nothing to do with the expropriation of the landlords or the condemnation of those who were executed. Just as the urban population were not permitted merely to submit, but must also confess, attend meetings, undergo re-education, and if possible, be converted to a full comprehension and approval of the policy of the regime, so the rural population must itself carry out Land Reform, not accept it from above. The people, although illiterate, must not be treated as incapable of thought or self-determination, they must be taught to understand what the regime planned to do, and why such policy was really desirable. The Party did not intend to create a vast majority of satisfied smallholders for whom the revolution meant nothing more than the acquisition of a plot of land.

The Communist Party must have known very well that a mere division of the land was not a Marxist policy, was in fact the very plan which enlightened opponents would propound as the best antidote to rural discontent, a policy which if the Kuomintang could have brought itself to apply might have, twenty years earlier, quelled the revolutionary ferment and established a firm basis for their regime. It was also, the Communists believed, an inadequate answer to the real problem of peasant poverty and rural development. The first stage of Land Reform could at best give every peasant a tiny holding, barely sufficient for the maintenance of one family, inevitably insufficient as the population grew, incapable of creating that surplus of production which was essential to sustain the programme of industrial development. It would be necessary before long to go far beyond this, but the Chinese Communist Party by virtue of its long period of close association with the peasants, understood the psychology of the rural population. It was not necessary here to learn from the mistakes of Russia, the Chinese Communists had already learned from their own experience.

Land hunger and hatred of the landlord class were deep and ancient motives, which for centuries had inspired the peasant rebellions, but had never availed to win a final lasting triumph. The absentee character of Chinese landlordism, accentuated in the disturbed period of the republic, had never permitted such co-operation and understanding as had mitigated the harshness of European feudalism. Landlords rarely improved their tenants' holdings; they exacted higher rents from greater yields; Lady Bountiful, the original Loaf Giver, had never graced the Chinese village. To enlist the co-operation of the peasant in the further, complex, and undreamed of stages of Land Reform it was first necessary to satisfy his ancient hunger and appease his old, hereditary grudge.

So the first stage of Land Reform was often a violent, almost a disorderly proceeding which provoked some overt resistance in remoter parts of the country where landlords had at their disposal private groups or gangs of retainers. These activities could be attributed to agents of the fallen Kuomintang and thus suppressed as 'counter revolution'. At no time a real danger to the regime such open opposition served to exacerbate the 'struggle' in the countryside and enlist the peasants in a fuller, more active co-opertaion with the government. The scene was thus set for the second period of Land Reform, the Lower Stage of Co-operative Farming.

This lower stage left the peasant holders with full title to their land, the farms still sub-divided into small plots, but now 'mutual help teams', co-operatives which took charge of marketing and introduced new seed, better tools, and persuaded the peasants to plant crops in accordance with a national plan, were introduced. Before long the peasants had been induced to treat all the village lands as one unit for purposes of planting and harvest. Production was increased and rationalized, central direction of agriculture became more possible.

Yet this was far from enough. Mechanization could not be considered so long as every village remained an intricate patchwork of smallholdings, nor could production attain the necessary level, even under the guidance of the co-operative, while individual management and the consequent uneven development of the land remained in force. After six years of Land Reform the time was ripe to go further, and set the vast organ of persuasion to proclaim the goal of the Higher Stage of Co-operative Farming.

Industrial advance had now brought the possibility of mechanized farming in the dry north within sight. The tractor factories were going up, the tractors themselves in three years' time will begin to flow out from these factories, and an immense transformation of the North China plain could be planned. But this would not be possible if the region suited to this development remained in the Lower Stage of Co-operative Farming, with individual plots still marked off, and holdings still minute. Mechanized farming requires that large areas of land be treated in a uniform manner, it cannot profitably be employed on a patchwork of tiny plots. There may well have been a further, political, reason for the change. If individual title and separate plots remained there was still nothing to prevent the slow regrowth of land holding, perhaps of landlordism. Some men would sell, others more successful, would buy. Peasant land-hunger would impel men along the old road to wealth and comfort. The basis of the proposed socialist society would be slowly corrupted by the private ownership of land.

But 'Russian mistakes', among which the rapid and forceful establishment of Collective Farms might well be reckoned, warned the Chinese to avoid the simple, obvious solution. The Higher Stage of Co-operative Farming is designed to secure all the advantages of large-scale farming without affronting peasant susceptibilities or wholly destroying the satisfactions of ownership. State Collective Farms exist in China; they have been established in the north east, where formerly Japanese land companies had developed large-scale farming in areas hitherto uncultivated. Reclaimed marshes, waste-lands which have been rendered cultivable by irrigation schemes, or areas where floods had wholly obliterated the old private land holdings have been developed in this way, run by managers paid by the State, and manned by wage-earning labour. Such Collectives are designed to act as pilot projects and guides to the Higher Stage Co-operatives in the development of large-scale agriculture. But they have at present rarely been established in areas of former private land ownership where the earlier stages of Land Reform had been carried out.

The Higher Stage of Co-operative Farming, now established in between 80 per cent to 90 per cent of the farm lands of both North and South China makes a radical change in the system of land tenure, a change which goes a long way towards the abrogation of private ownership.* In a Higher Stage Co-operative Farm two or three villages are united, some hundreds of peasant landholders forming the active voting membership of the Co-operative. All land is pooled; all boundaries are removed, all visible record of separate ownership or individual holdings disappears. The owners, now members, retain title to an equal share in the Co-operative's joint property, but not a share proportionate to the smaller or greater holding which they have pooled in the new organization.

Nor do the members draw an income from any calculation of what their former private property earns in the new Co-operative. They are remunerated on a sliding scale calculated from the number of days worked on the farm, with greater rewards for those days worked in the busy seasons of planting and harvest. It is also stated that if the Co-operative makes a substantial profit in the year, over and above what is needed for maintenance and improvements, the members will divide such profit among them as a bonus or dividend. It would seem that this is rather an unreal expectation, partly because the

* In November 1956 there were in all 764,000 Co-operatives including 116,740,000 peasant households. *Handbook on People's China.* Op. cit.

system is still so new that barely two years have passed since it was inaugurated (in many areas 1957 was the first full year of operation), partly because the demands of maintenance and improvement are likely to absorb all profits.

The members elect the working committee which directs the management of the farm; they can dismiss this committee, which is composed of members of the farm itself, without any outside, government appointed personnel. It is claimed that this right and power of control is real and effective; each co-operative is, in fact, an autonomous unit, managing its own affairs. It is also apparent that the managing committee always consists of former 'poor peasants', often Party members or wholehearted supporters of the regime. Ex-landlords do not seem ever to be elected to these committees, and when asked why this was so, the answer given is that they would not stand for election, nor receive many votes if they did. It is indeed improbable that members who belong to this once hated and still suspect class would willingly put themselves forward or undertake tasks which might bring trouble upon them if all did not go well.

The rapid establishment of the Higher Stage, even though strenuously advocated by all the pervasive, incessant pressure of the system of persuasion, is said to have surprised the government and Party. It was not expected that the peasants would so swiftly accept a drastic change of this character which strikes, it would seem, a final blow at the treasured right of private ownership of land. Great pride and pleasure is expressed at the ready co-operation of the peasant masses, their political maturity in understanding the value of socialist agriculture, the ease and smoothness of this major transition. It would certainly be unwise to discount the power of persuasion in bringing this change about, yet even allowing for the effect of such a constant and unremitting propaganda, some other factor must be postulated to explain the evident fact that the Higher Stage has indeed been achieved so rapidly and smoothly.

Outside observers will reflect, not unnaturally, that the government of China is very strong, commands an apparatus of enforcement far superior to any preceding regime, and will suspect that intimidation or even an open show of force has played a major part in establishing the new system. In China no such evidence is visible. There are no concentrations of troops or gendarmerie in the rural areas, far fewer soldiers are to be seen in the Chinese countryside than at any previous time in the past thirty-five years. There is no evidence at all that the establishment of the Higher Stage met with passive resistance, still less with open defiance. It is clear that the peasants, already organized in Lower Stage Co-operatives, have in fact not only voluntarily accepted the new system, but did hasten to join and establish Higher Stage Co-operatives ahead of the schedule expected by the regime. But this strange development still needs to be explained.

The Chinese peasant is a shrewd man; he has had a very long experience of governments of all kinds, mostly unfavourable to his interests. He, and his fellows, have also developed over the centuries a great capacity for organization, usually of a clandestine kind. The old movements such as the secret societies, the quasi-religious sects, and their overt manifestations in risings and rebellions, were all designed to protect the peasants against injustice, oppressive landlords, predatory officials and disorderly soldiery. There are now no landlords, no warlord armies, no bandit gangs. There is a very powerful government which exercises a control greater than ever before, presses forward with new and strange policies, but claims that these are in the interests of the peasants themselves. This claim can still be measured against the universal knowledge of the short-comings and oppressions of the previous regime. The government had given the peasants the land and despoiled the land-lords; now it wishes the peasants to pool their land, but still manage their own affairs. The first requirement may seem to many of dubious value, but the second is a great reassurance.

The Co-operative is in fact a legalization of that type of organization which the peasants themselves have so often tried to form. It has the advantage of combining the population of several villages, and as exactly similar organizations cover the whole province or region, it brings all the peasant population within an identical system, with the same problems, the same expectations, and, it may be, the same complaints. The power of the peasants to express their views, whether favourable or unfavourable, to the agricultural policy of the state is thus greatly enhanced. It is no longer a question of individual protests, made by persons who can be easily identified, and who can therefore be denounced or charged with some offence. The Co-operatives as a whole are more anonymous, are directed by elected committees, which must in turn satisfy their constituents, the members, several hundreds in each Co-operative.

Since the government wants it this way, why should the peasants not concur; the old system of private landownership gave but a poor return for much hard labour, the new system it is claimed, will benefit all and share the risks as well as the returns. It is at least worth trying, the more so as any reluctance would expose a recalcitrant or laggard community to further intensive persuasion; and it must be supposed that Chinese peasants, also, can weary of too much exhortation. By embracing the new policy voluntarily and swiftly the peasants gain the goodwill of the Party, are more likely to be trusted with the real management of the Co-operatives, can more readily influence the direction of agricultural policy if this seems to be moving against their desires.

It is also certain that the countryside has been affected by the great wave of enthusiasm and energy which now sweeps through all Chinese society. The old system, even when turned to their benefit, was still an old system; in the present atmosphere of revolutionary ecstasy a new system merely by virtue of its novelty has attractions, especially for the young and for those who suffered most from the old order. The managing committese of the Higher Stage Co-operatives are almost always composed of younger men—and women—to whom the landlord system is a bad memory of their youth, and for whom the new regime has an almost mystic value. They will gladly try anything which the Party recommends; the older people are less confident, both of the system, and also of themselves. A little bewildered, unable to keep up so easily with the swift changes of a new age, they are inclined to let the young men take charge, since the great government, the People's Government, as they are constantly reminded, wills it that way.

Whatever the cause, the face of the countryside, particularly the North China plain, has been transformed by the establishment of Higher Stage Co-operatives. The small fields have gone, the innumerable little dykes of earth which marked their boundaries have been ploughed out. The private graveyards which occupied space on every owner's plot, are swiftly going, to be replaced, an inquirer is told, by public cemeteries. Instead of the patchwork of fields, growing each a differing crop, one vast unbroken sea of wheat stretches to the horizon. Even the traveller can see that this must imply a very great increase in the production of the wheat-growing area. For if the boundary dykes were small, they were also ubiquitous and in aggregate amounted to a great acreage.

The great plain, featureless enough under any system of agriculture, has now lost most of the few distinguishing marks which alleviated its monotony. The villages are still there, one every mile or so, combined now in threes or fours to make a Higher Stage Co-operative. But the graveyards, the fine trees which shaded them, the varying pattern of crops and small fields are gone. Cleared and unified, still cultivated by millions of hand labourers, the North China plain now awaits the tractor, the millennium of mechanized farming, which the regime has held out as the real answer to peasant poverty and back-breaking toil. It is obvious that no area in the world could be better adapted to this type of development, if it were not for the fact that it is still encumbered by the habitations of a vast population which the tractor must render largely redundant.

Not all of China grows wheat, nor is all the country flat. If the Higher Stage has transformed the face of the North China plain and made mechanized farming possible, the application of this policy to South China promises no such radical development. With the exception of the area behind

Shanghai in the Yangtze delta, the similar region around Canton where the Pearl River flows to the sea, and limited zones in the middle Yangtze and in the Red Plain of Ssuchuan, there are no great plains in the south and west. Everywhere mountain chains dissect the country, valleys are narrow, levels constantly vary. This is the land of rice, which must be grown in water, on levelled, dyked fields, capable of irrigation from a higher source and drainage to a lower conduit. As contours vary the shape of the fields must follow the level ground, twisting along the sides of streams, climbing terrace-like up the higher steep heads of the valleys. Sometimes long and narrow, or square and short, curved like half moons, the varying rice fields, cut from the hillsides by the labour of long past generations have imposed upon South and West China an intricate man-made pattern intimately geared to the flow of water and the contours of the land.

Wherever possible the water is led from the higher reaches of a stream through field after field, irrigating by natural flow and draining away when no longer required. But when the land is flat and the river lower than the fields water must be pumped up, either by those beautiful, immense and skilfully constructed water-wheels of bamboo which line the river banks, or by treadmills operated by human labour, or again by simple devices turned by an ass or ox. Villages are built upon the hillsides so that no scrap of level land shall be wasted; where there is no hill they are scattered along the high banks of a river or canal or stand upon a mound, probably itself the accumulation of the rubbish of the settlement which has risen upon the debris of former dwellings.

The changes which the introduction of the Higher Stage of Co-operative Farming can impose upon such a countryside are more limited than those which have occurred in the dry north. Land is pooled, but must still remain divided by the necessary dykes which hold in the water. Rice was always the main crop, and must still remain so. No doubt unification and central management increase production, cut out waste, eliminate individual inequalities in efficiency and husbandry, but the effect of all this can only be limited. Above all, no one has yet devised any practical method of mechanizing rice farming in hill country. The small fields are not here the product of fragmented ownership, but of the contours of the hillsides and the slope of valleys. They cannot be amalgamated, they are too irregular in shape and size to be cultivated by machines—or at least by such machines as have yet been devised. The best that mechanization can yet do is to substitute power pumps for the treadmills and water-wheels, the ass and the ox.

Elsewhere, in some parts of the world, rice farming has been mechanized; but such areas were formerly virgin soil, which artificial irrigation has brought into use. They are flat plains which had no habitations upon them, which could be laid out in wide regular fields, irrigated with pumped water. In China these conditions are only found where some marsh or wasteland has recently been recovered and reclaimed; in the densely inhabited delta lands of the Yangtze and Red River, near Hankow or in Ssuchuan, the application of these methods would involve displacing a population literally counted by millions. Any expectation that this can be effected is clearly unreal. There is therefore no present prospect that the new stage of Land Reform can, in the rice lands of China, be the preliminary to the introduction of mechanized farming.

This means that in more than half of China, and the most populous half, the objective of the regime in introducing this system can not be identical with the aims pursued in the dry North China plain. No profound change can occur in a country which always grew rice in small fields, still does so, and must continue with the same means of production, even though land tenure be reformed, central management introduced for larger areas and machinery brought in to aid irrigation. In South China and in the mountainous west the new system must stand on its own merits, using the labour of the members of the Co-operatives in very much the same way as the landlords used the tenant farmers and the tenants used the landless labourers. The northern peasant may have been induced to enter the Higher Stage by the prospect and promise of mechanization, a new wonder which would ease his toil and make the sacrifice of ownership and private management worth while. No such prospect can be held before the eyes of the southern peasant.

It would seem probable that the existing division between north and south, the dry and the wet, the wheat and the rice, which has throughout Chinese history played a major role, will be perpetuated and even accentuated when to these difference are added the mechanization of the north while the south continues to be the land of hand labour. Such a situation, combined with the development of the mineral resources of the north-west and the creation of industrial cities in that region, will tend to create a significant reversal of the economic trend which has dominated China for more than a thousand years, the growth of the south and the decline of the north. To this must be added the problem of the redundant labour which the mechanization of the wheat lands will produce.

Already the architects of China are being asked to study and plan a new type of settlement suitable to the mechanized farm lands of the north. The existing villages are too numerous, too close together, too haphazard in their location. They will get in the way of the tractors. But there are thousands of them, inhabited by many millions, perhaps as many as two hundred millions of people. These people now cultivate the great wheat plains by hand, aided by a few animals. Ploughing, sowing, weeding and reaping are done by hand; Chinese agriculture has been a vast process of horticulture, the hoe and the sickle have been its basic tools. The advent of the tractor and the mechanical reaper must revolutionize these methods, rendering the labour of millions unnecessary.

When this point is put to those in charge of the programme of mechanization the reply is that the programme will take many years, at the very least a decade to reach fulfilment. During this period industry will grow rapidly, and the new factories will absorb the redundant farm labour. This appears to be a very optimistic estimate of the possible expansion of industry, taking little account of the concurrent growth of the population itself. Industrial revolutions elsewhere have always been associated with a very great increase in population, and there seems no good reason why China should prove to be an exception. It is at least possible, perhaps certain, that the new programme of mechanized farming may create problems as great as those it seeks to solve, and it is also probable that the universal application of the policy of Higher Stage Co-operatives will add to them.

Under the age-old system of Chinese agriculture, harsh and cruel though it was, a balance of population was roughly maintained by the operation of the system itself. Individual families knew well enough what their land could yield, how many persons could find a bare subsistence from the return it gave. When this limit was surpassed, the alternatives were starvation or emigration. For centuries past these two choices lay before them and interacted to keep the rural population within limits. Famines were frequent, millions of men and women moved away to new lands; from the north to Manchuria, in the south to lands beyond the sea or into the relatively thinly populated south-western mountain provinces. During the last two centuries of the Manchu dynasty the growth of population became more rapid, partly due to the long peace assured by the strong rule of the earlier Manchu Emperors, K'ang Hsi and Ch'ien Lung, partly as a result of the introduction of new crops, the potato, sweet potato, cotton and tobacco.

The limits of internal migration were already in sight before the end of the dynasty, with the major exception of Manchuria, which has received, since the turn of the century, a migration estimated at nearly thirty million people, coming for the most part from the nearby provinces of Shantung and Hopei. Migration beyond the seas has in recent years been checked or wholly arrested by the legislation passed in the foreign countries themselves. It can no longer be counted upon to relieve the pressure of population in the southern coastal provinces. There still remain large tracts in the south-west and north-west where new forms of husbandry, irrigation and conservancy can extend the area under cultivation, but measured against the magnitude of the problem these palliatives are meagre. Foreign observers have for years seen no other solution than family limitation, but until very recently the Communist Party derided this notion as capitalist defeatism, and would give it no countenance.

In 1956 it was already apparent that this attitude was beginning to change. No doubt it had been very difficult, on the morrow of a great victory won in the name of the People, by which it was claimed that they were liberated, to turn round and tell them that they were far too numerous and too fecund. Six years of an intensive campaign to improve public health and sanitation, the end of civil disorder and a perceptible, if slight, rise in the living conditions of the peasants have already revealed the ominous shape of things to come. The Chinese population, for the first time for centuries enumerated with careful accuracy, was shown to be, not the four hundred millions of which everyone had talked for years, but much nearer six hundred millions. It is now realized that nothing short of a world cataclysm can prevent China having a population of close on one thousand millions by the beginning of the twenty-first century.

In March 1957 the logical conclusion from these facts was at last acknowledged. Peking announced that an exhibition demonstrating methods of birth control, 'which had already been shown in a number of cities' was now showing in the Capital.* It may be expected that once this decision has been taken the full force of the system of persuasion and publicity will swing into action to implement the new policy and explain why it is necessary, correct, and wholly in accordance with the teaching of Marx, Lenin and Mao Tse-tung. It will be instructive, to students of the system of persuasion, to observe how this last gyration is performed.

* Reuter reported from Peking on 8 March 1957 that the Minister of Health, Madame Li Te-chuan, had appealed strongly for birth control and planned families to 'improve the welfare and health of the people'. Madame Li told the Political Consultative Conference that the population of China was growing by about fifteen million a year. Every effort was needed to break down traditional opposition to birth control which was especially strong in rural areas.

Undoubtedly one factor will assist the regime to make the practice of birth control effective; in China, as elsewhere, the liberation of women from the strict domestic subjection of an earlier social order has been observed to be one of the necessary conditions for a decline in the birth rate. This is already quite apparent in the educated class. The large families of ten or more children which were the rule, and the ambition, of the older generation have almost disappeared. Two or three children are now the norm. But among the mass of the population no such development is yet visible. Under the old conditions a heavy infant mortality was expected and accepted as inevitable. A peasant family needed all the labour which it could provide, and the labour of the sons was obviously the cheapest source. The fact that when these grew up and married there was no land for them and no hope of sustaining a further increase on the family plot did not inhibit procreation.

Under the system of Higher Stage Co-operative Farming the members are largely freed from this old anxiety. Any member who works is entitled to his remuneration, land is no longer individually owned, so no family need be dependent on the return of a limited holding. It would appear inevitable that if the present rate of increase is kept up and indeed raised by the fall in infant mortality and the elimination of many diseases the number of members on every Higher Stage Co-operative will rise annually, unchecked by any fear of famine. The agricultural surplus production which the system is designed to ensure will soon be eaten up—literally—by the members of the Co-operatives themselves.

Critics of the People's Republic, running rather ahead of the present facts, have already claimed that the condition of the peasantry, far from improving, has been depressed by the policies of the new regime, and in particular by the drive for industrialization supported by the surplus agricultural production of the land.* Such evidence as can be collected by an observer who visits China does not bear out this assessment.

* This is the theme running through the work of W. W. Rostow and others. *The Prospects for Communist China*. Chapman & Hall. London. 1954. See pp. 294, 311.

There are clear signs in the villages, not merely in those which are incorporated in 'show piece' co-operative farms, that conditions have actually improved. Except in certain very fortunate areas, far from the march of armies, and free from the menace of flood and drought, the rural villages of China have, during the past thirty years, displayed every sign of poverty and misery. Many buildings were ruinous, few had been repaired; the peasants wore ragged, patched and worn out clothing. The children had the swollen pot bellies which indicate malnutrition. The street or road was unswept, undrained and filthy; packs of hungry, mangy and ownerless dogs scavenged among the refuse for scraps of food and ordure, flies swarmed over the heaps of muck. There was no medical service available for the peasants, a few, very few, villages had a rural school attended by a small number of the children.

These conditions have changed, and show some improvement. The dilapidated houses have been repaired, new dwellings built, some even having a glass window, where no such luxury was ever seen before. The roads are kept clean, rubbish heaps and filth have been removed and are not allowed to accumulate, the dogs have gone, the flies amazingly diminished. The peasants now wear whole garments, simple enough, but not ragged. The children look healthy and fed, there is always a village clinic displaying a vivid collection of posters illustrating diseases, how they are spread, how avoided, urging simple necessary measures of hygiene. These conditions are not confined to large villages which are the headquarters of a Co-operative, but can be seen in any village visited by chance for some purpose quite unconnected with agriculture.

Such improvement, or amelioration, is not in itself profound; the standard of living in a Chinese village remains far below that of comparable communities in Europe or in Japan, but it is certainly not falling further below the level of the Nationalist and republican periods, it has in fact appreciably improved. Whether this improvement can be continued and accelerated by the introduction of the Higher Stage Co-operative, as the Chinese Communists claim, or must prove transitory and illusory as the critics of the People's Republic maintain, would appear to be a matter of opinion and prejudice, rather than well founded calculation. That such improvement as has occurred has won the support and enthusiastic approval of the people themselves is obvious enough to any visitor.

The present generation of peasants can compare their former misery with such amelioration as has recently taken place. Better houses, cleanly living conditions, the reduction of disease, medical attention, a better diet, less infant mortality, are all desirable, but are not fundamental changes in the pattern of life. Many of these benefits will bring new problems, above all a rapid increase in numbers. Even if the present standard of improved livelihood can be maintained, it would not for long satisfy a population which has been roused to a new political consciousness and promised much more than this. As in so many other fields the regime has so far profited by gaining the credit due for performing a necessary work of social salvage, which is in no sense an essential attribute of the Marxist system, but could, and should, have been done by any reasonably competent government of whatever political complexion.

If 'socialist agriculture' is to have a wider meaning than this it must imply coming to grips with far deeper problems and making an attempt to reshape the fundamental basis of Chinese society. Mao Tse-tung has claimed that this is, in fact, the intention. The 'old Chinese economy' together with the old form of government and the old culture must be replaced. But the old economy was precisely the methods and manners of an agriculture which sustained, in poverty no doubt, but still sustained, a population which has now attained six hundred million. Very few of this enormous mass of mankind yet live by industry; at least 80 per cent are peasant cultivators.

A reform of land tenure, even on such a sweeping scale as the virtual abolition of private landed property in the Higher Stage of Co-operative Farming, may improve production, but still leaves the economy as dependent on agriculture as it was before. It will still employ the labour of millions of peasants, unless mechanization is introduced to reduce the numbers so employed and lighten their toil. But mechanized farming on a very large scale has hitherto been successfully applied where the population was light, the lands open and almost virgin. If mechanization is to be employed in the agriculture of North China this involves introducing the technique used in open countries to a plain densely inhabited by millions of farmers, an area which has been settled for thousands of years. It may be possible to reconstruct both the economy and the society of North China in this way, but it is certain that no such gigantic undertaking has been attempted elsewhere.

If this is the answer to the problem of Asian peasant poverty and subsistence agriculture, a problem not confined to China, the experiment which the Chinese are planning will be watched with intense interest by her neighbours to the south. In all the rice and wheat lands of Asia the governments of the newly independent states are alike threatened not so much by the political message of Communism as by the doubt whether any other system can solve the problem of the peasant and his poverty. If once it becomes clear that the Chinese system offers an alternative more hopeful than any provided by private land tenure, it will be impossible to hold back the surge of support which local Communist parties will obtain.

In China the system of Persuasion has convinced the whole nation that the Higher Stage, and no doubt any further stages which may be planned, contain the whole answer to this problem. Once the system is in full operation, everyone will see for themselves that it possesses immense advantages, no one will want to reject it except a handful of selfish landlords. There seems to be no sound reason for doubting, as many foreign critics do, whether this belief is genuine and really held by the Chinese Communist leadership. No educated person in China can fail to know that the survival of all regimes has in the long run depended upon holding the consent of the governed, and that the vast majority of these are peasants. Every dynasty fell primarily because the land problem became too acute, the misery of the peasants insufferable. The Chinese People's Republic, a regime founded by men who have had twenty-two years of guerrilla, peasant warfare in their experience, and owe their power and their survival to peasant support, must make the solution of this problem the key stone of its policy, for if the support of the peasants is truly lost it would be doomed.

The disappearance of landlordism and the initiation of the era of co-operative farming thus presents the Chinese people and their government with three broad choices. If the system is allowed to operate for the benefit of the peasants, mechanization being introduced gradually and carefully, the support of the peasants will be secured, but their numbers will have to be controlled by an intensive policy of family limitation. Rapid industrialization will have to be confined to areas where exploitation of resources is easiest and least costly. The programme of industrialization as a whole will have to be restricted so that it will not be too great a drain on the production of agriculture. If, on the other hand, reasons of defence, or doctrinaire belief in the virtue of the industrial worker as such are allowed to outweigh the needs of the peasants, then the system will be strained and driven to build up an ever larger surplus at the expense of the peasant consumers, until the day comes when they will see no value in the new order, and the old cycle of rebellion and disorder will reappear.

Lastly, aware of this danger, but also unwilling to wait for decades for the millennium of an industrialized, socialist China, the regime may try to push forward the mechanization of agriculture wherever possible, and at the same time build up a giant industry to absorb the redundant peasantry. Such a task involves a co-ordination of resources and an accuracy of planning which no previous form of government or social order has achieved; the Communist Party, believing with dogmatic faith in the superiority of its own doctrines, may feel confident that even this high goal can be attained.

CHAPTER SIX

ART, LITERATURE AND ARCHAEOLOGY

'LET FLOWERS OF Many Kinds Blossom, let Diverse Schools of Thought contend.' In these fair words Mao Tse-tung encourages the artists of China to develop their individual styles, the scholars to propound their varying theories. Nothing could be more liberal, more promising, and more at variance with the conception of the Communist attitude to art and literature that has prevailed in the West. Before the Western observer is ready to take these promises at their face value he will want to know the answer to many searching questions. In what soil are the hundred flowers of art to grow and bloom, with what will they be manured; are they to be true wild flowers, sporting and cross-fertilizing as chance influences may decide, or are they to be well cultivated pot plants carefully weeded and trained with all the skill of an expert gardener?

It is already clear that the free contention of the scholars must be interpreted strictly within the limits of an overriding acceptance of Marxist philosophy. It may be true that debate can rage upon scientific questions, or upon interpretations of historical facts, but it is certainly not possible to publish freely controversial polemics directed to prove that Communism is a fallacy, or that Marx was mistaken in his analysis of society. China is in an age of faith; if a mediaeval Pope had urged upon the scholars of his day their right and duty to debate the finer points of theology, he would not have meant, nor have been taken to mean, that they were free to advocate the superior claims to truth of the doctrines of Islam or Judaism.

Consequently, some Western observers will, from the standpoint of their own beliefs, feel that the freedom Mao commends to his followers is the right to question religious truths while accepting materialist errors uncritically; others, having no dogmatic beliefs, will not recognize freedom in a system

122

which sets any firm frontier upon the range of the questing intellect. Once certain doctrines have been proclaimed and accepted as positive and immutable truths, they are no longer open to question; errors may be analysed and exposed, but such mistaken views must not be put forward as alternatives which the reader is free to accept if he finds them more convincing. During long periods of history, and in many parts of the world, this dogmatic outlook has prevailed; it has been thought that free intellectual inquiry into any and every question was unhealthy, tended to disrupt society and corrupt morality. This view is now held in China, and the system of persuasion and propaganda has been established to support it. There is therefore very little doubt that the freedom of the scholars to contend is similar to the right enjoyed by mediaeval scholastics who debated the question of how many angels could dance on the point of a pin, but never raised the previous question, whether there were in fact such beings as angels in existence to do the dancing.

The position of the plastic arts is different. It is not obvious that this or that style of painting or sculpture must necessarily conform with or contravert the economic and social doctrines of Marx and Lenin. To the outside observer there seems no real reason why abstract art should be out of favour with Communists for any cause other than that the leaders of the movement do not happen to appreciate this style. In conservative circles in the non-Communist world the same prejudice is often entertained, and 'advanced' styles are frequently believed to be associated with Left-wing opinions. One of the paradoxes of the revolutionary society of China is that the fervent opponents of nineteenth-century capitalism and imperialism are ardent admirers of precisely the style of painting which was held in high honour by the Victorian Empire builders.

A recognition of such disconcerting facts has led many critics to the conclusion that the whole of the old Chinese artistic tradition is in imminent danger of destruction. It is argued that Mao Tse-tung's own dictum that the old Chinese culture, together with the old Chinese economy and state, must be replaced by a new culture and a new economy can only mean that the old arts will be progressively neglected, discouraged and disparaged until they become the hall-mark of reactionary tendency and are formally condemned. Just as some vestiges of capitalist economy survive until the time is ripe for their elimination, so the old style of painting will be allowed to linger on until a new generation of artists has been trained up in the practice of social realism, and then extinguished. Language reform will enable the old literature to be discarded by the easy expedient of failing to issue new editions in the simplified script and failure to educate the rising generation in classical Chinese. No catastrophic burning of the books will be necessary, a slow process of neglect will, within two generations, make the old literature a dead language. The surge and sweep of the great programme of industrialization must destroy the charm of the old Chinese cities, eliminate the monuments and temples of the past, which to the new rulers are hateful reminders of the society which they seek to replace.

This is the case made out with a mixture of gloomy satisfaction and gloating grief by the Nationalist exiles in Formosa and many of their overseas supporters. It is designed to support the thesis that China is now nothing but a Russian colony, at least culturally, and that the destruction of an individual Chinese culture is necessary to secure the permanent domination of Russian influence and the Communist regime. Though no doubt stated with undue emphasis for propaganda purposes, this indictment needs to be examined and tested against observed facts: the transitory fashions of a revolutionary age must, if possible, be distinguished from the deeper and more enduring trends which are shaping the development of the arts in the new society.

It is first necessary to reflect that China is not a museum, and that the development of modern industrial civilization under any form of economic and political regime, not excluding the late Nationalist government, would inevitably lead to profound changes in the taste of the nation and in its artistic mode of expression. The decay of some aspects of the old culture was already fully apparent many years before the Communist Party came to power. Art critics, indeed, have sometimes seen little but imitation in the painting of the last two centuries, or even earlier periods. Few collectors of porcelain have esteemed the wares of the eighteenth century and later ages, except for the technical excellence of the workmanship. Nor can it be said that even under the Empire itself in its last age the monuments of the past were preserved with care and devotion. The movement to revive literature by abandoning the classical style and using the living speech of the people began in the years immediately following the First World War. Over a wide field of art and literature the present People's Republic has only carried forward movements which originated in the early Republic and reflected the general dissatisfaction with the stagnation which had become apparent in the cultural life of China.

In order to assess the true effect of the policies of the present regime upon art in China it is first necessary to consider the state of the arts under the previous regimes since the fall of the Empire and then examine the new departures and developments that have arisen during the past six years. A clear division between what in China is called the Western style and the traditional Chinese style of painting had already become established in the period between the two world wars. Traditional Chinese painting continued to engage the talents of the great majority of artists, and among these were men such as the veteran Ch'i Pai-shih, who could be accounted masters in any period. Virtually untouched by any Western influence this school produced, and still produces, works which conform to the long established techniques and conventions of classical Chinese painting. It would not be easy to claim that these works were superior, or inferior, to those of their forerunners the classical artists of the Manchu and even the late Ming period. The old tradition still continues, still meets with widespread appreciation and admiration, and in this sense has still a strong vitality which as yet shows no sign of diminishing.

Another school, regarded by older scholars as iconoclastic,

sought inspiration from purely Western sources. Although usually trained when young men in the classical manner, these artists went abroad to Paris, studied afresh at the Western schools, and returned to China to paint in oils in the Western style. It is doubtful whether their work received in their native land more than a very limited degree of appreciation, mainly from people of similar experience to their own. It must also be said that the Western critic, who on this ground can feel more sure of himself, found nothing in these works which struck him as truly original, nothing characteristic of any new interpretation, nothing which distinguished the work of the Chinese Western style painters from the average productions of Western artists of rather moderate talents.

There arose, towards the end of this period, especially during the war with Japan, a new school formed by men who had studied in Europe, at first painted in the Western style, but after returning to China had begun to experiment with a re-interpretation of the classical tradition, incorporating in their work some of their Western experience and also influences derived from a study of the earlier art of ancient China. The fact that most of these artists worked during those years in the remote western interior provinces, beyond the range of the Japanese invasion, had an important influence. At Tunhuang, the cave temple site in North-West China, many of them were able to make a first-hand study of the greatest collection of surviving early Chinese painting, the frescoes dating from the T'ang and slightly earlier periods (sixth to tenth centuries AD) which have been preserved upon the walls of the Tunhuang cave temples. This art pre-dated the work of the great Sung (eleventh to thirteenth centuries) masters, from which the later classical style of Chinese painting directly derives.

The art of Tunhuang may well represent what was in its period the popular, as opposed to the more sophisticated Court style of painting, which as known by early copies, has closer affinities with the later classical style. It is also obvious that the Tunhuang style has been influenced by or more probably may itself have influenced, Persian art and has thus some remote affinity with the art of Byzantium and the Italian primitives. These characteristics, and the strength and simple vigour of the style, appealed to the Chinese artists who had received a Western training. They began to paint in a style influenced both by this background and by the Tunhuang art. From this inspiration there has arisen a school of modern Chinese painters whose work has a definite link with the classical and pre-classical tradition in China, and also employs some of the forms of Western style, notably using perspective, which classical Chinese painting ignores. Men such as Wu Tso-jen and the late Hsu Pei-hung, both leaders of this school, can be said to have created a new era in Chinese painting, an art vigorous, alive, truly national and yet not directly imitative of any previous manner. The best known of these artists are now working in China, members of the Institute of Fine Arts in Peking.

Yet if this is the flower which to the Western critic seems to bloom best in the Chinese garden of arts, it would seem that the weight of official patronage and commendation, though not withheld from either the new or the classical Chinese styles, is still more fully bestowed upon the recent development of the pure Western manner, a style which now takes its models from Moscow rather than Paris. To the outside observer, at least, the effects of this enthusiasm for the Russian social realist school are unfortunate. Few Western critics would accept the opinion that Russia, either before or since the October Revolution, has stood in the van of European painting. The consequences of taking Russian work as the model and inspiration for the Western school of painting in China has been to substitute un-original imitations of inferior works for equally unoriginal reproductions of a style which was itself alive and powerful. No trace of any modern trend appears in these works. Not only abstract art but every other development which has diversified the European tradition since the end of the last century appear to be wholly ignored. Social realism is directly inspired, it would seem, by the mediocre work of the last decades of the nineteenth century; Every Picture Tells a Story, and the stories are banal.

Whatever may be the origin of this depressing development in Russia, the situation in China would appear to be an example of the working of one of the sterner laws of culture contact in every age and country. A Gresham's Law would seem to govern the exchange of artistic styles between peoples of widely divergent cultural traditions. The Bad always is preferred to the Good. Just as the Europeans, on reaching the Far East, began to collect with great enthusiasm the latest and least meritorious examples of Chinese porcelain, the modern, derivative, over-decorated and vulgar Chinese and Japanese bronzes, the curious and the quaint, the elaborate and the intricate, mistaking fine craftsmanship for great art, while ignoring or misunderstanding the real aesthetic values of an alien style which ran counter to their knowledge and experience, so the modern Chinese are all too apt to fall into similar errors.

There is, in the earlier stages of appreciation and collection of a foreign art, an inherent tendency to play safe. The significance and the conventions of the classical style, naturally the first to be studied, have been learned and understood; whatever departs from these must be regarded with suspicion, and anything which violently flouts them is condemned out of hand. Thus the Manchus, themselves a people who were on the periphery of the Chinese culture, enshrined the waning classical styles of China with a veneration and admiration which admitted of no qualification, and obstructed all advance. Refinement and clever craftsmanship could be accepted so long as this involved no departure from time-worn themes and traditional subjects. When the Western critics first began to understand something of the history of Chinese art they were almost equally intolerant. Having discovered the Sung, they despised the Ming and all that followed as imitative, degenerate or feeble.

It would seem very probable that the Chinese are themselves now passing through this experience. They have discovered the art of the West, they can appreciate and enjoy it in its classical form, but they cannot yet bring themselves to see the organic connection between this style and the later, modern developments, nor understand what the contemporary Western artist is seeking to achieve. It is far more likely to be the workings of this psychological law than the fiats of a political party that at present bans the modern trend in Western art from Chinese galleries and studios. The present surfeit of social realism is therefore a phase, perhaps a necessary and inevitable phase, in the adjustment of Chinese taste to the impact of the Western artistic tradition, which for the first time, is really widespread. The innumerable lifelike busts of Mao Tse-tung, and heroic pictures of the revolutionary wars which now adorn so many Chinese public buildings and factories are no more great works of art than the pot-bellied bronze statuettes of Maitreya Buddha and the *famille rose* porcelain which the Victorians so ardently collected. But both served to introduce an alien art to a larger and ignorant public. Only when this low-level introduction has been made, and accepted, can the slow process of education and true appreciation of a foreign art make its way upward into the aesthetic comprehension of the creative artists and the connoisseurs.

Is it therefore possible that so far from representing a collapse of the old Chinese artistic tradition the present pre-occupation with an outmoded style of Western art is a fallow period in which the seed of some future and original departure is gradually maturing; the paradox of apparent conservatism in art in the midst of revolution is only apparent, for the adjustment of aesthetic sensibility and the modification of taste may well need more time and prove a more delicate operation than political revolution or the transformation of the economy.

The sharp separation now observed in the work of artists and in the teaching of the art schools between the Chinese and Western styles in painting is itself a proof that this adjustment is still very far from complete; it indicates that the dominant attitude is still one of uncritical reverence for the classical tradition in both fields; each must be kept pure, free from what is clearly thought to be the contamination of the other. The relative unimportance of the school which has brought Western experience to a reinterpretation of the Chinese tradition proves that this approach is still esoteric and has not yet caught the imagination of the age.

On the other hand, there is no real evidence that the movement or lack of movement in art is directly related to the policy of the regime. It is certainly not true that the classical style is denied publicity or the facilities for reproduction and dissemination. The works of eminent painters in the old Chinese style are everywhere on sale, are reproduced very widely and frequently exhibited. Leading artists of the new school of modern Chinese style painting hold positions of importance in the Institute of Fine Arts and the art schools, and these schools and institutes receive an ample revenue from the government. The creative artist, no matter what style he works in, is a favoured being, well rewarded, assured of congenial working conditions, given facilities for travel and fresh inspiration from contact with other aspects of the national life. Foreign artists observing these conditions are rather inclined to wonder whether the Chinese artist under the People's Republic is not perhaps a little too comfortable and cared for, his life rather too institutionalized. The disappearance of the private patron and the collector able to pay an economic price for creative work, a consequence of the economic and social policy of the revolution, has been countered by the State itself, which has taken over both these roles and fulfils them with generosity. But this has perhaps meant not only that the artist has escaped from the garret, but also from the stimulus which only the garret could provide.

Examination of the facts thus shows that there is no campaign being waged by the Party or the government to destroy the Chinese artistic tradition and substitute an alien style. There is in China today a strong, and perhaps largely misguided enthusiasm for one style of Western art, a style which the artists and art-loving public of western Europe and overseas countries now regard as outmoded and lacking vitality. There is reason to think that this style is popular in China partly because it is believed to represent the true and orthodox European tradition, modern trends being disregarded as decadent or aberrant, partly because the popularity of this style in Russia has led the Chinese to think that the Russian social realist school reflects the taste of the proletariat, and is thus more in touch with the people than the modern schools, which it is thought, the people do not appreciate or admire. The Chinese masses, when introduced to an alien Western art, must be expected, according to this reasoning, to prefer the same style as the working masses of Europe.

On the other hand, the Chinese continue, at the same time, to perpetuate and to appreciate their own style of art: it is evident that no ideological objection to this traditional art is felt in Party or government circles, since very large sums of state money are expended on exhibiting, reproducing and disseminating such works, and on the art schools where artists working in the Chinese style are employed and trained. In so far as government action can be seen as a danger to the free development of art, the danger comes rather from too much care and fostering than from repression and neglect.

Mao Tse-tung has written that a new Chinese culture, which would involve new artistic styles, must be expected to rise from the new kind of Chinese society and economy. All history shows that such an expectation is almost certain to be fulfilled. History also gives very strong reasons to expect that any such development will take not less than two full generations, and perhaps much longer to materialize. The rise of Christianity ultimately transformed the art of the late Roman Empire, substituting the Byzantine, Christian inspired work of Ravenna for the weak copies of Greek models which had lingered as late as the reign of Constantine. In more modern times a major development in European art, the rise of the French school in the nineteenth century, occurred in the land where the French Revolution had run its course, transforming society in the years between 1789 and 1815. But it was in the second half of the nineteenth century, not in the first revolutionary years, that the great painters of the French school were most active and influential. Fifty years would not be a long time for the Chinese artists to adjust to a new society, and at the same time to arrive at a more intimate and balanced understanding of the Western artistic tradition. When that time is reached Chinese art may be expected to respond to the delayed stimulus originally imparted by the social and political revolution of our own period.

While it may well be true that the flowers of art may blossom in China today as freely as in any other society, it is not so clear that the contention of diverse schools of thought, as manifested in literature, is really so untramelled. On this point the official doctrine as expounded by Lu Ting-yi, Director of the Propaganda Department of the Central Committee of the Chinese Communist Party, is more ambivalent. On the one hand, 'History shows that unless independent thinking and free discussion are encouraged, academic life stagnates.' On the other, 'We can see things that are obviously pernicious. The stuff written by Hu Feng is one such example. Pornographic and gutter literature that debauches people and turns them into gangsters is another.'*

Western critics will whole-heartedly subscribe to the first of these dicta, but will wish to examine the second with more care. 'The stuff written by Hu Feng' is one thing, pornographic and gutter literature is quite another. The problem of how far 'horror comics' and suggestive sex-exciting literature should be prohibited, controlled, censored or supervised is very much alive and very far from solved in the Western non-Communist world; we, too, can see the things that are 'obviously pernicious', but we find it much harder to discriminate between the literature which is suitable for adults, and therefore to be freely published, and the borderline material which may avoid the charge of pornography, but fail to qualify as a work of art. We can admire the confidence which the Chinese display on this debatable ground, we can recognize the frankness with which they avow the real reasons for classing the 'stuff written by Hu Feng' as obviously pernicious, but we cannot share the view which makes this classification.

* Lu Ting-yi. Speech on the policy of the Communist Party of China on art, literature and science. Peking *People's Daily* (*Jen Min Jih Pao*). 3 June 1956.

Hu Feng, a well-known author, was no writer of porno-graphy, but his works are now regarded as counter-revolutionary. He is charged with having 'attacked the Party and the people's regime'. While 'we hold that there must be democratic liberties among the people, no freedom should be extended to counter-revolutionaries: for them we have only dictatorship. This is a question of drawing a political demarcation line. A clear political line must be drawn between friend and foe.'*

Nothing, indeed, could well be clearer. The contention of the diverse schools of thought must stop short of politics, must not attack the Party nor the people's regime. But in what way, by whom, and with what criteria attacks are differentiated from criticism remains obscure. Criticism is invited, encouraged. 'Anyone criticized should be allowed to answer back, and such counter-criticism should not be muzzled.' Also, 'a strict distinction must be made between the battle of ideas among the people and the struggle against counter-revolutionaries'. Finally, there emerges a more precise definition of the field of freedom:

'Letting flowers of many kinds blossom, diverse schools of thought contend, means that we stand for freedom of independent thinking, of debate, of creative work; freedom to criticize and freedom to express, maintain and reserve one's opinions on questions of art, literature or scientific research.'

It is thus politics which are left out of the list of subjects suitable for the contention of the schools of thought; a large omission, and one not easily defined, for on the one hand it is a rightist error to 'assume that art, literature and science have nothing to do with politics' and 'on the other hand it is one-sided and "leftist" to oversimplify things and equate art, literature and science with politics. This view is equally wrong'. It is hardly surprising that some of those who responded to this new policy by making criticisms found that they had over-stepped the narrow boundary and indulged in 'attacks'.

Among these were two of the leading members of one of the

* Lu Ting-yi. Op. cit.

Coalition parties, the Democratic League. Chang Po-chun and Lo Lung-chi are both vice-chairmen of this party, and as a consequence of the criticisms which they made they were accused of being 'bourgeois rightists' and of hatching schemes to stir up trouble. On this subject the chief organ of the regime, the Peking *People's Daily* (*Jen Min Jih Pao*), had some illuminating comments. After describing the 'sinister role' which the Democratic League, or some of its leaders had played in the spate of criticisms let loose by the policy of letting the diverse schools contend, it frankly avowed the purpose of this policy.

'The Communist Party foresaw that a class battle between the bourgeoisie and the proletariat was inevitable. For a long time in order to let the bourgeoisie and the bourgeois intellectuals wage this battle the press published few or no affirmative views and did not counter the frantic attacks made by the bourgeois reactionary rightists. . . . The reason was to enable the masses to distinguish clearly those whose criticism was well-intentioned from those with ill intentions behind their so-called criticisms. In this way the forces for an opportune counter blow amassed strength. Some people call this scheming, but we say it was quite open.'

Some people may, indeed, be inclined to agree with those in China who raised their eyebrows at this manoeuvre.

After pointing out that the number of those who had gone too far was small, and did not even represent the majority view in the Democratic League, the article considers what treatment the sinners should receive, and in spite of the violence of the language used to denounce their offence, comes down on the side of mercy.

'Should they be punished? As things stand this is not necessary, because the people's regime is very consolidated and many of them are prominent people: we can afford to treat them leniently without resorting to punishment. Calling them "rightist elements" in general is enough, it is not necessary to call them reactionaries.'

It would be ungracious to look a gift horse too closely in the mouth, but it is hard to avoid remarking that the logic which decides that those engaged in sinister schemes should be spared because they are prominent people is obscure, and the *Jen Min Jih Pao* itself, in the same article, had already fallen into what it finally decides is the error of calling the offenders 'reactionaries'.

These are not the only indications that in this controversy the force of the language used is a poor guide to the real strength of the indignation felt, or the degree of disgrace into which the too outspoken critics had fallen. A doctrine which in a Communist country comes very close to toleration of dissent is preached in the concluding part of the same article.

'There is another group of rightists who only talked but did nothing. Their talk was similar to that of these other rightists but they took no destructive action. With them it is necessary to be even more lenient. Their wrong statements should be criticized thoroughly and without mercy, but they should be permitted to reserve their views. Whoever they are they should still be allowed freedom of speech. There is no harm in keeping such a small group within the great consolidated state, now that the masses understand their mistakes. It is necessary to recognize that the rightists educate us in negative aspects. In this respect the poisonous weeds have had their uses. Their poison has already been set free (? dissipated) and the damage it has done among the people is also salutary.'*

The 'great consolidated state', that modern version of the universal Empire of the past, can also, now, feel confidence that Orthodoxy is not in real danger, and scholastic deviations and eccentricities are harmless irritants, like fleas on a dog, serving to keep the host animal mentally alert.

If the question of how far freedom to criticize really extends is still entangled in the thickets of Marxist theory, it is at least clear that the gloomy predictions of those who feared that the Communist regime must necessarily be hostile to the cultural heritage of the older China are mistaken. By implication it is admitted that such an attitude did in fact prevail in Party circles,

* *Jen Min Jih Pao*. 1 July 1957.

but it is now exposed as 'incorrect'. In some ways it may be said that the new policy towards the older literature is more liberal and understanding than the dominant trend in education and thought under the republican and Nationalist regimes.

The modern trend in Chinese literature long predated the triumph of the Communist Party; within a few years of the fall of the Empire in 1912 movements were afoot to adopt the colloquial language for literature in place of classical Chinese; the long neglected and despised novels of the Ming period were given the status of classics; a new literature of novels and criticism written in the modern vernacular and reflecting strong Western influence rapidly obtained a wide popularity. Some of the great literary figures of that age are now, like the novelist Lu Hsün, venerated by the Communists as a forerunner, others like the educationalist and philosopher, Hu Shih, execrated as a 'hanger-on of the American imperialists'. As a very great part of the new modern literature of the twenties and thirties was revolutionary in tone, influenced by European left-wing writers and later by Russian literature, it is natural that it should suit the taste of China today, and that the older literature, produced under the so-called 'feudal' social system of the Empire, should be suspect as reflecting the undesirable ideals of the past. Confucius, his works and those of his followers, were at first treated with scant respect and condemned as the linchpin of 'feudal ideology'. Those who feared that the old Chinese literature would be allowed to fall into complete oblivion, if not actually suppressed, had some evidence for their alarm.

It could be argued that without any active ill will the Chinese Communists and the new generation educated under their instruction would find little to interest them in the literature of pre-revolutionary China. Its approach to life, the emphasis on the values of family solidarity, the indifference to the community as a whole except in so far as unquestioning loyalty to an autocratic Emperor was concerned, the opposition to change and progress implicit in the outlook of its philosophy, the neglect of science and technology, were all attitudes repellent to the ardent modernizer and revolutionary. Even the vast range and bulk of Chinese historical material was permeated with a theory of moral values, or cyclical rise and fall, the present mirroring the past, the future predictable on a like pattern, which is antithetical to the theories of Marx and Lenin.

The real need for the study of the natural sciences and their application made it in any case certain that classical Chinese could no longer expect to hold exclusive domination over the mind of the rising generation. Even without any social revolution it was already clear that the Chinese classics, like the Western classics, would increasingly have to make room for modern subjects and for science. Such tendencies were already strong and increasing under the Nationalist regime; before the Communists came to power seven out of every ten university students followed science and technical courses in the universities of Peking. In the years following the Communist revolution it might be expected that the immense impulse which this event has given to the study of science in China would result in the virtual abandonment or utter stagnation of the classical learning.

In fact the policy of the new regime has not been destructive of the old literature and art, but on the contrary, has been directed to the 'critical acceptance' of the heritage of the traditional culture. In the same key speech addressed to artists, writers and scientific workers, Lu Ting-yi defines the attitude of the Party in terms a great deal more explicit than those employed upon the thorny problem of freedom of debate. The national heritage from the past is rich, it must be 'studied seriously and accepted critically'. 'Wholesale Westernization is misguided and must be opposed, there is still too much of the attitude of belittling our national heritage, and in some spheres this is still a really serious problem.' The tendency to reject the traditional culture without discrimination or examination is condemned, even while it is admitted that this trend is still strong. Much evidence of the actual activity of the government to foster and preserve the literature and art of the past shows that these words are not an empty gesture.

In so far as the traditional literature and philosophy of China is now to be subjected to an examination and revaluation in the light of the broader knowledge of human history and culture available to modern Chinese scholars, this process is, of course, far from new; it has been going on for at least thirty or forty years, but it is also true that the process is still incomplete. The scholars of the early Republican period and those of the Nationalist period were indeed aware of the wider horizons of Western history and literature, and deeply influenced by their Western learning, yet it was often a narrowing influence. Chinese scientists too readily accepted their Western teachers' opinion that all science had originated in the West, and took no interest at all in the achievements of their own civilization; Chinese humanists were either specialists in their own literature and history, or in those of the West; there was little contact between the two branches of learning and comparatively only a slight influence of one upon the other. Just as artists worked either in the Chinese style or in the Western manner, but very few attempted a synthesis or accepted an influence, so the humanities in Chinese education remained sharply divided between Western and Chinese studies.

Western non-Communist scholars will be inclined to feel grave doubts about a system which introduces the criteria of Marxism into the study of academic subjects but it must be admitted that, at least in the earlier stages of this process in China, something has been gained of real value. Since the Chinese Communists accept the theory of the world-wide unity of the masses, the People, it follows that they seek and find evidences of this unity, this common humanity, wherever they look. This tendency has therefore broken down the mutual exclusiveness of Western and Chinese studies, and has introduced a much-needed current of new thought into the closed world of Chinese classical scholarship.

It may be that the corpus of Chinese dynastic history is now subjected to a too minute search for evidences of popular unrest and an age-old dissatisfaction with the 'feudal' system of the Empire, but at least this leads to a serious study of the economic forces which were at work in different ages, an aspect of history for which the source material exists, but which fell outside the range of interest of the older generations of scholars. Present day pre-occupation with the precise ages which should be identified as those of slavery, feudalism and nascent capitalism may seem over meticulous to the Western student, but has served to break up for ever the old, unreal pattern of philosophic unity which Confucian thought had imposed upon Chinese historiography. The history of Chinese science and technology, almost untouched until today by Western* or Chinese scholarship, is now given pride of place in Chinese universities and research institutes, and if the reason for this preference stems from Marxist dogma, it none the less brings attention and research to a long-neglected and important field.

In their re-examination of the literature and poetry of the past the modern Chinese scholars are discovering that it did not always reflect only the sophistication and luxury of a privileged class, but also the enduring aspirations and frustrations of ordinary humanity, the People, who were never wholly cut off from the educated minority who alone could record their hopes and fears. It may seem an arbitrary criticism which decided that T'ang scholar officials such as Tu Fu and Po Chu-i should be hailed as 'People's Poets', but it destroys the doctrinaire assumption that such poets, on account of their class origin, can have no message for the liberated People; and it has the further very practical value that the works of these great masters of the old literature are republished in plentiful editions. The selection of the new culture heroes of the past may be directed by the precepts of Marxism, but this selection is no more arbitrary than the older discrimination based upon conformity to Confucian orthodoxy. The ship of Chinese learning had for too long been steered by a crew which looked out on one side only, and the ship had developed a dangerous list; now crew and passengers are leaning over the other rail in an endeavour to get on an even keel.

* Until the recent work of Dr J. Needham. *Science and Civilisation in China.* Cambridge University Press. 1954.

Those who feared that the advent of a Communist government would mean the end of the old Chinese literature have thus been proved wrong; but if that literature is unquestionably being preserved, republished, and respected, it is also being re-examined and criticized from a new standpoint. Every age will make its own valuation of the past, and every succeeding age will in turn discard some of the ideas which their forefathers cherished; what matters is that the records and works of these former times should be preserved and transmitted for the enrichment of future generations who can be trusted to make their own judgment without relying wholly upon the commentaries of the present period.

The drama in China, in its traditional form nearer to opera than to straight theatre, was the point of contact between the common people and the sophisticated literary culture of the educated class. It drew its themes and stories from authentic history, Buddhist legend, and classical literature, it often incorporates famous poems and prose quotations in the libretto; through this medium even the illiterate could claim their share in the heritage of the ancient Chinese civilization. It is, moreover, a secular art, not deriving from popular religion, as is the case in most parts of Asia, but originating in the Court of the T'ang dynasty (seventh to tenth centuries AD) and slowly percolating down through the society of later ages until it has become a truly national art appealing to all classes. Further, it had retained its ancient vitality and was hardly affected in any way by the modern influences coming from the West.

The Communists could not fail to acknowledge that the opera was thus both a national heritage and a people's art, in spite of its manifest links with the traditional culture and the Court. As the main recreation of the masses, including the rural population, whose knowledge of the famous operas was often extensive, the Party early adopted and patronized it. When they came to power the Peking opera and later the numerous provincial variations which flourish in all parts of China received the full favour and encouragement of the regime. It was without doubt partly as a result of their experience of the popular taste for the old drama which led the Party to realize that the policy of 'wholesale Westernization' would not make a wide appeal to the Chinese masses and would tend to divorce the Party from the People.

'In the theatre we have already had experience of applying the principle, "let flowers of many kinds blossom side by side, weed through the old to let the new emerge". That has been most valuable. What we must do now is to apply the same principle to all other branches of art and literature.'*

The experience has indeed been valuable, for there is some evidence which indicates that this appreciation of the popular taste and its love of the old culture was not at first widespread or approved in Party circles. When the regime first came to power in Peking some of the best-known Peking operas were banned as 'superstitious' or because their theme seemed too permeated with the 'feudal' sentiments of the older age. The provincial theatre suffered from a similar doctrinaire supervision by ardent opponents of the old order. This tendency has now been stigmatized as 'incorrect', and it is admitted that it is 'necessary to wage a resolute struggle against doctrinairism'. The theatre today is once more truly liberated, and it may be hoped that the cause of this change of policy, the realization that the doctrinaire approach to the arts was alienating popular support, will prove equally beneficial to the other arts and to literature.

The extreme doctrinaire Communist approach was a sign of lack of confidence; the fear that any and every influence from the imperial and 'bourgeois' past must undermine the new regime revealed a mistrust of that regime's real popularity with the mass of the people. Six years later in this, as in other fields, the Party can laugh at such fears, and tolerate, without alarm, the public performance of plays and operas which glorify the imperial heroes of old China and display the wealth of Buddhist legend in works written in an age when these legends were universally accepted as truths. Yet there is and must be a subtle

* Lu Ting-yi. Op. cit.

change: the old plays expressed an outlook and beliefs which were real and operative to the audiences for whom they were written. Now this outlook and these beliefs are increasingly only of historical interest to the audiences of today and to-morrow. There will always be room for plays having this interest, but the moderns will also demand others which deal with contemporary problems and express the feelings and viewpoint of the present age.

The regime has encouraged dramatists to supply this need, both by writing new operas in the old manner, such as the famous 'White Haired Girl', which treats the contemporary theme of landlord oppression and peasant resistance in the manner of the classical opera, and also the production of straight plays, owing much to Western and specifically Russian influence. These plays are popular and well attended; it is perhaps too soon to judge how many of them will find abiding acceptance and an honoured place in Chinese dramatic literature.

Archaeology is a science rather than an art, yet it has most important connections both with history and with the plastic arts. In China this branch of learning today enjoys a peculiar eminence and a degree of official support which the archaeologists of the capitalist world must perforce envy. It is not at first sight obvious why this science should find such favour with the Communist Party. It is true that some, though not all, of the eminent Chinese archaeologists of the present age were early converts to Communism; but there were many scientists and scholars in other fields of which the same was true. It is more probable that it is the nature of archaeological work itself which finds approval, on ideological grounds. For archaeology is essentially a 'materialist' science: it deals with artifacts, with objects found *in situ*, with ancient works of art and inscriptions, more with facts and less with theories.

Moreover what archaeology reveals, if attested and genuine, is indisputable. Such things were made by the men of such an age; such were their burial customs, barbarous or refined; these inscriptions and works of art, and these alone, certainly and authentically represent the ideas and the taste of bygone ages.

The purpose of some construction or artifact, the meaning of some obscure inscription, may be in doubt, and varying theories on these points may be put forward, but the dispute is without ideological content, it is a dispute about the interpretation of facts, not about the validity of ideas. In an age in which the 'correct' and the 'incorrect' in disputes about ideas can imply far-reaching consequences and dangers, there is something very satisfying both to the ideologists and the scholars in devoting attention to a subject from which these considerations are excluded. Archaeology is a safe subject: the scholar can pursue his research without fearing that it may lead him to a conclusion at variance with state policy; the Party can lavish its patronage on this research without any risk that some heresy or deviation may spring up from the excavations. The fruits of this fortunate situation have been impressive.

The field was very nearly unexplored. Although in a country with a long history of civilization, and in the more anciently settled parts a relatively dry climate, there was every reason to expect that much material of the greatest interest and importance lay concealed, but still preserved, little systematic archaeology had been possible in the troubled ages of the Republic and the Nationalist regime. The one important excavation, near Anyang, where science had verified the old tradition that here lay the capital of the early Shang dynasty, had for many years been interrupted by the Japanese invasion and the subsequent civil war. Elsewhere funds were lacking for anything more than surface surveys. South China, from the acrhaeological standpoint, was a *terra incognita*.

The new government was clearly not in the position to finance large-scale excavations or undertake an extensive and costly archaeological survey of so large a country; at first it confined its patronage to providing funds for the care and preservation of known sites and monuments, by which the depredations of curio hunters, grave robbers, and amateur treasure seekers were brought to an end. It was only when the programme of development and industrial construction got under way that it was realized that these measures would prove quite inadequate to preserve and study the immense quantity of valuable finds which were now constantly brought to light. The new railways run through the ancient historic provinces of China; the new industrial suburbs adjoin the famous cities of antiquity; as soon as construction work began, archaeological material, some of which was of the greatest interest and importance was unearthed almost wherever excavations were made.

This was not altogether unexpected. When the original railways of North, and particularly of North-West, China were built in the first decade of the twentieth century, a similar flood of finds, mostly from tombs, poured out; but at that time they went onto the curio market unrecorded, unattested, from unidentified sites which were destroyed as they were discovered. Archaeologists and art students had long bewailed this profanation which had revealed the riches of the past but had made any attempt to classify or determine a chronology speculative and unsound. The prestige which archaeology now enjoys has prevented a repetition on an even larger scale of this disaster.

A law was passed making any and all objects of archaeological value the property of the State, part of the People's cultural heritage. All construction workers and managers must report the discovery of such objects to the authorities and must leave them, undisturbed as far as possible, until the site has been investigated by one of numerous archaeological field teams which are scattered about the country to carry out this supervision. On major projects the team is present and works with the engineers in charge of the project. If the site must be built over or destroyed, the archaeologists first survey, photograph, measure and remove the finds. Where a minor diversion or alteration can save a really valuable site, the change is made.

The consequences of these simple but sweeping measures have been far-reaching. The museums are choked with new finds, which the overworked staff have scarcely time to list and store, only the most significant can be given preliminary study. The commercial curio market has virtually dried up. Discoveries of the highest historical value have been made, the supply of attested, identified and located material of all periods has immensely increased, making necessary a thorough re-assessment of the history of styles, techniques and cultural development.

The beautiful burial urns decorated with spiral patterns which had long been known to be a product of the Chinese neolithic age, the Yangshao culture, came, it was also known, from the north-western provinces of Shensi and Kansu. Much of this region is now rather barren, drought stricken and sparsely populated. When the new railway linking Shensi and Ssuchuan provinces was built, several thousands of these urns were found in a mere hundred kilometres of railway construction. Since a railway is but a narrow strip, it can be concluded with certainty that the neolithic population of this region was very large, quite possibly larger than the population of the present age. In the suburbs of the busy and fast growing city of Cheng-chou, in Honan, at the intersection of the main north–south and east–west trunk railways, construction work opened up what is probably an older Shang city than Anyang, containing bronze vessels of a more primitive type, a discovery which provides an important link between the neolithic and advanced bronze ages in China.

In South China, at Changsha, the capital today of the province of Hunan, and equally, in the first millennium BC, the capital of the southern state of Ch'u, which the classical authorities treat as half barbarous, recent discoveries have produced a rich harvest of sophisticated works of art, lacquer ware, inscriptions on silk and wood, which by themselves, even before full study, conclusively contradict the old assumptions that this region lagged far behind North China in the classical age. An exhibition of bronzes of the Chou period discovered in the year 1955 held in the Palace Museum at Peking in May 1956, assembled a collection which, for quality and quantity, equalled any exhibition of the same material which has been held in Europe. Many of these pieces were inscribed, and the inscriptions, so far as there has yet been time to study and decipher them, indicate that important additions to historical knowledge, in some cases at variance with traditional accounts, will result from these discoveries.

Another aspect of the interest in and patronage of archaeology is the care and preservation of known historical monuments and sites. No search is being made for unknown sites, nor is any attempt yet being made to excavate those which are known, but undisturbed. There is neither the personnel nor the time for large-scale archaeological exploration, but all such sites as have been identified, or are now discovered, are scheduled as national monuments and preserved undespoiled until the pressure of work caused by the chance discoveries of construction work has eased off and careful planned excavation is possible. A survey of all known monuments of historical interest is being carried out, and such relics are being preserved from further neglect and damage, and where urgently necessary, restored or repaired. Thus well-known sites which were rapidly deteriorating before the People's Republic was established, such as the cave temples at Yunkang in Shansi, Lungmen near Loyang and the Ming tombs near Peking, have been put under proper care, vandalism stopped and restoration undertaken. The archaeological survey has also resulted in the discovery and preservation of other, unknown places, such as the T'ang period (ninth century) temples in the Wut'ai area of Shansi, the oldest known brick and timber constructions in China, and the Buddhist shrines at Maich'ishan in Shensi.

Once again the programme for archaeological research and the policy of preserving and restoring monuments of historical and artistic importance is not an essentially Communist policy, but a task which all modern civilized governments in other parts of the world have undertaken and sponsored. Here, as in many other fields, it is the present regime which has been the first in China to do what should have been done half a century ago: the People's Republic is entitled to the credit for doing the work well, thoroughly, and without stinting funds for matters which might well seem less urgent than other pressing needs. This care for the past glories of the Chinese civilization does not in itself establish the merits of a Communist system of government and society; it does disprove the pessimistic belief that such a system must necessarily be inimical to the preservation, study and concern for the traditional culture of the Chinese people.

The belief that the Chinese Communists intended to undermine and finally destroy the traditional culture of their country was supported by alleged evidence that they also intended, as a means to this end, to reform the written language, abolish the use of the Chinese ideographic script, and introduce an alphabetic system, probably the Russian Cyrillic or some new form derived from that prototype. It is certainly true that some such reform was mooted in Communist circles and had its ardent advocates. However, this idea was neither new nor specifically Communist. Ever since the original revolution of 1911 against the monarchy there have been groups of Chinese intellectuals, usually the foreign educated, who urged such a reform. Many foreigners, who did not themselves read Chinese, and a few who did, supported the idea. It was argued that no real widespread popular education, and thus no true democracy, was possible if children had to spend years learning how to read and write; no scientific advance could be hoped for if all the literature had to be written in ideographic script which cannot employ foreign, and therefore scientific terms, except in a clumsy and inaccurate transcription into Chinese characters having only a vague correspondence in sound with the foreign words.

These are serious objections, and they were not the only ones. Chinese ideographs are often complicated and hard both to memorize and reproduce in writing. Their use has produced a double language, spoken and written, often very unlike. For the ideographs, standing for ideas and not for sounds, enable a sentence to be written very tersely, whereas speech is more diffuse, and thus written Chinese was widely different from the colloquial language, which in turn was never written as it was spoken. It was argued that only the innate conservatism of the Chinese made them cling to a system which was cumbersome and archaic.

Recent events have cast some doubt on the theory that the Chinese are an inherently conservative people: the objections to the ideographic script also ignored the very strong arguments in its favour. The first of these is that the script, standing for sense and not for sound, is independent of dialect variations in the spoken language. Just as the Arabic numerals, used by all European peoples, convey the meaning but not the sounds of the words which in the various languages denote the numbers, so the Chinese ideograph, on an identical principle, gives the meaning but not the sound of the word. A newspaper article written in Peking can be read with equal ease by those who see it in Canton or Foochow, although if these readers were to speak the words aloud the Peking author of the article would not understand a word of what was said. The unity of the Chinese people, in spite of very diverse dialects in the southern provinces and minor but important speech variations in other parts of a vast country, has been preserved very largely by the fact that there was but one written language equally intelligible to all who could read, even if utterly closed to all who could not.

Secondly, the written language was also very largely independent of time. The most ancient literature, of the first millennium BC, may indeed present considerable difficulty to those who have not made a special study of it, but even this archaic literature is more easily read by a Chinese scholar than Chaucer would be by an English student. The Chinese literature of the later ages, from the Han period (200 BC) onwards is substantially identical in style with the literary language used until modern times. Chinese literature has thus a greater and closer continuity than any other, and is more easily accessible to the modern educated person than the old literature of any other culture.

Further, it is not in fact necessary for children to spend many years learning the classical style of writing before they can read at all. If this was so under the Empire, it was because the educational system was designed to make reading and writing a difficult and distinguished accomplishment reserved to a scholar class. Since the Republic, and long before the Communists came to power, popular education had been modernized and simplified. It was found possible to teach children and illiterates one thousand, or even fewer characters in the first place, make books and newspapers which used this more limited vocabulary, and having thus started the pupil with a 'basic Chinese' enable him to increase his range by progressive exercises, or simply by reading more widely. Educational reform on these lines had already sharply reduced illiteracy, especially in the great cities where it was more fully operative, well before the Japanese invasion. The main handicap to universal literacy was not the ideographic script, but the lack of teachers and schools for the peasant millions.

It had long been accepted that the Chinese ideographs were often written in an unnecessarily complicated form, another consequence of the old exclusive attitude to literacy. In common practice, though not in print, people used many abbreviated forms, some of which had been current for centuries. There was no real reason other than academic conservatism, why these simpler forms should not be made general and used in all script. This might make the reading of old books more difficult, but new editions could be printed in the modern form and in fact in the third century BC Chinese script had at least once undergone such a major reform; the older form of script having since that time been reserved for seals and fancy inscriptions, much as Gothic script still lingers in English usage.

The disadvantages of abandoning the ideographic script were thus very formidable. It would mean a serious blow at the cultural unity of the nation. Whole provinces in the south would be divided from the rest of the nation, and from each other, even further among themselves, by new languages, written as well as spoken. It was obvious that such a development might have political as well as cultural consequences. The literature of the past would be lost: even if, at an immense cost of trouble and work, this literature was transcribed into a romanized or a Cyrillic script, it could not but be transformed in the process, since the old literature, in its terse classical style was simply not susceptible of transcription into modern Chinese. It would need to be paraphrased as well as transcribed, in a word, re-written. This made it obvious that no such immense task would ever in fact be accomplished.

The critics and opponents of the Communist regime were acutely aware of this problem; they feared that if the talked-of reform of the script meant the introduction of an alphabet, one of the great attractions of such a change for revolutionary Communists would be precisely the ease with which they could wipe out the literature of the past and only reproduce such small part of it as suited their purposes. Tocsins of alarm sounded across the strait of Formosa and were echoed in anguish in the universities of Europe and America.

Meanwhile the Communist Party and government were approaching this problem with wary caution. No doubt at all that they saw all the disadvantages of the ideographic script, and were also well aware of the uses for propaganda purposes of an alphabet. Equally, they cannot have ignored the dangers of provincial separatism, the threat to national unity—to the ideal of 'All China'—in any proposal to abandon the ideographs. How far they felt respect and affection for some part at least of the ancient cultural heritage can be gauged from their subsequent policy. After the capture of Peking and the establishment of the People's Republic they set up a commission of expert linguists to advise and report on the problem of language reform. The impression prevailed in Chinese academic circles that the commission had instructions to go very thoroughly into the question, to take its time—if not to waste it—and thus to allow a cooling-off period to elapse while the government took stock of the problem. The commission did not report for six years.

Long before that it was already clear that the main decision in favour of a less drastic reform had already been, in effect, taken. The campaigns against illiteracy, based on the established method of teaching a limited vocabulary, the 'Thousand Character Mass Education Movement' which had been initiated soon after the First World War, were pressed forward with the far greater resources and superior organization which the People's Republic could command. The movement to simplify the script and use abbreviated characters for all purposes arose first among the civil servants and secretaries of the administration, men pressed for time and working long hours. As a very eminent member of the government put it, 'My secretaries began using these abbreviated forms, and although I cannot always easily read them, it is no use protesting, so we thought it better to make them widely known so that they can become the established forms.'* The movement thus obtained official approval and was launched with all the weight and energy of the system of Persuasion behind it. The reform is not so radical as to make the older, elaborate forms of the characters wholly obsolete, although it is certain that the more complicated of these will fall out of ordinary use; future generations who are taught the new forms would find that an old text presented the same kind of difficulty as sixteenth-century spelling does to the modern English reader. Equally, there is nothing to prevent the re-publication of old texts in the new simplified characters, just as, say, a modern edition of the Paston Letters need not keep the original spelling.

The decision to retain, but simplify the ideographic script, did not remove the need to find some more practical method of rendering foreign words and names than the clumsy approximations used in the past. A system which could only render the word 'Russia' by using characters which are read with the sounds 'Ou lo ssu' has always been a grave handicap in Chinese historical and other literature, in which foreign words and names must be mentioned. The practice of interposing the foreign name in Latin script was sometimes employed, but the disadvantage which limited this practice was the fact that Chinese is normally written in vertical columns, from top to bottom, and from right to left on the page. The Latin script word had thus to be printed sideways, and the page turned round to read it: printers greatly disliked the inconvenience of this device.

* Chou En-lai, in conversation with the author, May 1956.

At an interview given to members of an Australian Cultural Delegation which visited Peking in May 1956 the Prime Minister, Chou En-lai, explained the policy which had been adopted to deal with this and kindred problems of language reform. It had been decided to use an alphabet as a secondary script for writing foreign names, words such as internationally used scientific terms, and as an aid to teaching illiterates the Chinese ideographs. The question of what alphabet to adopt had been thoroughly discussed, and the decision had been that the Roman or Latin script should be used, 'because it is the most widespread in the world today'. Some dispute still prevailed as to whether this system of romanization should employ all the twenty-six Latin letters, or discard some of them, or add a few to their number to meet the peculiarities of Chinese pronunciation. To facilitate the use of the romanized script for these limited purposes it had been decided that in future written Chinese would be printed in horizontal lines, from left to right, following the practice of Western literature, which the Prime Minister pointed out, had other practical advantages of speed and convenience. The new romanization, when finalized, would also become the official form in which all Chinese names and words would be rendered in foreign languages, maps and publications.

If any further reform should one day prove advisable, it could safely be left to future generations to decide, for no wholesale change of script was either possible or desirable in the forseeable future. He pointed out that a pre-requisite of further changes would be a unification of the spoken language, which was far from attained at present. It was the policy of the government to promote the use of what is now called 'Pu T'ung Hua'—'Standard Speech', which he defined as the educated speech of Peking. This speech is, in effect, what was formerly called 'Kuan Hua', 'Official Speech', or by foreigners, 'Mandarin'. The use of Standard Speech is spreading fast, and under the former name of 'National Speech' had already in Nationalist times made great headway among the dialect speaking population of the south and the Overseas Chinese.

Modern means of mass communication, the wireless and the cinema, which use Standard Speech, had greatly aided this development, and the fact that the Japanese forbade the teaching of it in the occupied areas of South China and South-East Asia, made the southern Chinese and their overseas relatives all the more enthusiastic pupils. Nevertheless, it will be many years, if ever, before the great southern dialects die out, or even before the huge rural population of those provinces become bilingual. The present policy of republishing the classical and historical literature of China in the new format, but with the ideographic script unchanged or slightly simplified, is evidence in itself that there is no expectation of a sudden change to a romanized script or any intention to allow the old literature to perish through neglect.

It is also significant that after consideration it was decided to employ the Latin, not the Cyrillic, alphabet as the secondary script for rendering foreign words and names. It suggests that those who imagine that the Chinese Communist Party is but the instrument of Soviet Russia have much to learn. Until very recently it was indeed Russian which had taken the place of English as the first foreign language taught in schools, while English had been relegated to second place, and was not taught below university level. Already in 1956 it was freely predicted that this priority must soon be changed. The use of English was, it was pointed out, far greater, and the number of those qualified to teach it far larger than was the case with Russian. It has more recently been decided that students may choose between these two languages, or take both. There can be little doubt that it is the growing realization that in the rest of Asia it is English, not Russian, which is the language of inter-communication which has been a potent factor in favour of English teaching.

Thus, step by step, the Chinese Communist Party has been led in the cultural field to follow policies far more moderate and enlightened than their opponents feared or their own ardent supporters expected. It was found that it was a source of strength, not a confession of weakness, to conform with the national taste in art and literature, drama and the ideographic script. The Party does not intend to take these things to itself unchanged and unreformed, but it clearly does understand that it is wiser to build the new on the foundations of the great tradition rather than sweep all away and substitute a foreign idiom.

There is a recognition of the strength and enduring force of national pride and the prestige of a great and ancient civilization, however misguided its former political system and social order is now deemed to have been. Small things often indicate the mood of a nation better than published policies. Formerly, the traveller in China saw many inscriptions in English; street names, shop names, directions, etc., were frequently written in English as well as in Chinese ideographs. Today, not only has every English inscription of this sort, even to the names of railway stations, disappeared, but no Russian inscriptions have been put up to replace them. The foreign traveller who does not read Chinese ideographs is wholly dependent on the interpreter who accompanies him, and this applies to the Russian adviser or expert just as much as to the visitor from the West.

CHAPTER SEVEN

RELIGION IN PEOPLE'S CHINA

'We Communists are athiests, but we respect all those who have religious belief. We hope that those with religious belief will also respect those without.' Chou En-lai.*

THE FACT THAT Communists are atheists is, for the majority of people in the West, the most disturbing aspect of the Marxist system. It appears to cut off these societies from the main stream of previous European civilization, to break the continuity of their ancient culture far more violently and more drastically than any change in the political or economic orders. The substitution of republics for monarchies, which was so revolutionary in the early nineteenth century, has now become an almost insignificant transition which in no way implies a major shift in the international alignment. Socialist governments have come to power in the Western democracies, and even put into operation programmes which were once regarded as ultra-revolutionary without world-shaking consequences. It is no longer the hostility to private property and capital which is felt in the West to be the source of conflict with the Communist world, it is the ideological difference which is now emphasized, and the heart of this difference is the materialist interpretation of the cosmos.

The Western intellectual may frequently be agnostic, vaguely deist, not a church member, or a rare attender, but his values are still very largely Christian values, his outlook is intimately related to the Christian background of his society. Even when he questions these values himself, or criticizes the assumptions of the Christian Western civilization, he assumes

---

* Speech by Chou En-lai, Prime Minister of the Chinese People's Republic, to the Asian-African Conference, Bandung, April 1955. *The Facts of the Bandung Conference.* Australia-China Society. Sydney, 1955.

that most of his fellow men hold such values and were moulded by the conventions and beliefs of this civilization. To declare oneself an atheist is still a challenge, to advocate the dissolution of organized religion is still a rare and unpopular attitude. On the other hand, many Christians, faced with the Communist atheist opponent, are now prepared to sink ancient enmities and find common cause, in the name of God if not of Christ, with Moslems, Buddhists and Hindus.

But these attitudes and assumptions are altogether alien to the Chinese outlook. Not only was there no ancient, all-embracing religion in whose bosom the Chinese civilization was nurtured, but on the contrary, there were three, conflicting, irreconcilable theologies which were none the less easily accepted, practised or neglected, without becoming the cause of violent controversies or persecutions. The educated Chinese had, in effect, been not merely agnostic but atheist for many centuries. During that long period no body of religious belief commanded the respect and authority which revealed religion has held in the West. Confucian ethical teaching might be the orthodox doctrine of the empire, but it was not a religion, it was indeed expressly disinterested in religion. The ancient rites which the Emperor performed on certain occasions in honour of the Supreme Deity, Heaven, were in fact ceremonies, honoured and cherished for their antiquity and tradition, but requiring little belief and no participation from the educated class.

Buddhism had always been mainly a popular religion, and always under the stigma, in the eyes of the educated, of being an alien religion also. If Buddhists could get their religious beliefs 'respected' it was certainly very much incumbent upon them to respect those who were without such beliefs, the Confucian scholars. In actual practice, throughout the last thousand years and more Chinese scholars and officials had from time to time sharply criticized Emperors who favoured Buddhism, denounced that religion as an alien superstition, and only grudgingly accorded it tolerance as a system dear to the people, and apt to keep them contented with their lot. The attitude that religion, the belief in the supernatural, and the existence of divine beings, was uneducated, rustic and unsophisticated, was inherent in the outlook of the educated Chinese.

These views were even more strongly, and more justifiably felt in respect of the inchoate system of ancient polytheisms which had taken refuge under the name of Taoism. True philosophic Taoism, the quietest philosophy of Lao Tzu and Chuang Tzu, was buried under an age-old accumulation of doctrine and rites, superstitions and pseudo-sciences, ranging from simple country customs like the worship of mountain gods and fertility rites, to astrology, magic, geomancy and the quest for the elixir vitae. The Taoist priest in later centuries had sunk to the status of a mountebank, and the ill repute which his practices inspired had cast an unfortunate and harmful slight on true scientific inquiry.

There were, in addition to these native or long acclimatized cults, the foreign religions of Islam and Christianity. The former counted many millions of followers, mostly in the north-west part of China, and it was accepted that they descended, in part at least, from foreign, west Asian settlers. As such they were always regarded as a minority people rather than as Chinese Moslems. This was, of course, largely a fiction, for both by blood and long assimilation, the Chinese Moslems were in every respect except their religion, truly Chinese. But conversion, except by violence or by the purchase of famine refugee children, was so rare as to be negligible or unknown. In the sense that no ordinary Chinese would think of conversion to Islam as a spiritual alternative, it is true that the Moslems were, and are, a people apart and not only a minority religious group.

The Christians, both Catholic and Protestant, numbering at most three millions, oscillated uneasily between this peculiar status, proper to the Moslems, and that of the more invidious position of being converts to a foreign creed, and thus in some way 'un-Chinese'. The old-established Catholic communities, particularly in North China, had acquired some of the coherence and status of the Moslem minority and might, with the passage of a few more centuries, have become a recognized 'peculiar people'. The Protestants, having nowhere formed such compact communities as the Catholic peasant villages of the north and north-west, but having remained small isolated groups of converts very largely in the cities and towns, had not obtained similar recognition and acceptance. The common attitude to Protestant Christians was one of suspicion, the feeling, often clearly expressed, that such people were foreign sympathizers, almost disloyal. The main factor modifying this popular sentiment was the educational standing of many Protestant Christians, which was high. As members of the 'book perfumed' scholar class they were respected, even if their beliefs were considered a strange foreign aberration by the mass of their countrymen.

This being the religious situation in China, the Communists did no great violence to the national tradition by openly proclaiming their atheism. They merely explicitly claimed or admitted a position which had long been the accepted attitude of the greater part of the educated class. So far from breaking sharply with the main cultural tradition of China, their standpoint rather reaffirmed it, or at very least, fitted naturally into that tradition, and continued it. It is unlikely that any Chinese feels that the avowed atheism of the Communist Party is a violent break with the culture of the past or that this fact is to anyone, except the tiny minority of Christians, a potent objection to Communist teaching and doctrine. In so far as the Protestant Christian outlook had spread among a small minority of the educated class, this outlook is identified with the 'bourgeois ideology' which an American or European education was considered to have instilled. As such, it is undesirable and incorrect, and the Protestant Churches are urged to rid themselves of the foreign influences which have corrupted some of their members. The religious beliefs of Christians will be respected provided these do not connote political opinions opposed to the regime.

In any objective consideration of the People's Republic's policy towards the religions of China and their followers it is, therefore, essential to remember that China was not only a pagan society, but a multi-religion community in which no one faith dominated all the others, and moreover, where such domination as existed in this sphere was exercised by an agnostic ethical system, Confucianism, garnished with some picturesque and very ancient ceremonies. But almost all this side of the Confucian system had fallen into desuetude at the end of the empire, thirty years before the Communists came to power. The attitude of the imperial gvoernment had always been in theory rather contemptuous and hostile to revealed religions, such hostility being frequently moderated in practice by the personal predilections of individual Emperors, but none the less remaining the orthodox and official attitude. Whereas in recent centuries in the West all statesmen paid lip service to Christian beliefs, even if notoriously lax in practice, in China all the ruling class overtly professed Confucian agnosticism even if quite a large number of them privately practised the Buddhist religion.

The essential meaning of the remarks of Chou En-lai can be deduced from these considerations. The Communists are atheists; because they are Marxists and also because this is the natural and accustomed outlook of the Chinese educated class. Yet they respect those who have religious beliefs. That, too, is traditional to this class, which for centuries had been used to equating religion with superstition and tolerating it as the inevitable result of the illiteracy and ignorance of the people. But they hope—or expect—that those with religious beliefs will respect those without them. They can also make sure that these people show this respect, and apply sanctions to the disrespectful. 'Respect', it is clear, must here be interpreted as 'non-interference'. The Communists promise to permit those who have religious beliefs to avow them and practise their religions, but only if they in turn make no attempt to oppose the atheism of the Communists or engage in an evangelizing campaign. That would not be 'respect' for the unbelievers, and will not be permitted.

The old standpoint of the Confucian scholar is still there,

reinforced by the militancy of Marxist materialism. Religion may be tolerated as an inevitable manifestation of ignorance, but must not be propagated, may be expected to decline with the spread of literacy, and must not become the cover for hostile political action. The Confucian official never forgot that peasant rebellions very often were associated with some variant of Buddhism or Taoism, that even Christianity had lent fervour and cohesion to the T'ai P'ing rebellion. Religions were tolerable as long as they were inactive, decadent, or carefully controlled, subsidized and devitalized by official patronage. Once they became popular and aroused zeal, escaped from imperial protection and appealed to the masses, they were highly dangerous and must be firmly suppressed.

It would not be pushing the comparison too far to see in the present religious policy of the Communist Party in China a modern inheritance of this point of view. Religion is still widespread, but mass education will gradually weaken its hold. Religious schools are not permitted, religious instruction may only be given privately, or in a few permitted seminaries devoted to training priests and clergy. Churches, temples or mosques must be, as it were, licensed, exhibiting outside their gates a placard announcing that they are recognized places of worship for such and such a religion. Evangelization, open-air preaching, or any other activity likely to arouse popular interest and excitement are forbidden. No Church or religion must have any association with a foreign organization. Churches and religious organizations must no longer enter the educational field, must not run hospitals, orphanages or other institutions which would give them a character other than that of a strictly religious community devoted to worship and ritual, and to nothing else.

No doubt there is a further motive behind this policy. The imperial official was mainly concerned lest some form of popular religion roused the masses to rebellion, or gave organization and leadership to their discontent. The Communist Party itself exists to provide this organization, leadership and driving power. It is the Party which must animate and arouse the people, not merely keep them quiet. Communism must provide the very stimulants which popular religions fitfully and imperfectly supplied. No one expects that every Chinese can become a member of the Party, any more than every Christian should become a priest, but it is expected, and hoped, that in time all men will accept the leadership of the Party, believe in its teaching, follow its instruction. Communism is in the religious field not merely as an umpire, it is a competitor.

Viewed in this light, and taking into consideration the fact that the standpoint of the Party in this sphere is not, as it is in Europe, directly opposed to the traditions of the past but in fact closely conforms to those traditions, the application of the Party's policy must be examined. It immediately becomes clear that the treatment meted out to different religions in China varies widely, and that the reasons for this variation have little or nothing to do with the beliefs themselves, but are determined by social and political considerations.

Although Confucianism was not in the ordinary accepted sense a religion, yet it had associated with it a number of rites surviving from the early religion of China. There were temples to Confucius in every major city and ceremonies commemorating the Sage were carried out at these places on certain anniversaries. The imperial cult of Heaven could be regarded as a Confucian cult in that it was certainly commended, or accepted by Confucius. Certain other cults associated with the Throne and the State had the same standing. The advent of the republic brought all these to an end, and shrines such as the Altar of Heaven, the Altar of the Gods of the Soil and others in Peking became public parks or historical monuments. The temple of Confucius himself continued in use and the rites were annually performed.

With the triumph of the Communist Party this last stronghold of the most ancient religion of China was overthrown. The teachings of Confucius were treated as the main inspiration of the 'feudal system'—by which is meant the social order of the Empire and the rule of a landed gentry. Confucianism thus fell finally from all esteem. It was counter-revolutionary;

historians might still study the works of Confucius and his disciples to assess the political institutions and economic background of the feudal society, but as a philosophy or a system of ethics they were condemned and derided. Recently a more objective approach to the work of the ancient Sage himself has been shown, but it is unlikely that this will go further than to re-establish him as an important thinker and influence in a remote age, a figure of historical significance, but without value for the modern world.

Just as it was the popular, mystical pagan religions which offered the most obstinate resistance to the triumph of Christianity in the Roman Empire, not the refined intellectual philosophy of Stoics or Platonists, so Confucianism, lacking a popular appeal or a supernatural sanction, has easily succumbed once the educated class embraced a new doctrine. When Justinian closed the Schools at Athens Greek philosophy, as a system opposed to Christianity, swiftly vanished. The popular religions even though persecuted and forbidden, retained a large following for several centuries. It seems possible that this story will be repeated in China.

Taoism is not unlike the popular polytheisms of the late Roman world, it is equally despised by the educated, lacks any central organization and coherent doctrine such as distinguish the higher religions, but has a great hold, in its innumerable local cults and superstitions, on the mind of the people. It is comparatively simple to take over the large temples and turn them into schools, museums or institutions; it is much more difficult to prevent the peasant population from carrying out rites to the local gods of the soil or crops, the spirits of the rivers and mountains. This kind of Taoism is likely to linger for some generations yet; and just as paganism got its name from the old-fashioned beliefs of secluded rustics, Taoism may come to stand for the superstitions of the least educated and most backward sections of the people. As such it cannot hope for any patronage or consideration from the regime.

Two of the traditional 'Three Ways', Confucianism and Taoism, were native to China, and virtually confined to the

Chinese people, or, in the case of Confucianism, to peoples strongly influenced by Chinese civilization, such as the Japanese, Koreans and Viet-namese. Buddhism was alien, Indian in origin, but naturalized after a long period. Buddhism also has many millions of adherents beyond the borders of China, and is, alone of the Three Ways, truly a world-wide religion. It might be thought that this international character, and its still apparent alien aspects, would have prejudiced the Chinese Communists against Buddhism. It is evident that it is the foreign links and international character of the Church of Rome, and to a lesser extent of the Protestant churches also, which have brought the Christians into disfavour. Buddhism has these characteristics also, and the foreign Buddhists are much closer to China than the main communities of foreign Christians.

But Buddhism has not received the same treatment as the Roman Catholic Church. Buddhism enjoys the favour of the government, and is certainly not undergoing any persecution. The reasons for this difference are worth consideration, for they will serve to illuminate the policy of the regime towards religion in general. In some respects Chinese Buddhism did not resemble the other religions of foreign origin practised in China. Firstly, its followers numbered many millions; secondly, the foreign connections were all with Asian countries, either recently freed from colonial rule, or small and weak. Thirdly, Buddhism in China was disorganized, decadent and declining. It was also, although foreign in origin, long established and an integral part of the later Chinese culture.

Viewed from one aspect it might be said that all Chinese, unless very modern revolutionaries or exceptionally austere Confucian scholars, were in some sense Buddhist. Almost all families practised some Buddhist rites, called in Buddhist monks for marriage and funeral ceremonies, were conscious of Buddhist theology as part of their background and culture. They were Buddhist just as much, and no more, than many Western agnostics are Christian. If, on the other hand, only the real, active fully believing and practising Buddhists come into the reckoning, these faithful would still number well over fifty millions in China. This appears to be the figure which the government accepts as valid in calculating the actual strength of Buddhism today. It would include not only the monks but also large numbers of laity who are enrolled in societies of a pious character, taking vows of abstinence from meat and wine, and many millions of peasant families, especially in southern and western China, who remain devout Buddhists.

The reasons for the varying strength of Buddhism in different parts of the country are rather obscure; it is certainly a common matter of observation that in the north this religion is weak and declining. Temples, unless preserved by the government as historical monuments, or put to other uses, are deserted and decaying. Monks are few, novices very rare. The great shrines of the past such as Lungmen near Loyang and Yunkang in North Shansi are no longer either active centres of religion or even places of pilgrimage. Nor is this decline new; at least since the fall of the Empire the phenomena of rapid decay have been all too evident. An observer who knows only the north might conclude that Buddhism was virtually dead in China.

In South China, and particularly in the lower Yangtze provinces he would receive a widely different impression. Temples, even in urban centres such as Shanghai, are well maintained by funds provided by the faithful, pilgrimages are extensive and draw thousands to the famous monasteries of the south. Monks are numerous, their numbers do not seem to be declining, and young men are commonly found in the monasteries. Although the Chinese are a people with a common culture and history, there are marked differences in the character and temperament of the inhabitants of varying regions. Some difference of this kind may account for the apathy of the north and the ardour of the south.

The Buddhist religion in China was, none the less, and as a whole, disorganized and weak. It had no real central authority, each temple or monastery stood by itself, dependent on its own lands and on the contributions of the faithful. Where the lands were rich and the people devout, it thrived; where war or decline had impoverished the monasteries and the people had grown indifferent, it decayed. No significant attempt had been made to rekindle national enthusiasm or faith, no interest was shown in re-interpretation of doctrine to make it more acceptable to modern minds, little or no active intercourse with foreign Buddhists was maintained. Extinction might be a long way off, but decline was steady; few foreign Christian missionaries felt that Buddhism was the real opponent or a serious challenge.

Buddhism in China got little or no support or assistance from Buddhists overseas. In Japan, where the religion was more alive and influential, traditional factors had tended to impose barriers between the faithful in the two countries. For nearly three centuries Japan had been closed to foreigners, including Chinese. Since her emergence from seclusion Japan had more often been the enemy than the friend of China, and the climate of intense nationalism on the one side and resentment tinged with envy on the other had made intercourse, except for commerce and professional purposes, uneasy. The Chinese who went to Japan either went on business or to study at a Japanese university; neither class of visitors was likely to be disinterested Buddhist pilgrims. Japanese in China came as business men or on military service; they, too, were uninterested in or contemptuous of Chinese Buddhism.

Japan and China at least had shared the same branch of Buddhism, the Mahayana, but the Buddhist countries of South-East Asia were followers of the older, and in their view, the purer teaching called Hinayana by their opponents, but more properly known as Vairocana. A difference in doctrines and practices at least as wide as that between the Protestant north and the Catholic south of Europe, even if without the history of strife and bloodshed which has embittered the Christian tradition, made intercommunication fitful and co-operation rare. There were, moreover, important language barriers between the Chinese Buddhist and his Thai or Burmese co-religionist. Few Chinese Buddhists could read the scriptures except in their Chinese translations, works centuries old. It can be said that probably no southern Buddhists could read Chinese, and very few on either side could have conversed in any language with each other. Relations of any kind with these countries were slight; Burma, Ceylon, Cambodia and Laos were under foreign colonial rule, their governments took no interest in promoting the inter-communion of Buddhist communities. Weak and disorganized China, under the late Empire or the Republic, was equally indifferent.

The third major form of the Buddhist religion, the Lamaist branch, practised in Tibet and Mongolia, was well known to the Chinese, since it had been introduced to China by the Mongol rulers of the Yüan dynasty (AD 1278–1368) and had been patronized by the Manchu Emperors, for political purposes. It had always retained an alien character, its monks were Mongols or Tibetans, and its shrines, in Peking or other centres, had been maintained by imperial favour to gain the goodwill of the Mongol and Tibetan tributaries of the Empire. Lamaism was thus not only foreign, but, to the Chinese, rather barbarian. Since the fall of the Empire, the main centre of this religion, Lhasa, had been in political opposition to the transient regimes of the Republic, and the second centre, Outer Mongolia, had fallen as early as 1924 under the domination of a Communist government supported by Russia.

Such being the state of Chinese Buddhism when the Communist regime came to power, it is not surprising that the policy of that government towards it has been almost the exact opposite of that pursued towards the other foreign religions, Catholicism and Protestantism. Whereas it is the foreign connections of these latter which the government has been at pains to sever, it has fostered and revived the foreign relations of Chinese Buddhism. At home the government has sought to organize the native Buddhists, and has assisted them in the repair and maintenance of some famous shrines. So far from seeking to emphasize the differences between Chinese and South-East Asian Buddhism, the People's Republic tends to treat all Buddhists alike, to promote pilgrimages to foreign centres, and return visits by foreign Buddhists to China, to assist the movement, largely originating in Burma, to give unity and cohesion to the Buddhist world. The facilities given by the Chinese government to convey the precious relic, the Tooth of Buddha, to Rangoon for the celebration of the second millennium of Buddhism in 1955, are an example of this policy.

From the point of view of the Communist Party the Buddhists are not only harmless, they could be an asset. They have no organization capable, or desirous, of opposing the government. Their economic power, such as it was, was due to the possession of lands attached to monasteries. These are subject, like other landed property, to Land Reform and the temples are thus reduced to complete dependence on the contributions of the faithful or the bounty of the government. Communists may regard Buddhism as a superstition, but it is a quietist creed, teaching men to accept the evil of this world as the penalty paid for their own former crimes or failings. Buddhists, as such, are never moved to revolt, for such a protest would be a denial of their beliefs.

On the other hand, the religion still retains the allegiance of several million people in important parts of the country. It would serve no useful purpose to embitter and alienate these peasant masses, people who, in other respects, are sympathetic enough to the new regime, and ready to do its bidding and implement its policies. Communists may expect that the spread of education and technical knowledge in the rural population will weaken and finally destroy the faith of the peasant Buddhists. There is no reason to force the pace.

Meanwhile a sympathetic, tolerant and respectful attitude to Buddhism is an important asset in dealing with the peoples of South-East Asia. These nations are now once more free and independent. Their Buddhist religion is central to their culture, a unifying bond which is showing remarkable vitality and powers of recovery. Almost all of these countries—Siam excepted—are neutralist, or non-aligned in the Cold War. If the impression spread amongst them that China was hostile to Buddhism, persecuted the religion, and aimed at its extinction, this would be a very potent propaganda weapon in the hands of the opponents of China and Communism. If the contrary impression is created, and China is seen as sympathetic, helpful, well-disposed and tolerant, the argument that Communist regimes must be hostile to religion is discounted and fails to convince. Chinese acceptance of Buddhism and respect for that faith proves, too, that China is still Asian in outlook, feels solidarity with her southern neighbours, shares in the great revival of Asian culture, which in these countries means Buddhist culture. There is every reason to tolerate Buddhism at home and favour it abroad.

Buddhism will thus survive, will not be suppressed by persecution, and may even revive and grow stronger, provided it remains within the organizational framework which the Party has encouraged it to adopt. The Communist Party does not like unorganized, diffuse, and independent bodies. 'All China' must be the keyword in religion as in other matters. So the Chinese Buddhists, after close on two thousand years of muddling along, are now to be streamlined into the Chinese Buddhists' Association, organized in June 1953, under a Board of Directors consisting of ninety-three eminent Buddhists representing every branch of the religion found within the borders of the People's Republic. The major and historic differences between the schools and sects need no longer divide the faithful; Lamaism shall lie down with Mahayana; the four presidents of the Chinese Buddhists' Association include the Dalai and Panchen Lamas, the Chagan Kogen, a Mongolian Lama, and the eminent Hsü Yun, a leading Chinese abbot.

Islam is also a foreign religion; it, too, has an international range, connections with foreign countries, and a much more intransigent record than quietist Buddhism. But Islam in China is a far-off outpost of the Moslem world, the most easterly region in which large numbers of Moslems dwell, and a small minority among the Chinese people. There were formerly some widely ranging estimates of the number of Moslems in China. Some authorities put the figure as high as fifty millions, others much lower. The All China Islamic Association, founded in May 1953, which now speaks for the Chinese

Moslems, does not claim more than ten millions, and includes in this number the minority peoples of Sinkiang, Uighurs and Kazaks. If these figures are correct the number of Chinese Moslems, as distinct from non-Chinese peoples of Moslem faith living in the People's Republic, is probably not more than six or seven millions. This is a figure about three times the total of the combined Christian communities, Catholic and Protestant, but it is still only just over one per cent of the Chinese population.

The Communist regime, it may be thought, might well disregard so small a percentage of the nation, or compel it without discrimination to conform to the general pattern of the new society. This has not been the policy which has been followed. Instead, the government has chosen to emphasize the separate status of Moslems and to distinguish this community from the rest of the Chinese people. It is true that in its far-off origins the Moslem community was bred of alien stock. No fully authentic documentation of the introduction of Islam to China has survived, for the subject did not engage the attention of the orthodox Confucian historians.

It is generally accepted on Moslem tradition and indirect evidence that Islam was introduced to China in the T'ang period, seventh to ninth centuries AD, and that it came both by means of Arab traders to the south coast, and by the intrusion of central Asian mercenary soldiers and merchants by the land route to North-West China. The oldest mosques in the country are the Kuang Ta mosque in Canton, alleged to be founded in AD 627 (a date only five years after the Hegira); and the Hua Chueh mosque at Sian, the ancient Ch'angan, which also claims to be a T'ang foundation. Whether either of these are really quite so early may be doubted (the existing buildings are of much later date), but the tradition at least supports the belief that there was an introduction of Islam both by the sea and land routes, of which these two cities are the respective terminals.

In any event it is certain that the first Moslems were foreigners and that for a long period the Muhammadan community was alien. Very slowly, by unrecorded degrees, these foreign settlers lost their identity, their language, and their alien looks, but retained their religion. The ordinary name for Moslems in Chinese, 'Hui', which has now been adopted as the official name for them as a national minority, is said to be derived from the Chinese pronunciation of the tribal name 'Uighur'. Uighurs were Moslems, so Moslems were Uighurs. It is also known that the Moslems made it a practice to buy up the children of famine refugees, orphans, and victims of war and massacre, and then bring up these children in their own faith as members of the Moslem community. In this way their numbers grew, but their foreign blood was much diluted. In modern times the Moslems in China proper are in no sense an alien people, but Chinese adherents of a foreign faith. The Communist Party and government has not chosen to regard them in this light, and in this conforms with an old attitude common among the Chinese people; for to the ordinary Chinese the Moslems are still foreigners. They are not classed as 'Han' but as 'Hui', and this means of another race as well as of another religion.

The treatment of the Moslems differs from that accorded to the Buddhists by virtue of this insistence on an alien origin. Chinese Buddhists are still in all respects Chinese, 'Han' Chinese. Moslems are Hui, a national minority people, provided with special schools, an institute of higher learning in Peking, and, in the north-west and south-west where they are really numerous, autonomous districts and autonomous regions carved out of the provinces in which they dwell. Policy is directed to stressing the alien origin. the right of such people to foreign customs, including religion, to their 'national' culture and separate identity.

The purpose is clear; it is not desired that the Moslem community should be seen as a religious group, which other Chinese might join, nor is it desirable that Islam should be thought of as a rival ideology which might appeal to non-Moslem Chinese. Islam is to be respected, Moslems are free to follow their religion; even the lands attached to mosques are exempt from Land Reform:* because Moslems are a national minority, having their own rights distinct from those of Han Chinese. But equally, Han Chinese cannot become members of a national minority, any more than an Englishman can become a Welshman. Moslems must be born, not won by conversion.

The Moslems, like the Buddhists, have links with foreign nations. Like the Buddhists also, these foreign nations were for the most part recently under colonial rule, weak, or very distant from China. There is no threat of 'foreign imperialism' contained in the association of Chinese Moslems with Pakistanis or Indonesians, still less political content need be feared in the pilgrimage to Mecca or cultural relations with Egypt and Syria. On the other hand, there is valuable goodwill to be gained in these far-off Islamic nations if it becomes known that the Moslems of China, a minority of an infidel land, are none the less respected, free to worship Allah, masters of their own small communities, educated in their own schools. At one time both Britain and France liked to claim that they were 'great Moslem powers'—by virtue of the millions of Moslems over whom they ruled. The Chinese People's Republic has not advanced this somewhat peculiar notion, but it does no harm to remind the Moslem nations of Asia that China also is, in some respects, a Moslem nation, and respectful to the Faith.

There are also internal reasons for treating the Moslems with restraint and respect. They have long been known as a turbulent and warlike group, which, in the provinces where they were numerous, did not hesitate to rebel. In the nineteenth century the Manchu dynasty had to contend with two formidable Moslem uprisings in China proper, and a secession movement among the non-Chinese Moslems of Sinkiang which for several years detached that province from their Empire. The Moslems of Yunnan, in South-West China, also looked abroad for aid, proclaimed an independent state and sought (but did not obtain) the alliance of Queen Victoria. The Nationalists had their

* Speech of Burhan, Chairman of the All China Islamic Association, 18 October 1952. Reported in *Moslems in China*. Foreign Language Press. Peking, 1953.

Moslem problem; rebellions in Sinkiang, and a remedy almost worse than the disease, the handing over of the military power in North-West China to Moslem warlords who virtually ignored Nanking.

When the Kuomintang was *in extremis* great hopes were placed in these Moslem generals of Kansu, Ninghsia and Ch'inghai. They, at least, would really fight. Moslems were utterly opposed to Communism, with which they could have nothing in common. The Moslem soldiers were tough, hard fighters, who would be a match for the People's Liberation Army. It did not prove true: the Moslem generals were as keen to save their wealth and their liberty by flying to Hong Kong or America as any Nationalist commander. The peasant Moslem soldiers had no greater love for Moslem landlords and militarists than had those who were not Moslems. The resistance of the north-west was, if anything, more ephemeral than in other parts of China.

Yet the Communist Party was also aware that Moslems, although not inclined to defend landlordism and corruption, were sensitive about their religion, would not easily abandon it for Marxism, would indeed fight well and long if they really feared that the new government meant to dragoon them into apostasy. When, in the first flush of victory, propaganda squads went round Peking posting every door with a picture of Mao Tse-tung, foreign consulates included, the Moslems promptly protested that the Mosque door had been profaned by this action. Within the hour other squads appeared to remove the offending representation of the human form.

As a national minority, protected in the exercise of its national religion, enjoying some autonomy, its Moslem culture fostered, indeed revived, displayed as an advertisement to the wisdom, restraint and tolerance of the People's Republic, Islam in China has a future. It is not a wide horizon of progress and growth which opens before it, but a secure, sheltered existence peaceful and insignificant.

In the light of the treatment meted out to the two larger of the foreign religions established in China, can Christianity expect anything better, or, indeed, anything as good? The Buddhists are a large community, deeply penetrating the whole fabric of Chinese society. Their religion has been practised in China for nearly two thousand years. The Moslems are of alien origin, but long established, in certain regions an important local minority, even a local majority community. The Christians, in all not exceeding three or perhaps four millions at an outside estimate, are in fact sharply divided into almost equal moieties, between the Roman and Protestant churches. In Chinese eyes this division has appeared even more fundamental than it does to Western observers.

The accidents of missionary rivalry led to the adoption by the Roman Catholics and Protestants of Chinese terms and names for Christian beliefs and institutions which are quite different and, in Chinese ears, have no apparent connection. Thus the Roman Church is called *T'ien Chu Chiao*, the Religion of the Lord of Heaven; Protestantism—in all its forms—is known as *Yeh Su Chiao*, the Religion of Jesus. To the average, moderately educated Chinese, without foreign background or knowledge of English, these two religions seem to be quite distinct. The general term *Chi Tu Chiao*, Christianity, is not in ordinary day to day use, and is largely unknown to the mass of the common people.

It was, further, a widespread popular belief that the two branches of the Christian religion were respectively the national religions of France and England; that missionaries, who enjoyed, under the extraterritorial system, immunity from Chinese jurisdiction and protection of their Consuls, were the paid agents of these two Powers. The fact that not all Catholic missionaries were French nor all Protestant missionaries British, made little or no impression upon the popular understanding of the subject. The missions, separated from each other by doctrinal beliefs and also by a language barrier, rarely had any intercourse and still less co-operation. The Chinese people saw nothing in common between them, except that both were foreign. A people who still regarded their fellow citizens of Moslem faith as foreigners after more than a thousand years, were hardly likely to accept new alien religions with enthusiasm or treat converts without suspicion.

For several years before the advent of the Communist regime the missionary societies and churches which supported them had become increasingly aware of these formidable obstacles to the acceptance of their evangel. It was now seen that the reliance on extraterritorial rights, and the political and military power of the Western nations which had first forced open the door to the Christian missionaries, had proved a liability rather than a benefit. It had left Christianity in all its forms under the stigma of being the instrument of foreign aggression. Yet without this assistance the imperial government would never have permitted the missionaries to enter the country and carry on their work. The best the missionary societies could now do was to disclaim the desire or the need for any further protection and press forward with a policy of training Chinese clergy and ministers to take their places.

This policy had already in the years between the Nationalist revolution of 1926–27 and the triumph of the Communist Party in 1949 made great progress. It had been helped, unintentionally, by the Second World War which forced those missionaries of allied nationality to leave the large regions occupied by Japan, and those of Axis allegiance to quit the areas still under Chinese authority. In both the Catholic and Protestant churches the era of the missionary was drawing to a close, the establishment of churches served exclusively by Chinese clergy and priests was already in sight. Yet many missionaries, with long and wide experience of the country, deep knowledge of the people and their prejudices, feared that this change was coming too soon. They saw that the churches were numerically still very small, financially often very poor, still under strong social pressure and the suspicion of being foreign organizations. They doubted whether they were yet strong enough to stand alone without veering into heresy or yielding to worldly, political, influences.

These doubts, many will think, have in part been justified by the event. The Communist revolution—Liberation as it is called in China—no doubt accentuated all the difficulties which the Christian churches had to contend with, but this event did not in itself create all these problems. The Nationalist regime, even though some of its leading members were Protestant Christians, was often swayed in its policy, particularly in educational policy, by nationalist sentiment, which tended to be anti-Christian, especially with regard to the foreign connections of the Chinese churches. In the churches themselves, as foreign missionary influence declined, there began to appear some signs of a specifically Chinese approach to problems of dogma and doctrine, which were disturbing to Western Christian observers.

It was natural that the foreign missionary, of every church, had brought with him to China his own tradition and religious background. In every Western country there was an old, historical opposition between the Church of Rome and those churches which had arisen since the Reformation. The two religions were in competition at home, and continued to compete in China. Protestant missionaries felt it their duty to warn their flock against the errors of Rome: Catholic priests were equally on guard against the sin of heresy. The Chinese, who had only a hazy understanding of the history which lay behind this quarrel gained a clearer idea of the matters on which the two churches disagreed than on the great range of doctrine common to all Christians. But these subjects of disagreement, to a Chinese, seemed secondary and hard to comprehend. Popular belief, taking the more familiar Moslems as a guide, held that the Protestants could be distinguished from the Catholics by such customs as Protestant opposition to smoking tobacco, drinking wine or attending the Chinese theatre, while the most conspicuous Catholic characteristic, familiar from Buddhist practice, was that the priesthood was celibate. Catholic activity in founding orphanages and rescuing abandoned children was compared to the Moslem practice of buying up the children of famine refugees, a practice which the non-Moslem Chinese disliked and resented.

Among the Protestant churches there were, in China, the

same divisions which a long train of historical events had produced in the home countries. Anglicans, Presbyterians, Methodists, Baptists, Seventh Day Adventists and smaller esoteric sects, competed for the conversion of the pagan Chinese. Some of these churches did indeed enter into agreements which zoned their activity, avoiding the open competition of two missions in one city; others refused to limit their work in this way. The Chinese had no knowledge of the complex theological history which lay behind these divisions, no understanding of the social forces at work in the Western countries which had tended to perpetuate them. The points in dispute seemed to them fine, difficult, and obscure. In face of the massive fact of the overwhelming non-Christian majority these doctrinal divergences also seemed irrelevant and unimportant. As the Chinese Protestant churches gained their autonomy from the missions there arose a marked tendency to ignore or slur over the doctrinal disputes which the Chinese churches had inherited from their Western missionary founders.

In 1949, when the People's Republic was established, the churches were confronted with a situation which sharply emphasized all these problems. The Catholic hierarchy, although far from enthusiastic supporters of the Nationalist regime, which if in any way touched by Christianity tended to be under Protestant influence, still felt that Communism was a greater enemy, and moreover one which the Vatican had explicitly and unreservedly condemned. They could not co-operate with Communism; their duty was to oppose it, consequently they promptly incurred the charge of being counter-revolutionary. The leading bishops, the Chinese cardinal, were forced to flee the country; others were imprisoned, or expelled. Orphanages and schools were closed, and if the churches themselves remained open to worship, it was only on sufferance and under the obligation to accept the regime, refrain from preaching against it, and abandon the social work of the Church. Those foreign missionaries who remained were progressively eliminated, by expulsion, imprisonment followed by expulsion, or refusal to permit the return of those who were out of the country.

The Protestant churches, having no central organization which had adopted a clear anti-Communist stand, were not exposed to the same pressure. The missionary bodies decided that their presence in China would henceforth do more harm to the churches than good, and ordered the missionaries to withdraw. The Chinese government in turn made it obligatory upon the Protestant churches to sever their connections, financial and otherwise, with the parent churches overseas, and the missionary societies which had supported them. Protestants, like Catholics, were soon debarred from running schools and other institutions, which were taken over by the State. Deprived of their overseas financial support they could not, in any case, have continued to maintain such work. The churches were forced into independence and reliance upon their own followers, and they were at the same time confined to purely religious activity.

The Common Programme of the Chinese coalition government, in which the Communist Party plays the predominant role, assures all law-abiding citizens of the right to practise their religion. In the sense that churches remain open, the clergy (provided they are Chinese) can continue to officiate, and that no person is compelled to renounce his faith, this programme is being implemented. But policy towards the Christian churches is also directed firmly at destroying their dependence on foreign assistance, severing their links with foreign organizations, eliminating any influence they exercised upon education, social policy or foreign relations. The question arises whether such a situation is in fact compatible with the survival of the Christian churches in China, what future lies before them. Remembering the direction of policy towards Buddhists on the one hand and Moslems on the other, to which of these solutions can Christians aspire?

The Christians are a much smaller community than the Buddhists but they are, on the whole, a better educated sample of the population. This is especially true of the urban Christians, both Protestant and Catholic, many of whom are the products of missionary schools. As a well educated group strong in the professions and technical sciences, the Christians were relatively much more important than their numbers indicated. They dominated the Chinese medical profession, which owed its origin to missionary hospitals. They were influential and prominent in academic life, where many of the modern universities had been missionary foundations. They were, inevitably, the group most directly influenced by Western ideologies, and the links they maintained with Western Christian countries were not merely religious but also cultural in a wider sense. The educated Christians are thus the section of the scholar class most prone to the new sin of 'bourgeois rightist' or reactionary ideas.

On the other hand, the Christians were all, undoubtedly, Chinese. They were not of alien descent either remotely or recently. They could not be given the status of a national minority and placed in a special category insulated from the general stream of Chinese social life. The Moslem solution is not really open to the Christians for this reason, and also because, except in very few instances, they do not form compact communities living to themselves in their own villages. Although like Buddhists and Moslems they are members in a world-wide religion with the vast majority of their co-religionists living in foreign countries, these foreign lands are not Asian, are not recently liberated colonies, but the homelands of the 'imperialists' from whose yoke the Communists have delivered China. So far from the Christian connection with foreign countries being an asset, it is their greatest liability, and the source of their troubles.

Very recently, since the Protestant churches have been reformed and pruned of all foreign support and assistance, their value for assuring contacts with the West has been cautiously explored. It is now seen that if the Protestant Church in China can be shown to be free and untrammelled (in its religious activity) this is a valuable counter to the propaganda of the opponents of the regime and the critics of the People's Republic. The Chinese church can be allowed to resume some contact with foreign churches. Visits of Western churchmen may be permitted; the fact that many Western Protestant clergy are active in the movement for peace, opposed to military policies and critical of the boycott of China organized by the United States, gives the Chinese Protestant Church a new value. Since it is in any case only a very small minority of the nation, and its members include a valuable group of highly educated, patriotic and technically qualified men and women, it may be given religious freedom and exhibited as a proof that such freedom really does exist, in the strictly religious context, in People's China.

The Protestants have thus won their place, and seem assured of tolerance; but the prospect of further growth and expansion is not so clear. All education is now secular, government controlled, and has no religious content. Those who wish for instruction in their religion must obtain it privately, out of hours, and only a few seminaries for the training of clergy remain of the educational endeavour of the Protestant churches. Christians, it may be said, must thus 'contract in' to their religion, rather than acquire it automatically in their school years. It is obvious that the regime, itself atheist, believes that this will lead to diminishing returns, that the educated of the next generation will fall away from the church, and that the evangelization of the non-Christian masses will make no further progress, since such public campaigns are not permitted. The Protestants, a useful and now harmless group, may be left in peace because no one in the Party really thinks they will thrive or expand to any significant degree.

This expectation may be falsified in the event, for there are signs that the Protestant churches are taking steps to adjust themselves to the new world in which they must henceforth live. A movement to form a united church, transcending, or ignoring, the doctrinal differences which have separated Protestant Christianity into many sects is now very active and powerful in China. It appears to have the encouragement, or at least the approval, of the regime. This need not surprise, for a very similar unity has been imposed upon, or accepted by, the Buddhists. The Party likes to deal with larger entities, and an 'All China Federation of Protestant Churches', or better still, an 'All China Protestant Church' would be welcome. On the other hand, such a union can only be accomplished by doing some violence to the accepted tenets of the constituent churches; it will tend to draw the Chinese Protestants further from their foreign co-religionists, and to encourage the growth, in time, of a Chinese church with its own peculiar doctrines.

As the movement to overcome or pass by the divergent doctrines of the parent churches was already apparent in China before the Communists came to power, and does represent a Chinese response to this problem, freed from prejudices taken over from the West, it may be expected to make a wide appeal among the Chinese Protestant community; it will also be acceptable to the regime, and there is thus every reason to expect that this is the future development of Protestant Christianity in China.

The situation for the Catholic Church is different. It is much more difficult for the Chinese hierarchy to make the kind of adjustment which would win the tolerance and approval of the Communist Party. There is allegiance to the Vatican, which has made its attitude of hostility to all Communist regimes crystal clear. On the other hand, the Roman Church is already a unified body, and as in China no one thinks of the two branches of Christianity as being closely akin, there is no pressure to force Roman Catholics into unity with the reformed churches. The problem is how to reconcile the existence of a coherent and well-established Catholic community with a regime which cannot admit the authority of a hierarchy loyal to the Vatican, while the hierarchy, in turn, cannot admit the legitimacy of an atheist state which the Vatican has condemned. Logically it should be impossible in these circumstances for the Catholic church to operate at all, or for the regime to tolerate any part of its activity. Fortunately neither side has pushed logic to extremes.

The Chinese Catholic laity are the oldest established group of Christians. In some parts of the country, notably Peking and Shanghai, the Catholic community dates back to the Ming period, the seventeenth century. The proportion of recent converts among the Catholics is very much smaller than among the Protestants, the proportion of Christian families of many generations standing much higher. Protestantism was not preached in China until the early part of the nineteenth century, and not widely known until after the Opium War of 1844. Catholicism had been introduced to China in the early seventeenth century, and by the end of the Ming period, in 1644, was already making considerable headway. The Catholic community is thus more close knit, stable, and united than the Protestant community. The response of the Catholics to the present situation is however also characteristically Chinese, and stems from the very fact that they are an older and more traditional group.

Like other, non-Christian Chinese, the Catholics also see the Protestants as quite unlike, separate and distinct from themselves. They, too, cannot enter into the background of European history which has conditioned the attitudes of Western Christians. They have never been an important political force in China, they have not in the past had the same influence in educational, academic and scientific life as the educated section of the Chinese Protestants. Far more of them come from long-established Catholic families, often poor, far fewer from intellectual conversion at school or university. They are not really interested in the political struggle—as they see it—between the Vatican and the Communist regime. They are very much interested in keeping the churches open, in having priests available to say Mass and serve the churches; they are determined to practise their religion, they do not much care how it is controlled at the highest level.

The consequence of this attitude among the laity, and the expulsion, flight, or imprisonment of the hierarchy, has been to leave the Catholic Church in China served only by the parish clergy, and largely controlled by the laity themselves. To be allowed to officiate and carry on religious work a priest must make a declaration of loyalty to the People's Republic. Such a declaration is forbidden by the Vatican, but the Catholic laity have induced or compelled most of the parish clergy to take this step, and thus assure the continuity of services and the toleration of the government. On such terms the regime is quite prepared to admit the Catholics to the same freedom of worship as any other religion enjoys; the same, but no more.

The church must confine itself to religious services, no social work may be undertaken, no political attitude other than that of submission to the state will be tolerated. The spiritual link with Rome is accepted, and permitted, but neither financial support nor control in any but matters of doctrine and dogma can be allowed. For some years the Catholic Church in China has carried on in this uncertain, ill-defined status; a situation which could not be expected to endure without bringing further complications. For as there are no bishops left at liberty, it is not apparent how any further priests may be validly ordained. Those members of the lower hierarchy who have announced their acceptance of the regime's requirements, and have thus been enabled to exercise authority over the Church in China, have been excommunicated by the Vatican. The impasse appears complete, for any leader acceptable to one side is thereby rendered obnoxious to the other.

Recently, under what pressure, whether from the regime above or the laity below, or from both, the Chinese Catholic clergy have in their turn formed an association which, while declaring its allegiance to Rome in all matters spiritual, accepts the authority of the People's Republic in all matters temporal. That this body will henceforth be the effective organ of control in the Catholic Church in China seems inevitable. No other organization can function. But this situation, while it may be satisfactory to the Catholic laity who are not much troubled by the problem so long as the churches remain open and the priests can officiate, in fact amounts to a schism, yet not to a heresy, since the Chinese Catholics accept in every respect the doctrines and dogmas of the Church. It could lead to the rise of a schismatic church such as the Old Catholics of Europe. Such an outcome would not be unwelcome to the regime, for it would allow the Catholic Church to be exhibited as free in matters of religion, though forced into independence by what would be treated as the intransigence of the Vatican. It would also assure the regime of the loyalty and peaceful submission of the Catholic laity.

If Christianity has a future in China, it would seem probable that it is only on the condition that it resigns one of the principal functions which that religion has hitherto performed, that of being the spearhead of Western civilization. The Chinese, if not prepared for 'wholesale Westernization', are determined to modernize their country, and in doing so accept and employ all that the West has contributed in science and technology, much of what the West has given of political science, economics and sociology. But they are not willing, under the present regime, to take any of these things from the religion of the West; they wish to divorce religion from all social activity, leaving it as the private spiritual exercise of those who are inclined to practise it.

This view of religion is in accordance with Chinese tradition, and harmonizes with much Buddhist practice, but it is fundamentally opposed to the habitual outlook of the Western nations. Critics from these nations find it difficult to understand what is meant by freedom of religion if the social side of religion is banned. They tend to regard the Chinese promise of freedom, or the claim that it exists, as mendacious and meaningless. This is a failure to take into account the major difference between the role of religion in the Chinese and in the Western society.

The key to that difference lies in the second half of the sentence quoted from Chou En-lai's speech at the beginning of this chapter. '. . . We hope that those with religious belief will also respect those without (it).' The idea that those who denied the Christian faith were entitled to respect, or indeed even to life and liberty, is so very new in Europe, barely two to three centuries old, that it is still quite alien to the inner convictions of Western people. Religion was the central pillar of our civilization, the unifying force, the mainspring. It was never anything of the sort in China. Firstly, there was no one, accepted, universal, and therefore true religion. There were several systems, mutually contradictory, all time-honoured, all followed in some degree by most people, or all ignored by the select few. 'Three Ways to One Goal', the Chinese complacently remarked, meaning that every religion had some good in it, all would tend to make men better, no one was sure which was right, no one thought any one system had a monopoly of truth. The 'Goal', moreover, was not Paradise, but the good, sober, balanced conduct of life here on earth.

This view was traditional and sanctioned by ancient authority. In the early seventh century, when Nestorian monks from Syria came to China and sought permission to preach their faith, the Emperor, the great T'ang T'ai Tsung, issued an Edict, the terms of which have been preserved on the monument which the Nestorians erected, and which still survives.

'The Way has more than one name. There is more than one sage. Doctrines vary in different lands, their benefits reach all mankind . . . after examining these doctrines We find them profound and pacific: after studying these principles We find that they stress what is good and important. This teaching is not diffuse and the reasoning is sound. This religion does good to all men. Let it be preached freely in Our Empire.'

If religion strayed beyond the limits of teaching men how to live the good life, and the service of the Gods, and began to meddle in social and political problems, the attitude of the Chinese ruling class changed abruptly. Then religion became a pernicious superstition disturbing the people and subverting the orthodox ethical system on which government reposed. As such, it must be suppressed. There seems to be good reason to think that the attitude of the Chinese Communist Party towards religion is very similar to that of their imperial predecessors: it is not, in China, a revolutionary attitude, and consequently the religious question has not in China any of the urgency or importance which it assumes in eastern Europe, or is believed to possess by critics of the Chinese People's Republic.

CHAPTER EIGHT

CHINA'S FOREIGN GUESTS

OLD CHINA HAD a reputation for the milder forms of xenophobia: Western foreigners were known to the populace by the unflattering nickname of 'foreign devils'—said to be due to the unfortunate coincidence that devils of the Buddhist Hell were often represented as having light coloured hair and eyes, a pigmentation unknown among the Chinese. Small boys followed foreigners in the street making sounds imitating the bleating of sheep, for 'yang', the Chinese word for 'foreign' (literally 'ocean') is a homophone of the Chinese word for 'sheep'. It was said, too, that foreigners smell of sheep. Many of these popular pleasantries passed over the unconscious heads of the Western foreigners concerned, because they in turn, with an equal conviction of their own superiority, omitted to learn the language of the people among whom they passed their lives. The Old China Hand lived in a world of his own, dependent, indeed, on the services provided by Chinese labour, but conceding only the minimum to the exclusive civilization which made him such grudging welcome. Strangely enough he accepted, perhaps unconsciously, the term 'foreigner' for himself, and proudly talked of 'foreign food', 'foreign style', etc., meaning his own, Western, manners and customs.

The Chinese were not any more gracious to Asian than to Western foreigners, but saw very many fewer of these. Indians were usually called 'black foreigners'; Japanese were still called—behind their backs—by the old contemptuous term 'foreign dwarfs'. Mongols and other northern nomads had for centuries been known as 'hu', a word having roughly the same connotation as 'barbarian'. Western Barbarians was an expression used for western Asians. The various non-Chinese peoples of southern China and beyond the borders were usually treated, in popular speech, as if they were savages, and the names of these peoples written with the 'dog' element in the ideograph. If this was the underlying attitude towards foreigners displayed by the Chinese people, it might have been expected that when the new regime, claiming to be the People's Government, came to power, the ancient xenophobia would be given more formalized expression.

The Chinese people, moreover, and their new government, had very little sympathy with the main categories of Western foreigners who had made their living in China. The diplomatic corps, representing the 'imperialist nations'—for very few of the smaller countries of Asia or Europe maintained missions in China—was no doubt a necessary evil, but one which was at once rapidly diminished by the fact that only a few of the Western nations recognized the People's Republic. The Christian missionaries, one of the largest and most pervasive foreign groups, was at once halved by the withdrawal of the Protestants and speedily liquidated by the expulsion, or imprisonment prior to expulsion, of the Catholics. The merchants, concentrated in the Treaty Ports, were in the eyes of the Chinese Communists basically an undesirable community of capitalists. It might be necessary to leave some, representing shipping firms, more or less unmolested, but for the most part the foreign trading community was put under such pressure and restriction that it swiftly disappeared. Demands for arrears of taxation, unemployment contributions, discharge bonuses for workers and other devices ensured that the foreign merchant, when he left, took very little with him, and abandoned his capital equipment.

The smallest group of foreign residents had been those engaged in university education and other academic activities. These were for the time left in peace, even sharing with their Chinese colleagues the new privileges of being classed as 'workers'. They were probably the only group of foreign residents genuinely welcomed by the Chinese, and some very few of them still remain at work. Most were permitted to fulfil their current contracts and then leave, with the minimum of inconvenience or impediment.

Early accounts of Communist China by returning foreign residents tended to reflect very closely the impression produced by treatment at departure. Missionaries who saw their life work interrupted, their faith in jeopardy and their future obscure, were natrually overwhelmed at the catastrophe, and felt little but foreboding. Merchants and business men who had lost heavily and must now start again in circumstances far less propitious and comfortable, were bitter and resentful. Diplomatists of the non-recognizing countries felt keenly the loss China must suffer from their absence. The educationalists and specialists who had lived on for one or two years under the new regime, and suffered hardly at all from its policies, were much more objective and sometimes quite enthusiastic.

For some years the only travellers in China were, or were judged to be 'fellow travellers'; and the only Western residents, with very few exceptions, were the small number of diplomats representing the recognizing countries, and the not very large group of avowed Communists working with or for the People's Republic. It seemed then that the clock had been put back two hundred years to the days of the early contact at Canton, when the Western trader was an object of suspicion to be held at arms length, the Western diplomatic mission was surrounded with frustration and obstruction, the Western traveller, if he got into China at all, liable to expulsion, arbitrary arrest or detention. The non-Communist foreign press was banned, and no correspondents could travel or reside in China.

There are no doubt a number of reasons, as yet unknown, why the new policy of exclusion was modified from the year 1954 onward. One reason is, however, quite obvious; in 1949 the condition of China was such that the government can hardly be blamed for wanting to eliminate as many foreign observers as possible. Firstly it was felt, perhaps unjustly, that all Western non-Communist residents were hostile critics, who would malign the People's Republic. The less they saw of it, the better. Secondly, conditions were still disturbed, communications poor, security uncertain. The Communist regime certainly feared that foreign residents might get into trouble in the provinces, that incidents would occur, and that these would be used as pretexts by hostile foreign governments. The foreign resident, if not an enthusiastic Communist supporter and co-worker, was a nuisance, an encumbrance, and could be a danger. Those foreign residents who did not carry out some essential function soon found their passports marked 'useless'—and were asked to make arrangements for prompt departure.

It is now clear that behind this policy of exclusion there lay, not an intention to cut off all intercourse in future, but a plan to re-shape the pattern of such intercourse on new lines, having first removed all traces of the old system. The Treaty Ports and the Christian missions, seen as twin symbols of Western 'imperialism', were to be eliminated and with them the foreign communities they had nourished. The Old China Hand must go, because he was obnoxious to the Communists in himself, and also because his continued presence might exercise a pre-judicial effect upon the Western visitors who were soon to be invited to come to China in increasing numbers. It was hoped that the 'New China Hands' would acquire an untainted impression of the People's Republic, and transmit this more favourable report to their home countries. The great merit of the 'New China Hand' is that he has no stake in the country, does not gain his livelihood by residing there, is a bird of passage who can never become a problem.

Under the new policy anyone is welcome to come to China, but for a visit, not as a resident. Trade is promoted, by means of visiting trade delegations, missions and private journeys, but no foreign firm is encouraged to set up its own office and bring in a resident staff. The foreign community in China at any given date is probably as large, or larger than it was in the heyday of the Treaty Ports, but it is composed of transients. It is also made up of elements very different from the old community of pre-Communist days. The diplomatic corps, which alone has some permanence, is no longer dominated by the missions of the Western Great Powers; of these, only the British remain.

The major part of the diplomatic corps is now provided by

the missions from the Communist states, headed by the Soviet Union, with East Germany, Poland, Czechoslovakia, Hungary, Bulgaria, Rumania, Albania, North Korea, North Viet-nam and Mongolia in support. Not one of these states except Russia (and for a brief period, Poland and Czechoslovakia) has formerly had diplomatic relations with China. Next there is a fringe of states such as Yugoslavia and Finland who bridge the two worlds. The United Kingdom, the Netherlands, Sweden, Norway, Denmark and Switzerland are the only western European nations with missions in China. South America has no representation at all: but neutralist or non-aligned Asia supplies the third large component of Peking's diplomatic community. India, Pakistan, Burma, Ceylon, Indonesia, Afghanistan, Nepal, Egypt and Syria maintain embassies or legations in Peking. The diplomatic world of the Chinese capital is, as one of its members pointed out, made up of three parts, Protestant western Europe, Communist eastern Europe, and neutralist Asia. It is, moreover, very much larger than the diplomatic corps of the Nationalist, Republican or Imperial periods.

The only other large group of foreigners who can be described as even temporary residents are the Russian and eastern European advisers. It is not easy to assess the size of this community, for it is scattered over the whole of China, whereever some major construction project or institution requires the presence of an expert, an adviser or technicians whom China cannot at present supply. It is suggested by resident Western diplomats that the number of Russian, Czech, Polish and Eastern German advisers and experts with their families may be not far short of the number of similar experts and technicians, mainly from Western countries, who formerly worked in China for varying periods of time. On the other hand, the old White Russian community, once one of the largest in China, has now greatly diminished, and will soon disappear altogether. These people have been permitted to leave China in large numbers, and it is uncertain how many now remain, even in northern Manchuria, where at one time (1940) the Russian population was 70,000.* On balance, therefore, it is more than probable that the Russian resident population in China has greatly declined.

The new element in the transitory foreign population of China are the visitors invited to tour the country by one or other of a large number of Chinese organizations, mostly of a semi-official character. Delegations of all sorts are constantly travelling through China; they include trade missions, trade union delegations, religious groups, cultural and academic missions, scientists and specialists. They come from every country except, conspicuously, the United States, which has hitherto not permitted her citizens to enter the People's Republic. China has developed a large tourist trade, of a peculiar character, for the great majority of the new tourists are guests who enjoy the hospitality of their Chinese hosts, and are put to no expense at all. So far from acquiring foreign exchange by means of this tourist trade, it is obvious that China expends very large sums in bringing these visitors to the country and entertaining them when they arrive.

In most of the great cities of China comfortable hotels fitted with every convenience have either been erected to cater for these visitors or been taken over from private ownership. Peking has two new hotels in addition to those which already existed, in Shanghai the great luxury hotels which were once occupied by wealthy Chinese business men and Western travellers are now assigned to the unremunerative but generous entertainment of the visiting delegations and missions. The problem of what use these buildings could be put to in a socialist society has been solved by reserving them for the accommodation of visitors, who for the most part come from the capitalist world and are not themselves either Communists or 'fellow travellers'. An enterprise so bizarre and seemingly unprofitable needs to be examined and explained.

It must first be observed that these visitors are predominantly from Asian and African countries. Western missions and dele-

* See Walter Kolarz, *The Peoples of the Soviet Far East*. George Philip & Son. London. 1954. P. 38 footnote.

gations, though numerous, are rarely so large or so frequent as the groups from the former colonial world. The absence of all American visitors would in any case greatly reduce the normal proportion of Western tourists as found in any other country. The presence of large groups of Sudanese, Ethiopians, Syrians, Arabians and others from parts of Asia and Africa which send very few tourists to other regions affords a strikingly different composition from the normal tourist trade. Moreover, whereas there was a considerable tourist trade from the West in Old China, the peoples of Africa and western Asia were very rarely seen in China. The new tourism has opened for these peoples a world hitherto almost beyond their knowledge.

The great majority of these visitors have therefore never been in China before, have no knowledge of the former state of the country, no basis for comparing the present situation with the days before 'Liberation'. When they are shown cities such as Shanghai or Mukden they cannot easily discover how much of what they see has been created or improved by the present regime and how much was inherited from the past. For Western visitors, who have access to a literature which gives ample record of the previous condition of China, this difficulty is less, but still exists. It would be false to say that the Chinese are not willing to permit return visits by those who knew the Old China; on the contrary, no obstacles are placed in their way, nor is their participation in delegations or missions objected to. Yet they are, at best, few: for many of them it was not possible, when they were formerly in China, to travel to the places they now visit; their previous experience may have been more concentrated, but also more limited than the view obtained on a tour today.

In actual fact, it is probable that the Chinese gain more real credit for their present achievements from those who did know Old China than from those who only see the country now. To the New China visitor it is not remarkable that he should travel in reasonable comfort and perfect safety by train from Canton to Peking, or from Shanghai to Lanchou in the far north-west. He may find the railways slower than those at home, though he will probably acknowledge that they are cleaner and perhaps better maintained. But to the returning traveller who knew Old China, especially China in the immediate post-war period, these things are little short of miraculous.

Even in the pre-war years train travel in China was at best an uncertain operation. The railway might be cut by the sudden outbreak of one of the civil wars between provincial warlords, or rebellions against the Nationalist government. Occasionally, though more infrequently, trains were held up by bandits. Military interference was felt in other ways, almost equally inconvenient. The trains swarmed with soldiers and officers who had not paid any fares, but occupied the best seats. They were careless and even reckless with their firearms. They interrupted the normal schedule of the service, commandeered trains and rolling stock, behaved with arbitrary arrogance to the ordinary passenger. It was unwise to rely on booked seats, unless a servant could be sent to occupy the seat hours in advance.

In the post-war years conditions deteriorated much further. The railways, especially in North China, were reduced to spasmodic and unpredictable schedules. Every journey partook of the nature of a minor military operation. The railway was heavily guarded by blockhouses, trenches and fortified stations, but was constantly, sometimes almost nightly, interrupted. If the journey, however short, could not be completed in the daytime, the train withdrew at night into the fortified perimeter of a railway station. The fitful sleep of the weary travellers was frequently disturbed by bursts of gunfire, and the dull roar of demolitions. When, if it were possible, the effects of the night attack had been repaired, the train would creep on for a few more miles. A railway journey involved all the uncertainties of a voyage by sea in a primitive sailing vessel. The start and the arrival depended on factors which neither the crew nor the passengers could foresee or prevent, the duration was unpredictable, the discomforts certain, the danger great.

These hazards far from reducing the number of passengers who ventured to travel, seemed merely to add to the overcrowding and deplorable conditions. Those who could not find any standing room inside the carriage rode on the buffers, the roof, the footplates. They were in great danger of being swept off by passing trains, or falling off from exhaustion and cold. At every stop those on the roof leaped up and down in the hope of reviving their circulation sufficiently to survive until the next station. The stations were indescribable. Passengers camped upon the platforms for days in the hope of getting a train. When one arrived it was assailed by a furious mob determined at any cost to battle its way aboard without the least regard for those who wished to get off, who, in turn, must force their way out using their luggage as battering rams. Only a very modest improvement was needed to impress the returning China resident.

The train service in China today compares favourably with any but the most luxurious expresses of other parts of the world. It is, on average, very much better than the ordinary services in other countries. There is no overcrowding, punctual schedules are observed, the military forces do not use the ordinary services, order and discipline are maintained at stations, the trains are kept scrupulously clean. The attendants, charged with the education of the travelling public, exhort them over a public address system to obey the rules, behave with courtesy and consideration, report any slackness or inefficiency on the part of the railway service.

The visitor who did not know the old conditions may well take all this for granted, as normal, if often rather better than what he expected from experience elsewhere. Yet in this matter the contrast between the New China and the Old, on which the system of propaganda is often too apt to harp, cannot be overstressed. If the Chinese were to include among the many visiting delegations one composed of Former Railway Travellers they would undoubtedly score a propaganda victory of major value.

In the immediate post-war period all who could afford to do so travelled by air. Apart from the discomfort and danger of railway travel there was the essential advantage that air travel could only be interrupted by bad weather, whereas train travel might be discontinued altogether. The Nationalist government retained control of the major cities until a late stage in the civil war, and air travel became the only means of communication between them.

In People's China air travel holds a much reduced importance. The air services are relatively few, the aircraft small and not of recent design. Great caution is employed in conducting air travel, services are suspended if weather is not perfect. It is clear that few private travellers take to the air, and it is often quicker to travel by train from Peking to Canton, four days, than to fly. It would appear that the effort in this sphere of communications is reserved for the international lines linking China with Russia, and services to Sinkiang, regions which are not yet served by the railways. It is also probable that the high cost of aviation spirit, and indeed of oil in general, has imposed a limitation on the development of air travel, whereas the abundance of coal in most parts of China has always made railway operation cheap.

Having restored the railways, the Chinese hosts are now able to transport their numerous guests around the country in comfort and with adequate speed. It is also clear that for the greater part of the visiting delegations and missions, the route is well marked and follows a set pattern. Visitors enter the country through Hong Kong, proceeding by train from Canton to Peking, thence to Mukden and the industrial cities of Manchuria. Returning they travel to Tientsin, Nanking and Shanghai; pass a delightful week-end at the famous beauty spot, Hangchou, and so return to Canton by the railway linking Hangchou and Changsha in Hunan. Some delegations may visit the west or north-west of China, others will be taken for part of their tour by river steamer down the Yangtze from Wuhan to Shanghai.

In Peking they will be shown not only the institutions and installations in which they are professionally interested, but also the famous monuments of antiquity, the Palaces, Temple of Heaven, Great Wall and Ming Tombs. In Manchuria they will see the steel foundries, the coal mines, the factories of China's rising heavy industry. They will be shown a Higher Stage Co-operative farm near Peking, and another, where the agricultural technique differs, in the ricelands of South China. They will see the new housing projects in Shanghai, and visit the Sino-Soviet Exhibition Hall to see whatever current exhibition is displayed. From all these experiences they will derive much pleasure and interest, and on returning to their own country will be told that they have been taken over the beaten track, and shown only the fair face of the People's Republic.

Most of them, being new to the country, and knowing very little of its history, geography or characteristics, will not be able, when asked by their courteous hosts to suggest a route, or name places they would specially like to see, to make any suggestions, but will gladly leave such difficult problems to the competent organizers of the tour. If, however, they should have special and unusual interests, in art or archaeology, ethnography or some other branch of learning or of industry, and suggest that they would like to visit some remote region, famous for a Buddhist shrine, or for the beauty of the scenery, or perhaps for the development of an ancient craft, they will meet with every co-operation and assistance. There is, no doubt, a beaten track for those who cannot suggest an alternative, but for those who can there are no restrictions, no evasions.

As it is now possible to travel anywhere in China with safety and reasonable comfort, conditions which have not previously prevailed, the Chinese are very willing to show the traveller anything he wishes to see, confident that if he is able to draw comparisons with the past they will not be disadvantageous to the present. Abruptly reversing the policy of restriction followed in the early years of the People's Republic, the authorities now invite resident diplomats to make tours in the provinces, and give every assistance to travellers or members of delegations who want to see some special or unusual activity or place. In certain cases such visitors have been the first for many years who have come from any Western country.

Archaeological monuments, or special craft industries are more often found in out-of-the-way rural places, far from the large cities and main lines of communication. Visits to such sites enable travellers to compare the rural conditions in these unselected villages with those which they were shown at model Higher Stage Co-operative farms near Peking or Shanghai. It must be recognized that the comparison is not unfavourable to the less visited and unfrequented places. It becomes apparent that there is no objection to visitors seeing these villages because they will not find in them features markedly inferior to those of the show co-operative farms.

The chance visitor to a village near which some site of interest is located is no better able to judge from his contacts with the peasants there than with those in a model co-operative whether they are satisfied with the changes that have come over their lives, whether they feel a lack of freedom, regret the passing of private property, or dislike the dominance of the Communist Party and its cadres. He can, however, see whether the village is in good repair, whether the people are decently clad and adequately fed. He can note the presence or absence of a clinic and a school, observe if the streets are dirty or well kept; he can also see whether there are troops quartered in the village, or none at all, and look for other signs, such as fortified bridges and police stations, which would denote the existence of unrest.

The Chinese can be confident that such travellers will not be in a position to test the views and thoughts of the people, but that they can certainly see and will report favourably on the material aspects of their lives, the perceptible rise in the standard of living, the absence of any outward signs of repression or unrest. What the traveller sees may not be, to him, evidence of any great advance, or impress him with the excellence of conditions, but it is unlikely that such a traveller can fail to report that some progress is being made, that things are better than they were, and that there is no sign that the regime is actively opposed or needs to maintain itself with a display of armed power. Yet these relatively negative and

modest signs of tranquility and contentment run counter to
the widespread beliefs of most of the travellers' fellow countrymen, and flatly contradict the propaganda of the opponents of
the People's Republic. Thus the most cautious and guarded
report is likely to appear as 'Communist propaganda' to the
convinced opponent—and to be welcomed as valuable publicity by the regime itself.

The Chinese authorities are in a strong position in this field
and there is every reason for them to welcome and promote
visits and travel. If the visitor has been to China before
'Liberation', he cannot fail to be impressed with the magnitude
of the changes, and the real improvement in conditions. He
will be, no matter what reservations he feels on other questions,
inevitably a witness speaking favourable things. If he has never
been to China before, but has formed some opinions about the
country from the newspapers and public opinion, he will be
surprised, much less impressed than the returning former
resident, but will still testify that what he saw was better than
he had been led to expect, that conditions seemed normal and
peaceful, that he could go where he wished, see what he wanted
to see, and meet those whom he hoped to meet. He, too,
must inevitably appear as a favourable propagandist.

It is probable that the Chinese authorities are not very much
interested in the type of unfavourable criticism which travellers
will make on ideological grounds. The visitor who admits the
material improvements, but suspects the system, dislikes persuasion and propaganda, disapproves the restrictions on publi-
cation of dissenting opinion and the absence of an open legal
'opposition', is still valuable, because he must admit the material
achievements of the regime, and these are actual, concrete
facts. His opinions are his own, and in the Communist view,
mistaken; he held these views before he came to China, will
continue to hold them after he has returned home; but he will,
in all honesty, have to recognize the reality and scope of the
changes that have occurred, and his evidence will have all the
more value as coming from an ideological opponent.

Seen from this point of view the new facilities for travel, the elaborate organization for invitation of delegations and missions is all money well spent, effort which is repaid by useful publicity. The achievements of the regime are made known abroad to an ever widening audience; an audience, moreover, which not only or even mostly consists of the Western peoples, but of Asians and Africans who bring to China much less suspicion and prejudice and take away a far greater cargo of favourable impressions and pleasant memories. The chief impression which they certainly receive, and are intended to acquire, is that under Communism China has made a swift, sensational advance from misery to prosperity, from disorder to peace, from technical backwardness to modern proficiency. The conclusion which some at least may be expected to draw from these facts is that this is the system which most efficiently lifts a backward country from the ruck to the van, and is therefore an alternative which all backward countries must take into account, and must observe without prejudice. If this idea is diffused among even a minority of the Asian and African visitors, the visit has been very well worth while to the People's Republic.

It might be expected that however generous the hospitality offered to those foreign guests, it would still reflect the austere standards of the Communist ideal, rather than the luxury which capitalism provides for those who can afford it. Railway accommodation, which is not intended solely, or even mainly for foreign visitors, but for the population at large, does indeed follow the simple division into 'hard' and 'soft' classes, and although 'soft' is adequate, clean and sufficiently comfortable for long journeys, there is no attempt to emulate the luxury of 'Golden Arrows' or 'Vista Domes'. Hotels, however, are not the simple, clean, plain-living establishments which travellers might expect, and of which most would feel no inclination to complain. Except in out-of-the-way places, where visitors are put up in the hostels provided for Chinese official travellers, the hotels built for the new tourists, or taken over from the old regime, offer a standard of comfort, indeed of luxury, which compares well with any European country, and considerably exceeds that prevalent in, for example, Australia. The guest finds a choice of Western and Chinese food, both excellent and ample, clean bedrooms with private bathrooms, attentive helpful service, and a total prohibition on the giving or acceptance of tips. It may be an exaggeration to say that the average Western visitor from a capitalist country 'never knew how the rich lived till he came to Communist China', but it is not very far from the truth.

The effect of this unexpected profusion on the foreign guests is not perhaps always quite what the host intended. To many a Western visitor it appears almost indecent that he should find himself surrounded by a standard of comfort and service which he cannot afford and does not expect at home. That this should be provided by a Communist country, from funds raised by taxation, levied upon a population whose own standard of living is manifestly far lower than that of the wage-earner in the West, seems embarrassing, uncalled for and excessive. It rouses the suspicion that the hosts are trying to dazzle their guests with a display which will distract their attention from some other, less desirable aspect of the Chinese scene. Visitors of right-wing opinions are somewhat antagonized by what they feel to be a hypocrisy, those who at home are Labour supporters inclined to deplore what they regard as an unnecessary extravagance.

It is rather to be doubted whether these reactions are shared by the visitors, of any political faith, who come from Asia and from Africa. Most of these may be even less familiar with the comforts of life than Western professional men and trade union leaders. To them, however, these comforts typify what they wish to see made possible in the daily lives of their people. These are the standards which they knew, at second hand, in the old colonial days, reserved for their masters, but here offered to all comers; a concrete testimony to what the People's Republic has achieved and what it is willing to provide for its guests be they black or brown, rich or poor. To most of the Asians and Africans, luxury is not an indulgence which some of their countrymen have enjoyed and abused, and which they themselves have consciously renounced, it is the privilege which was formerly confined to an alien ruling class, which is now within their own grasp and is their rightful inheritance. If China can afford it, even if only for the few foreign guests, then this is a proof that China has truly progressed, and is giving an example to the world of equality of treatment and true hospitality.

It is certainly this impression which the Chinese hosts would like to convey to their guests, and it is also probable that it is this view of the matter which they themselves share. In the opinion of Communists there exists a very clear-cut difference between luxury derived from exploitation of the working class by capitalist wealth, and luxury offered as hospitality by the working class themselves. In the theory of the Chinese regime the People own everything; it is their government, their money, their hotel, and the foreign visitor is their guest. From the abundance of their resources it is really only a little offering that is made in hospitality and friendship, and it is only decent and right that this entertainment should be on the level of the best that capitalist exploitation could provide. For is not the Communist system superior to the capitalist system? And should not its standards of hospitality be at least as high? Higher, in fact, for they must be free from the taint of servility, of private gain and personal privilege which mars the pleasures of the rich.

There is thus a double character to this official hospitality to the 'New China Hands'; on the one side it displays and affirms the progress made in the modernization of China under the leadership of the Communist Party. China can, if and when she chooses, provide and afford the best. The system can beat the capitalist at his own game, for it can given as much comfort and luxury without depending on profit and private payment. On the other side it is a new, and for a nation, a very inexpensive and useful system or publicity; a new essay in foreign relations conducted on a mass level, reaching out to the peoples of the world behind their governments, affecting foreign public opinion, gaining friends who may not at the moment be in political authority, but who will exert influence on those who are in authority, or may later acquire it. The aims and possibilities of this new kind of foreign policy are worth examination.

Firstly, it must be recognized that the Chinese have a great advantage over their Western rivals in this sphere. A large number of young Chinese, and a majority of the senior academic and professional men, speak English or another Western language with facility. It is easy to provide a corps of competent interpreters to conduct tours and even individuals across the length and breadth of China. The experts whom they will want to meet are able to converse with them and entertain them in their own languages. In the case of the Asian and African visitors, this is not of course true, but English affords a common language with which both hosts and guests are familiar. Even if a Western government wished to compete with China in a similar programme it would be very difficult to provide a large number of competent Chinese speakers, only a very few experts could converse with Chinese visitors in their own tongue, and thus those whom the West could profitably invite would have to be the Western educated Chinese to the virtual exclusion of all others.

Yet it can hardly be denied that to the Chinese one of the merits of the new type of visitor is that he can rarely read or speak the language. Although contacts are remarkably free and unsupervised it is still true that most visitors must rely on the interpreter and are rarely left without one. The aspects of the Chinese society of today which are unwelcome or disturbing to a Western visitor are not so conspicuous to one who cannot read a word of the language. It is one thing to be told that the Press and publicity are instruments of a system of persuasion which permits the expression of no contrary view, it is another to read these organs for oneself and mark the profound difference between the Chinese and the Western Press. The gaily coloured slogans in their beautiful Chinese script are pleasing to the eye, but not necessarily so appealing to the sense of those who can read them.

Secondly, it has to be recognized that not only does no

Western government seek to emulate the Chinese programme of invitation and inspection by foreign visitors, but most of these governments show considerable dislike and suspicion of the very idea of introducing large numbers of Communist or Communist-indoctrinated foreigners into the country and then giving them full liberty to travel through it. So far from feeling confidence that the merits of the Free World will speak for themselves and the evidences of liberty prove convincing even to hardened opponents, the general attitude seems to be a contrary conviction that the visitors might corrupt the allegiance of the natives, spread subversion and unrest, give aid and encouragement to the native Communist Party. On the other hand, few governments except that of the United States of America raise any objection to their own citizens going to China in any capacity.

The Iron Curtain has two doors: one marked 'exit' opening out from the West, one marked 'entry' opening into China. Just as it is obvious that Western governments are highly selective in those whom they will permit to enter their countries, there is reason to think that the Chinese government is equally selective in those whom it permits to travel abroad. There has indeed been an easing of restrictions on both sides. Chinese theatrical companies, athletes, purchasing missions, trade union and student delegations, have been allowed to tour in the West—except in the United States. Chinese universities have sent representatives to international scientific and academic congresses. But there is a significant difference between these visitors from China and those whom China accepts. The Chinese abroad go on behalf of their own institutions and are paid for by them, not invited to tour the Western countries at the expense of the latter.

It might seem therefore that while Western governments feel little fear that their citizens will be beguiled or corrupted by what they see in China, they greatly fear the effect that large numbers of Chinese visitors might have upon their citizens who stay at home. The Chinese are not worried at all by the possible subversion or loss of faith that might come to their stay-at-homes from contacts with Western visitors, but are much more cautious about permitting large numbers of their people seeing the West at first hand. It must be recognized that in this situation the United States administration alone is logical; to them all and any contact with 'Red China' is anathema, at home or abroad.

It would probably be nearer the truth to see the contrasting policies of China and the West as proofs of confidence in their respective systems rather than of doubts and fears. The Chinese are now satisfied that the reconstruction and modernization of the country during the past six years has made such striking progress that they can afford to show it off to foreigners with the assurance that the facts will make a deep impression, and that those aspects which the foreigner may not like will be the least in evidence to him, due to his inability to read Chinese. They are confident also, that for the mass of the people the presence of a few thousands of delegates and tourists has no importance and makes no unfavourable impression. As evidence of China's new status and prestige it is indeed valuable at home also, for any Chinese can see that these 'New China Hands' are not at all the same people either in their practices or their pretensions as the former residents of the Treaty Ports. The Foreign Devil has gone, the Foreign Guest is welcome.

Equally, Western indifference to any such policy of mass invitation, and also to the visits which their own citizens pay to China, springs from confidence in the superior moral value of Western institutions and ways. It is not believed that large numbers of Chinese (or Russian) visitors would gain sufficient understanding of our system in a rapid conducted tour to impress their own countrymen with its merits when they returned home. It is unlikely that any Communist government would wish to pay for such visits themselves, and it is politically difficult or even impossible to propose to a Western legislature that public money should be lavished on the entertainment of hosts of convinced foreign Communists and sympathizers.

On the other hand, there is very little apprehension that the majority, or many, of the Western visitors to China will return converted Communists. Of those who go to that country some are already supporters of Communism, and will no doubt return with faith refreshed. Others may appreciate what the regime has done for China without feeling any conviction that similar institutions would be of benefit at home, or prove superior to the system which has been evolved by a long series of peaceful constitutional changes. Some will continue to discount material advances which are not accompanied by those forms of freedom of thought and action which they regard as the core of civilization. On the other hand, to those states which do not recognize the People's Republic and have no diplomatic mission in Peking, there is an undoubted advantage in permitting unofficial delegations and groups representing various professions to visit China and gather first-hand information on the nature and scope of the changes now transforming that country.

The Chinese have, whether wittingly or not, provided the means for a new kind of international relationship between their country and the Western world. The Western peoples from their own experience have tended to believe that diplomatic contact and formal recognition was the first step which has to be taken, without which relations of any kind are precarious and hazardous. For these reasons the policy of the Powers in the nineteenth century was to force an unwilling Chinese Empire to accept diplomatic missions whose duty was to safeguard the interests of the traders and missionaries. The experience of the Canton factories maintained by the East India Companies seemed to prove that trade was insecure unless buttressed by diplomatic representation. The varying fortunes of the early missionaries in China also indicated that without formal recognition of their right to preach and convert, and diplomatic missions to ensure the exercise of this right, religious freedom could not be secured.

Now the attitudes have changed; many of the Western nations, led by the USA, see no advantage in diplomatic representation in a country pledged to Communism. It is believed either that no trade is worth while, or desirable—the attitude of the United States—or that what is possible and necessary can just as well be carried on without recognition of the government of China. The Chinese themselves have made the continuation of missionary enterprise either impossible or unwise, consequently there is now no religious problem needing the aid of a diplomatic mission.

This, of course, was precisely the point of view held by the Manchu Emperors and their predecessors of earlier dynasties. Foreign merchants could come to China to trade, if they so desired; China did not particularly want them, or need them; in any case it was not necessary or desirable for foreign officials to reside at the Court in order to meddle with the matter. As for foreign religious teachers, they must always be regarded with some suspicion as potential trouble makers; it was clearly most undesirable that they should be protected by a mission from their own sovereign.

The reversal of positions is indeed complete. If the doctrine once held by the Manchu Emperors, that diplomatic recognition of an alien and perhaps hostile government merely enhances its prestige and power for harm without conferring any benefit upon the nation that accords such recognition, is now held by the United States Government and certain other Western powers, the Chinese People's Republic has adopted the contrary point of view. China not only actively seeks to obtain recognition from foreign countries many of which never had any relations with China in the past, but now expends large sums on a system of international relations which by-passes the diplomatic blockade. But it is evident that the main purpose of this new system is still to enhance the prestige and authority of China in the outside world, not to enter into a two-way traffic which could bring foreign, modifying influences to bear upon the social and political system of the People's Republic.

It is very probable that the Chinese Communist Party, whatever it may say in public for the record, is in fact aware that there is very little prospect of spreading Communist convictions among the peoples of the Western nations. Unofficial relations with these countries, even when official relations do subsist, is principally a method of publicity, designed to advertise the growing strength of China and deter possible enemies from adopting or adhering to intransigent policies. The consequences of a wider knowledge of China's industrial advance and material progress may be to alarm these countries, to arouse fear where there was before only indifference: but it also induces respect.

It cannot be denied that the attitude to China has changed in the past few years; the voices that argued for compulsion and for assistance to the opponents of the regime have grown silent, the emphasis is now on the need to organize defensive measures against possible Chinese pressure, either military or economic. It is significant that it is only in America, which has been cut off from all contacts with China, that there are still found responsible statesmen who say in public (even if they possibly doubt it privately) that they believe Communism in China to be a passing phase, insecurely established, and unlikely to endure.

Elsewhere the pre-occupation is not with the possibility of a change of regime in China, but with the growing power of that regime and the range of its ambitions. Confident that their own citizens are not likely to embrace Communist opinions in large numbers, and resigned to the prospect that the people of China are equally unlikely to desert that system, the Western nations of Europe and the Pacific feel no such confidence about the future trend in Asia and in Africa. In this they certainly, for opposite reasons, concur with the Chinese themselves. In respect of Asia and Africa the Chinese system of mass international relations is not merely designed to advertise the progress of the regime and deter foreign governments from rash courses, it is an invitation in a wider sense, an invitation to imitate and to adopt a system which is represented as more effective and swift in achieving the common aim of modernization.

It is recognized everywhere that, however inapplicable the Chinese Communist system may be to Western nations with an advanced industry and evolved political institutions, these factors are rarely found in Asia or Africa, where conditions often closely resemble those which existed in China when the regime came to power. The possibility that having common problems, the Asian and African peoples may be tempted to adopt similar solutions is real, and well understood in the Asian countries themselves. The greater part of Asia and Africa share with China two recent or continuing conditions. They are or were colonial or 'semi-colonial' countries, under the control or domination of Western powers.

Opposition to such control, nationalism, and racial feeling are the most powerful political forces in all these countries. No regime can survive in them which does not seek to satisfy the aspirations for independence, racial equality and economic progress. For the second common condition of all Asia and much of Africa is that it is heavily populated by people who are in the main poor. The standard of living is far lower than in the West, resources are undeveloped, capital is lacking for such development, technical knowledge and professional skills are in short supply. In some of these countries weak and venal governments have been unable to keep order or maintain their undisputed authority in the national territory.

All these evils abounded in pre-'liberation' China. The 'Unequal Treaties' imposed upon the country a number of limitations to full sovereignty; poverty and economic decline were universal. An unhealthy concentration of such capital as the country possessed in the Treaty Ports had produced a lop-sided and distorted development. Professional skill was often unemployed and intellect frustrated. Disorder and civil war were endemic. China's standing in the world at large was low, her claim to be a great power a legal fiction, which no one seriously accepted.

The Chinese, demonstrating to their new visitors from Asia and Africa the disappearance or rapid elimination of almost all of these evils, attribute the improvement without qualification to the adoption of the Communist programme and the leadership of the Communist Party. It is a powerful argument, and it is not yet adequately countered by any alternative which can be shown to have achieved the same results in the same short period. Western statesmen may, and do, point out that there is a price to pay for all this progress: the loss, or suppression of those liberties which the West has won for itself and prizes so highly. But the Asians rarely enjoyed these liberties; in the majority of cases they were not freely accorded by the Western colonial nations, and only painfully won in others. 'If you understood freedom, you would not wish to imitate the Communists', is a poor argument on the lips of those who themselves denied or delayed the gift of freedom.

Nor do the majority of Asians believe in the second Western criticism, that Communism merely substitutes a new foreign domination for the detested colonial regimes of the past. No one travelling in China can accept the suggestion that the Chinese people are now under Russian colonial control. Such a proposition is so manifestly contrary to the facts that it tends to cast deep suspicion on those who assert it. By over statement the value of the real evidence for 'Communist imperialism' is discounted. Chinese control of Tibet, Russian authority in the Moslem region of Central Asia, could be cited with some justice as clear cases of foreign rule over alien peoples. But the suggestion that the regimes in North Viet-nam or North Korea are alien dominations imposed by force from without is generally rejected.

To the Asian peoples the issue is seen in other terms. Can this system, or some alternative really deliver the country from its troubles, bring it out of the ranks of the backward nations and make it a modern state? Whichever system first shows an unmistakable lead in achieving these goals will win their allegiance. Invitations to bodies of professional men and intellectuals from these countries help to spread the belief in those circles that China has found the answer which they seek. They may not be convinced that the full programme of a Communist society is essential, and it may not be from the Chinese point of view necessary that they should be so convinced. What is desired is that they should see in China a country like their own, struggling out of the troubles and deficiencies of the past, asking only that she be allowed to try out her own solution without being condemned and harried by the former Western colonial powers or the pressure of American capitalism.

This picture will not be accepted in the West as fair or true; in Asia it is at the very least a view which finds many supporters. The idea that both rival systems, the Communist and the democratic capitalist, should be free to contend without political and military pressures is widely held. The suspicion of colonial ambitions still latent, or once more arising is intense; any programme of military aid directed against Communist expansion is seen rather as a threat than as a proffered protection. Co-existence, based on the Five Principles* which have been accepted by the non-aligned Asian countries as the basis of their foreign policy, is regarded as the proper relationship which should subsist between the Communist and non-Communist Asian countries. Any attempt to wean neutralist Asia from this policy is resented, any suggestion that on the Chinese side it is a cover for long range plans of expansion and subversion is disbelieved.

The Chinese have certainly come to realize the great value of this new solidarity among the formerly estranged and indifferent peoples of Asia. It may not be possible, or even desirable to promote Communist revolutions or governments in the countries of Asia; the creation of a majority opinion hostile to Western influence, opposed to Western and above all to American political and military groupings is in itself a major objective which secures for China very solid advantages. Her neighbours will refrain from joining such alliances as SEATO. Those countries which lie further off will become before long valuable markets for her industrial products. The embargo upon trade with China will collapse, has indeed already virtually collapsed as far as the Asian countries are concerned.

The economic motives associated with the policy of mass international relations are perhaps as strong as the political.

* See Chapter 10, p. 256.

If China can show her visitors that she now produces industrial goods for export which were formerly only to be obtained from the West, they will be glad to welcome an alternative source which frees them from too great dependence on the powerful industrial capitalist nations. This prospect is already a reality. China now produces textile machinery which she offers to the countries of South-East Asia at prices with which even Japan cannot compete.*

China is also in the market for the exports which the countries of Asia have to offer. Rubber from Ceylon, Malaya and even Thailand, which hastened to swallow its professed anti-Communism in favour of profitable trade when the embargo on rubber exports to China from Malaya was relaxed. Viewed in this light the gingerly approach of the Western nations to trade with China, the attitude that some such commerce may be admissable, but care must be taken not to let it go too far, or stray into fields where China might acquire 'strategic goods' is clearly unrealistic. China is in the race for the trade of Asia, both import and export, and her capacity for engaging in this competition increases year by year. Her policy of invitation and showmanship is designed to prepare the minds of influential sections of Asian professional opinion for the acceptance of China as a major source of supply for their industrial needs and a major market for their raw materials.

These are the objectives which an examination of the policy of mass international relations reveal. Publicity for the progress made under the new regime; a warning to potential enemies that China can no longer be disregarded; promotion of the solidarity of Asian peoples in their opposition to colonialism and Western leadership: a demonstration that co-existence is practicable and can be profitable, a means of circumventing the diplomatic impasse which still bars China from normal relations with a large part of the world. The objectives are such as foreign policy normally seeks to reach, but the technique is novel, effective and attractive to those to whom it is applied.

* *Information Bulletin.* Published by Embassy of Japan, Canberra, Australia. No. 11–B–57. 15 November 1957.

CHAPTER NINE

TWO CHINAS?

'WE WILL CERTAINLY liberate Taiwan.' All over China, on
hoardings and walls, placards and banners, this challenging
slogan reminds the Chinese people that the civil war is not over,
final victory has not been completely achieved, and that—the
corollary—this prolongation of the nation's division and suffering is all the fault of the 'American imperialists'. The question
of Formosa and the Nationalist regime of Chiang Kai-shek
still functioning on that island is indeed the key question in
Chinese foreign policy; it is this problem which divides China
from the West more truly than any question of regime; it is
the complication of the Formosa government which bars China
—Communist China—from the United Nations, which prevents recognition by many American and European nations,
which exacerbates relations between China and the United
States. If the Formosa question did not exist, the world would
long ago have accepted the Peking government, with regret,
or indifference, or alarm, but accepted it none the less,
just as the government in Moscow has been acknowledged
for close on forty years as the legitimate government of
Russia.

For there is not one China but two; there is the government
in Peking, and the government in Taipei, capital of Taiwan or
Formosa. The former is acknowledged and recognized by all
the Communist states, most of the non-Communist states of
Asia, by Britain, Holland, Switzerland and Scandinavia. The
Nationalist regime in Formosa, styled still the Republic of
China, is recognized as the sole legal and existing government
of China by the United States, Siam, the Philippines, South
Viet-nam, South Korea, Japan, and the majority of the South
American republics. Canada, Australia, New Zealand and
South Africa maintain a quasi relationship with the Nationalist

regime, receiving the Chinese diplomats and consuls but sending no missions to Formosa. Finally, and above all, it is the Nationalist regime which occupies China's seat at the United Nations, it is the delegate of Chiang Kai-shek who speaks for China on the Security Council.

A large number of states, including most of those of southern Europe, have avoided this question as far as possible by discontinuing any direct relations with the Nationalist regime, but refraining from recognizing the Peking government. France took this course because Peking supported the claims of Ho Chi-minh and backed the Viet Min revolution in Indo-China; Italy was probably more influenced, like Belgium and Ireland, by the attitude of the Catholic Church towards Communism and Chinese Communism in particular. Spain has recognized the Nationalist regime, which long ago, in a more liberal age, broke off relations with that country when Franco overthrew the Republic. Among the Arab states there has been since Bandung, a steady drift towards recognition of Peking, and the same tendency is visible among such states as Morocco, Ghana and Tunisia, which have only achieved independence in very recent years.

The diplomatic world is thus divided, the line of division following an uncertain and devious, but revealing, crack through the face of the non-Communist world. It may be observed that it is only where American aid is essential to the rehabilitation or survival of the regimes that the American policy of whole-hearted support of Nationalist Formosa is accepted. Where American aid in defence is important, but the local economy is itself strong and flourishing, as in Australia and New Zealand, a half-way policy of partial recognition of Formosa is followed; where American aid in defence is vital, but the problems of East Asia secondary, as in southern Europe and Turkey, a solution is found by ceasing all relations with either Chinese regime. Finally where, as in Western Europe, it is realized that America is in any case committed to the defence of the region, it is possible for these non-Communist countries, such as Britain, Holland and Scandinavia, to consult their own interests and those of their traders, and recognize Peking.

The consequences of these diplomatic evasions and expedients have been strange. The Nationalist regime is established on the island of Formosa, in the Pescadores or P'enghu group which is a dependency of Formosa, and in the islands of Matsu and Quemoy, close to the coast of the mainland province of Fukien, to which they belong. Formosa and the Pescadores were annexed by Japan after the Sino-Japanese war of 1895. Matsu and Quemoy have never at any time been detached from Chinese sovereignty. At the Cairo Conference during the late War, when Mr. Churchill, President Roosevelt and Chiang Kai-shek conferred, it was announced that after the defeat of Japan, Formosa and its dependencies would be restored to their rightful owner, China. The Chinese, considering that the inhabitants of this island, with the exception of a minority group of aboriginal hill people, are descendants of Chinese settlers, and that the island had been part of China's territory for upward of six hundred years, held that such a restoration was only elementary justice, and needed no legal ratification by Treaty to take effect.

At the Japanese surrender the island was occupied by Chinese forces, and, although still legally only Japanese occupied territory, was administered and accepted as a fully Chinese province. Several years passed before the allied powers felt themselves prepared to sign a peace treaty with Japan. In the earlier period, no one questioned for a moment the right of the Chinese to occupy and administer Formosa, nor the eventual destination of the island. The maladministration of the Nationalist authorities was indeed regretted, and by the Formosans themselves, who rose in protest in 1947, but were pitilessly repressed. When the Nationalist forces were driven from China at the end of 1949, several of the best units were withdrawn to Formosa. The government itself finally fled there, and with it a large number of officials and others who feared to remain under the new Communist regime. The attitude of the foreign powers to these developments was negative. Britain recognized Peking;

the USA declared that the defence of the Nationalists on Formosa was not an American interest.* Most states formerly in relations with China refrained from sending diplomatic missions to Taipei.

It was generally believed that the Nationalist regime, corrupt, demoralized and defeated, would prove no more able to hold Formosa than it had proved able to hold the other large Chinese island off the south coast, Hainan. The fact that the Nationalists still occupied the off-shore islands such as Quemoy and Matsu, and that they actually repelled a Communist assault on Quemoy soon after the Communist forces had taken the nearby port of Amoy, was not much observed at the time. It would seem possible that, had the Chinese Communists mounted an all-out invasion of Formosa in the early months of 1950, they would have carried the island by storm.

No full explanation of why they did not do this has yet been revealed. At the time they had virtually no air force, while the Nationalists still retained a number of serviceable aircraft. The Nationalists also still had the greater part of the small Chinese navy. It is eighty miles from the nearest point of the mainland to Formosa, and more nearly a hundred at other points on the Formosa Channel. It is a rough sea, notorious for bad weather. The Chinese Communists were almost wholly lacking in steamships, but they could have found very large numbers of junks in the southern ports. An invasion would perhaps have been possible, but costly.

The unanswered question is rather whether it was on account of these considerations that it was postponed or whether it was because the Chinese Communists had prior knowledge of the impending Korean War, and did not wish to commit their forces to what would have been a trap. The latter thesis, which is not of course accepted at all in China, is alleged to be supported by the evidence that early in 1950 the Chinese began to transfer their military forces from South China to Manchuria and the north. It is argued that these movements betrayed foreknowledge of the Korean crisis which broke in June of that year.

* United States White Paper. 5 August 1949.

The Chinese point out, on the other hand, that by the spring of 1950 the war in South China was over, Hainan island had been captured, the majority of the troops were northerners, and the southern summer is notoriously unhealthy for north Chinese. It was natural that these troops, who had been campaigning without respite for four years, should be moved back to their home provinces where they could be given recreation leave during the hot summer months. Both explanations being equally applicable to the situation, and equally impossible to prove or disprove, the problem of Chinese motivation in this matter must be left to future historians.

What is, however, quite certain is that the outbreak of the Korean War fatally involved the Formosa question, and transformed it. When the North Korean and South Korean forces were still the only ones in the field, within a few days of the outbreak, President Truman declared that in order to localize the conflict the US 7th Fleet would be charged with the duty of preventing any Chinese Communist invasion of Formosa, or any Nationalist attack upon the mainland. It is evident that the President and his advisers, aware of the fact that the US forces available were not even sufficient to defend South Korea, realized that they could have done nothing to save Formosa, if once invaded. The invasion must be prevented in advance, and the sea power of the United States afforded the only means of achieving this end. Hence the declaration, which was made without reference to the United Nations, or to the allies of the United States.

It is also apparent that the prospect of a Communist conquest of South Korea which would bring Russian power within striking distance of Japan was very real, and that if this was combined with a Chinese conquest of Formosa, Japan would be virtually at the mercy of the two mainland Communist powers. It was this strategic verity which had, long before, induced the rulers of Japan to annex first Formosa and later Korea. Forced willy-nilly along the path of empire by the consequences of her own conquest of Japan, America was finding it necessary to do the same things, even if it was still possible to disguise the hard necessities of strategy in the respectable garments of Freedom and Self Determination.

For the essence of the American intervention in the Formosan problem, an intervention which only a few months before had been declared to be unnecessary, was strategic. No one at this time had either faith in or fondness for Chiang Kai-shek and his regime. They were wholly discredited in America as else-where. But they were in Formosa; and that island is the last and most important bastion of the island chain of the Liuchiu group which links Japan with the Philippines, and thus strategically contains the whole eastern coast of Asia. It may very well be true that these considerations have no longer much importance; the intercontinental missile, the 'space rocket', may well have made, or be about to make, all rules of strategy relating to the surface of the earth and its geography out of date. But this was not the case in 1950.

Having gone into Formosa, or rather having declared that no one else should be allowed to go in, America had to find some legal argument to cover these actions, which might otherwise be thought to smack of direct intervention in a Chinese civil war—an act from which the United States had carefully re-frained when that war was still being fought on the mainland and the issue in doubt. It was remembered that, although the Cairo Conference had promised Formosa to China, the Japanese had not yet legally renounced their sovereignty, and need not do so to anyone in particular. So Formosa was still Japanese territory. When the Peace Treaty was signed a year later (8 September 1951), Japan renounced her sovereignty, but did not specify to whom. Formosa ceased to be Japanese; but did not become the territory of any other state.

This strange procedure had to be adopted to overcome a very serious difficulty, the fact that Britain had recognized Peking and had given that regime *de jure* recognition over the whole territory of the Chinese Republic. So 'China' meant one thing to Britain and another to America: Peking for Britain, Taipei for the United States; Two Chinas. Clearly it was not desirable that Britain should find herself legally bound to consider

Formosa as rightly belonging to the Peking regime, which America was determined to keep out of that island. Equally America was not anxious to recognize Formosa as part of China, since had she done so, it was very hard to see how her action in guarding the Nationalist regime on that isle could be held to be anything but the direct intervention in a Chinese civil war which Peking already claimed it to be. So Formosa could not be legally China at all, or any part of China; it must exist, like the legendary isle of P'enghu, which Chinese folklore locates in the same area, in a state of shimmering unreality, unattainable by the people of the mainland.

Unfortunately, these legalities do not, and never have, interested the Chinese of either party. Chiang Kai-shek and his followers at least agree with Mao Tse-tung and his Party in this; that Taiwan 'liberated' or 'free', is a Chinese province, inhabited by Chinese citizens, with a long history of Chinese rule, temporarily interrupted by 'Japanese imperialism'. To the Chinese the only question is whether the Nationalist regime should and can continue to exercise authority in what is to them a remnant of their former domain. Chiang must take this view, for does he not claim to be the legal government of the Republic of China, seated at the United Nations? If he has no territory which is truly Chinese over which to rule, how can his government make such a claim?

While the international diplomatic tailors were busy cutting the Formosan cloth to fit the awkward angular frame of the strategic facts, they tended to forget the existence of a still more anomalous situation in the 'off-shore islands', Quemoy, Matsu and others. These were not, and never had been, Japanese territory, occupied, ceded or receded. They were parts of the Chinese provinces of Chekiang and Fukien. They were thus metropolitan Chinese territory: over which the British had recognized the *de jure* authority of Peking, but the United States and others still held to be rightly under the authority of Chiang Kai-shek. And they were in fact under his authority, and military occupation. Some very remarkable gyrations have had to be performed to meet these conflicting theories.

Britain has distinguished—in sufficiently vague terms—between Formosa and the off-shore islands. The United States caught in the dilemma that if the islands are not Formosan, then they must be Chinese, and to defend them from Chinese Communist attack would unquestionably be intervention in civil war, yet to leave them outside the American commitment is to invite their loss, has taken refuge in obscurantist pronouncements concerning 'certain islands which are necessary to the defence of Formosa' without specifying whether these islands are in fact the Formosan Pescadores or the Chinese off-shore isles. Towards the end of 1954, when the Chinese Communist forces captured the island of Yikiangshan, one of a small group called the Tachen islands, off the Chekiang coast, this ambiguity in American policy came very close to causing war.

The United States, as it is said upon the personal initiative of President Eisenhower and against the views of his military advisers, refrained from intervention, and indeed counselled the Nationalists to withdraw from the now untenable Tachen group and the island of Nanchishan, to the south of it. This evacuation was carried out under the cover of the 7th Fleet, but without any opposition from the Communist forces. The Nationalists still retain Quemoy and Matsu, islands of much greater importance. Since that time there have been no further serious hostilities; from time to time Quemoy is bombarded and its batteries reply; British and other shipping is intercepted by Nationalist warships, but released through the prompt intervention of the Royal Navy. The war slumbers, but the problem remains as intractable as ever.

At the Bandung Conference in April 1955 Chou En-lai made a famous and significant declaration. He announced that China had no quarrel with the American people and that he was ready at any time to negotiate with the United States Government to achieve 'relaxation of tension in the Straits of Taiwan'. As a consequence of this announcement Chinese and American envoys have met at Geneva over a space of three years and discussed not only the Taiwan question, but other issues which divide the two countries. Yet very little result has come from these prolonged negotiations.

Some few American citizens, detained or imprisoned in China, have been released; the American Government claims that others, equally innocent of crime, are still detained. Some Chinese living in the United States have been permitted to return to China; the Chinese claim that others have been denied this freedom. The Chinese assert that those Americans whom they still hold have been convicted of espionage, acting as Nationalist agents, or were engaged on clandestine intelligence missions. The Americans assert that either the Chinese in the United States do not wish to return to China, or are convicted criminals serving sentences in gaol. On the wider issues of Formosa, the United Nations, the trade embargo and recognition, no progress whatever has been registered.

Since it is these questions rather than the unfortunate plight of a small number of Americans and Chinese that really cause the tension and danger of war, it is worth making a careful examination of the conflicting standpoints in order to assess the risk and the chances of a settlement in the future. No one doubts that if the major issues could be satisfactorily disposed of, the detained Americans and Chinese would be speedily released in one way or another.

The two views of the Formosa question, the central issue, can be briefly stated. In Chinese eyes America is intervening in the last stages of the civil war, protecting the Nationalist regime from certain destruction, denying the Chinese people peace, and in effect occupying a Chinese territory, Formosa. It is well understood by informed opinion in China that there is now no prospect whatever of Chiang regaining power by an invasion of the mainland: it is privately acknowledged that America would not back him in such a venture, the consequences of which could well be a Third World War; but this fact only increases Chinese indignation at what is considered to be a pointless and futile provocation, a merely spiteful interference in Chinese affairs, which can achieve no real purpose.*

The American view, as frequently stated by the Secretary of State, Mr John Foster Dulles, and his subordinates in the State Department, is that China's ambition to take Formosa is 'aggression'. It is denied that the People's Republic has any claim to the island, and although no such denial in respect of the off-shore islands is, or could be, plainly stated, it is asserted that these strongholds are essential to the defence of Formosa, that if they were abandoned Chinese Communist prestige would be enhanced, the morale of the Nationalists and neutral Asians depressed.

It is further argued that America has the duty to safeguard Formosa as a refuge under the Chinese flag for those Chinese who renounce Communism, and as a rallying point for the large communities of overseas Chinese in South East Asia who would otherwise have no allegiance open to them other than that of Peking. It is no longer officially stated that the United States expects Chiang Kai-shek to regain power, and it is not suggested that America should at any time help him to do so. But the view is still aired that the Chinese people given the chance would prefer his authority to that of the People's Republic. It is therefore claimed that America has the duty and the right to keep this alternative alive and available to them. In short, the Chinese Communists take their stand upon the unity and inidvisibility of the Chinese state; the Americans are being gradually forced to advocate a partition of China, to adopt the policy of accepting Two Chinas.

---

* Mr William Worthy, the only American newsman to defy Mr Dulles's ban on visits to China, has the following comment on this aspect of American policy:

'In citing the many advantages that would accompany American recognition of China the Indians (the Indian Embassy officials in Peking) say that normalization of relations would constrain the Chiang Kai-shek evangelists in the Pentagon, State Department, and Central Intelligence Agency to curtail our highly provocative air force flights along the China coast and our agent dropping, arms parachuting operations over the mainland. The Chinese were not so ungentlemanly as to throw these indefensible policies in my face, but in discussing American forces on Formosa and the off-shore islands, Chou En-lai did ask me pointedly how far Long Island was from the New York coastline.'

W. Worthy, Jr., 'Communism Chinese Flavor'. *The Progressive*. Vol. 21, No. 9. September 1957. Madison, Wisconsin.

Foreign attitudes to the policy of the People's Republic spring from the acceptance or rejection of either the Chinese or the American view on the Formosan question. If, as India and the non-aligned nations of Asia believe and announce, there is no justification for regarding the Communist intention to extend their authority over all Chinese territory as aggression, then there is very little other evidence of Chinese aggression in different places. The Indian view is that the Korean intervention was provoked by the counter invasion of North Korea by the forces of the United Nations. India refused to join in the UN condemnation of China as an aggressor. Equally, the support given to Ho Chi-minh in Indo-China is seen in non-Communist Asia as a justified assistance to a people struggling against colonial domination. These issues are in any case now closed. No one seriously expects the Korean War to be resumed by either side, no one fears further open hostilities in Viet-nam unless as part of a wider, major war.

Formosa remains; and on this question the opinion of the Asian states, except those which are close allies of America, is decidedly on the Chinese side. Elsewhere public opinion is more uncertain. The Left in Europe and in Australia and New Zealand tends to accept the Chinese standpoint, but would like to see the question settled by some compromise which would not imperil the freedom and lives of those Chinese Nationalists who would never accept the rule of Mao Tse-tung. It is often suggested that the Formosan people themselves should be given the chance to express their views freely and that the United Nations should guarantee that these views would be implemented.

This is a utopian idea of the power and independent authority of the United Nations, which nothing in past experience gives any cause to endorse. Much liberal opinion in the West would accept an evacuation of the unquestionably Chinese off-shore islands as a first step, while reserving Formosa to some future accommodation. Those Western governments which have not recognized Peking are inhibited from doing so by the complications which such a step would cause with

America, due to the question of the legality of the Nationalist regime: those, like Britain and Holland, which recognized Peking, before the Formosan issue became acute, do their best to exclude it from consideration in order to avoid being faced with a clear conflict of policy between America and her Western allies.

America's Western allies have not endorsed her policy or her view of China's claim, but they avoid saying so in public, and do their best to keep the question off the agenda of the United Nations and other major conferences. Japan, caught in the dilemma of her need for trade with China and her dependence on American aid, twists and turns uneasily, aware that her present recognition of the Nationalist regime is a blind alley which can lead to no solution, but unable to reverse her policy and still retain American friendship.

Thus gradually, almost imperceptibly the problem is changing. It is no longer, as in 1950, a purely strategic question on which the Western allies could reluctantly agree that America must be the judge and her decision binding upon her friends. It is now primarily a political matter, the question of whether there are to be in the forseeable future Two Chinas or One. It is also becoming plain that the ultimate answer to this question will be given not by America or Peking, but by the Chinese people, both inside and outside Formosa itself.

The realization that 'liberation' could be effected without war, by peaceful penetration, seems to have followed in China upon the crisis caused by the last open hostilities on an important scale, the capture of Yikiangshan and the evacuation of the Tachen islands. The fact that America preferred to advise her protegés, the Nationalists, to evacuate a Chinese territory, rather than assist them to fight for it, indicated plainly enough that the official view that Chiang would soon regain power no longer influenced actual policy.

For clearly, if it were true that Chiang and his forces, re-armed and trained as they were by American military missions, were getting ready for the long promised counter-invasion, it would be most improbable that they should begin by giving up two of their jumping-off points. The fact that at the same time America gave renewed evidence of her intention to defend Formosa itself, really only underlined the profound change of policy. America was now not contending for a Nationalist restoration, but for the acceptance of Two Chinas as a permanent solution. American suggestions that the negotiations for relaxation of tension in the Straits of Taiwan, proposed by Chou En-lai, should begin with a Chinese renunciation of any intention to use force to take Formosa, while at the same time Chiang was compelled to accept the doctrine that only with American permission could he attack the mainland, made the new line of policy perfectly clear. America wanted a settlement of the war which—though this was never said—might mean the evacuation of the off-shore islands, but would guarantee the continued existence of Chiang's Republic of China in Formosa.

Chou En-lai has refused to give this pledge; but he has none the less changed his policy also. The slogans still proclaim the impending Liberation of Taiwan, but now a new note is struck. Liberation can come by peaceful means. The Chinese people see no purpose in this conflict; are they not all brothers, what quarrel have they with the misguided followers of Chiang Kai-shek? Let these strayed sheep but show that they are willing to return to the fold and no old grudges will be borne, no former crimes remembered. Just as Li Chi-shen, once the butcher of Canton, can be forgiven and made a Vice-President of the People's Republic, so too the present Nationalist leadership can repent, can come home, can be given honourable employment and end their days in their own country. Even Chiang himself need not be beyond redemption. Long ago he fought against the northern warlords; he resisted the Japanese; if he will now reject the American protectorate and accept some appropriate office under the People's Republic, all will be forgotten.

Such is the present theme of the system of Persuasion and Propaganda. It would be very unwise to discount its strength and effect. It plays, very skilfully, on two deep feelings common to all Chinese; national unity and dislike of foreign interference. It is often said, or used to be said, that the Chinese people did not understand patriotism as it is practised in the West or idealized in Japan. This was in one way true, but misleading. The Chinese having had little contact with foreign foes who were not barbarian tribesmen, whom no one would prefer to his own rulers, had not that sharpened sense of national identity which the long conflicts of sovereign states in Europe had aroused in the West. The Chinese were the only civilized people—in their estimation—in their world. China was the Empire, the civilized world; beyond that pale was barbarism. No one needed to stress what was completely obvious; that civilized men will prefer civilization to barbarism.

But this unconscious acceptance of China as the only Empire, the one civilized land, meant in practice a solidarity among her people on essentials which fervent patriotism does not always achieve. No Chinese ever thought, few now can think, that they could become other than Chinese. The concept of changing nationality was so alien to their experience and tradition that it had no real meaning for them. A man might accept this or that dynasty, in times of division, pay loyalty to this or some other prince or leader; but all were Chinese, or accepted by China as such. It has been the constant complaint of foreign governments, both colonial and sovereign in Asia, that the overseas Chinese minorities will not renounce their innate allegiance to their ancestral country and its culture. They remain within their new home an alien people, still consciously, proudly and unalterably Chinese.

When in the nineteenth century and later the Chinese were forced to realize that other strong and mighty empires existed beyond the seas; that foreign nations as powerful as China, indeed for the time being far more so, were pressing their claims and demands upon the Empire, they reacted with strong hostility. Riots, massacres, incidents succeeded each other as the missionaries penetrated the land and the traders opened up the Treaty Ports.

At the time the favourite thesis of these foreign residents was to attribute all such troubles to the machinations of the 'mandarins'—the sinister and powerful officials who ruled China. Modern research shows that, on the contrary, the officials, only too aware of China's weakness and the use which aggressive powers would make of these incidents, did all in their rather limited power to restrain the hostility of the people. Their concurrent failure to restore the might of the Chinese state, their yielding to force, their humiliation in the eyes of the people, were the first causes of the Chinese Revolution which swept away first the Throne and then the entire ancient fabric of society.*

Thus to hint that any Chinese Party is subservient to the foreigner, dependent on his friendship, swerving from the true course of Chinese national aspirations, is damning and dangerous in the extreme. Both Parties are now engaged in blackening the other in this way. To Chiang and his propaganda department the Communists are the servants of Russia, the traitors who have surrendered the country to a foreign overlord. The Communists, not so insensitive to this charge as they would appear, are careful to emphasize the Chinese character of their regime; its care for the past, its independence of Russian methods, its freedom to 'learn from the mistakes of the USSR'. Chiang, accused in turn of being the 'running dog of the American imperialists' proclaims his violent nationalism, writes in his *China's Destiny* a passionate condemnation of Western imperialism, and in his new book asserts that Western aid to reconquer China would be useless and worse, that all his men need are the arms and they will do the job.†

Neither side can afford to incur the charge of being 'Han chien', that peculiar Chinese expression for which 'traitor' is an inadequate translation, since the essence of the phrase is the meaning 'traitor to the Chinese (Han) race'. But to admit that there could be Two Chinas, 'two suns in one sky' as the old Chinese saying put it, is to deny the unity of the Empire, the

* See *The Last Stand of Chinese Conservatism*. Mary Clabaugh Wright. Stanford University Press. Stanford, California. 1957. Pp. 147, 296.

† Chiang Kai-shek, *Soviet Russia in China*—A Summing Up at Seventy. Farrar Straus & Cudahy. New York. 1957.

solidarity of the Chinese people, to take the shameful path which makes one in the end 'Han chien'. Equally, to accept foreign domination, direction or even protection, is a denial of the fundamental postulate underlying all Chinese thinking; that China and the Chinese are the true superiors; outclassed, it may be, temporarily, in some new skill or art of war, but the one really civilized society, the most ancient, most numerous and best of mankind. Such claims are not now made, perhaps not intellectually supported by educated men, but the appeal to these underlying half-conscious beliefs can be a very potent instrument of persuasion.

For the Nationalists it is thus an inescapable necessity that they should claim not to be separating Formosa from the mother country to make a second China, but to be preparing to reconquer and reunite the one and only China. They cannot for one moment acknowledge the real nature of contemporary American policy, and they strongly maintain the imminence of the counter-attack, the urgency of the task of preparation, the high hopes they claim to feel for a favourable reception on the mainland. Yet this tune begins to pall. The years go by; the soldiers age; Communist China grows stronger, America shows no willingness to support an invasion, hope fades.

The immediate consequence, not far below the surface, occasionally erupts in violent manifestations, not of anti-Communism, but of anti-foreign, of anti-American sentiment. The fear that the charge is true, that they are in fact dependants, protegés, unable to pursue their own policy, not from their own weakness but from the restraint placed upon them by a stronger alien power, gnaws at the mind. When a rather clumsy attempt to shield an American serviceman from local justice was made in the summer of 1957, the world was startled to learn that the Taipei mob had sacked and wrecked the American Embassy offices, while the police looked on. Yet no one even pretended that this incident was the product of Communist infiltration or intrigue.

It was, on the contrary, the outcome of frustrated nationalism, of disappointment and disillusion. It is on this climate of opinion that the Communist system of Persuasion has now set to work. It has the two essential themes; 'you are dividing China, unnecessarily, we will welcome you home: you are submitting to foreign domination, at home and in your policy abroad. Reject it, be Chinese! Chinese do not fight Chinese!' There is every reason to expect that such a propaganda, countered as it is by nothing more positive than unreal, fading hopes, and considerations of American policy which have slight appeal to Chinese of any party, will steadily gain ground. This is clearly the expectation and the plan. There is to be no armed attack, which could only provoke war and alienate China's Asian friends. But by a constant emphasis on reconciliation, illustrated by the fortunes of some notable men who have gone back, it is expected and believed that the internal situation in Formosa will slowly be undermined and the ground prepared for one of those sudden political transformations which have characterized the whole course of the Chinese Revolution.

It is certain that such a revolution, perhaps occurring as a consequence of a struggle for the succession when Chiang Kai-shek dies, would place America and her allies in a very difficult diplomatic situation. A peaceful, or at least an internal Formosan movement to accept the People's Republic, could not be labelled 'Chinese Communist aggression' with any prospect that such a label would stick in the United Nations. The Asian-African block would most certainly reject any such suggestion. The Western nations who have recognized China, and many that have not yet done so, would be embarrassed and unwilling to intervene in what was unquestionably an internal Chinese affair. Many of these nations are at present fighting off such intervention in their own colonies by the champions of anti-colonialism; they could not afford to provide these opponents with a perfect *tu quoque* argument. Nor would the general public in either Asia, Europe or Australasia relish the risk of a general war to prevent what would appear to be the desire of the Chinese people of Formosa for union with their own kin on the mainland.

The attitude of these Chinese inhabitants of the island,

hitherto largely ignored by both sides, will become before long the paramount factor in the destiny of Formosa. They are of Chinese descent, number nearly eight million, but were for over fifty years under Japanese rule. While this experience did not give them any great affection for the Japanese, it did give them an understanding of the meaning and advantages of orderly honest government, public education, material progress. When the Kuomintang occupied the island at the Japanese surrender a horde of mainland officials swarmed into Formosa, intent on enriching themselves, ignorant or incapable of sound administration. Disillusioned and outraged, the Formosans rose in a mass, but unarmed, peaceful protest. The Nationalist governor suppressed this movement with a barbarity and ruthless cruelty which profoundly shocked the native Formosans, many of whose leaders hastened to escape abroad. A second foreign conquest seemed to have begun.

Profound distrust now divided the natives from their mainland rulers; when Chiang and his army and government retreated to the island, no posts of the least importance were entrusted to Formosans. The government and the army were exiles from China, living as strangers in what they too felt to be a foreign and a hostile land. At this time the Formosan Exile Committee, in Hong Kong, was engaged in a fruitless but persistent attempt to obtain United Nations intervention, not to bring the island under Communist rule, but to liberate it from the Nationalists and give it self government under a United Nations guarantee. Such a solution, ideal though it might be, had no hope of implementation. The Korean War soon determined America's policy in favour of the Nationalist regime, and no heed was paid to the views of the inhabitants of the island themselves. This fact has, in the view of many observers, cast a curious light upon the American claim to be defending in Formosa a last haven of freedom and democracy.

Time, none the less, has steadily worked in favour of the Formosan Chinese. They are the people of the land, they multiply and increase, the mainlanders age and die. Chiang's army, although reinforced by the Chinese prisoners taken in

Korea, many of whom chose to join the Nationalists rather than be repatriated to China, has ceased to be a purely main-land force. Formosans have had to be recruited to fill the gaps left by age, long service, or death.

As yet the command remains in the hands of those generals who did not, when still fighting in China, display conspicuous military ability. But there must soon come a time when not only the ranks but also the officers are recruited from the natives of the island. In civil life and government administration the same slow change must profoundly alter the composition of the public service. No one yet knows what these Formosans feel about their rulers, nor what aspirations they may cherish in the future. They, too, are Chinese; the generation which knew Japanese rule and learned the language of their masters is slowly ageing and passing away. It is already obvious that if some future crisis shakes the Nationalist regime, the attitude of the Formosans themselves will be decisive. If a real democratic regime were installed, the overwhelming voting strength would be native, and there is no reason to suppose that their suffrages would be given to Nationalist politicians whose past record is unimpressive.

The Chinese people are fond of searching their own history for precedents and parallel situations. Anciently, history itself was seen as serving this purpose above all others; the mirror from the past which could be held up to the present. They have not failed, no matter which Party they adhere to, to observe that in the history of Formosa there is a very striking parallel with the present situation. After the fall of the Ming dynasty, a Chinese regime, in 1644, the Manchu rulers gradually ex-tended their authority over the whole mainland. In the south Ming partisans long resisted, especially in the mountainous coastal provinces. One of their leaders was a certain Cheng Ch'eng-kung, whom the Ming pretender ennobled by granting him the imperial surname, Chu, from which he was commonly known to his troops as 'Kuo Hsing Yeh', Lord of the National (Imperial) Surname. In the south Chinese dialect which he and they spoke this is rendered Kok Sing Ya.

Cheng (for history has preferred to remember him by his own real surname) was finally driven from the mainland, but he had built a fleet and the Manchus had no sea power. Cheng found that the then almost savage and unsettled island of Taiwan had, in the confusion of the times, come under the domination of the Dutch, who had built a fortress at Anp'ing, inheriting this from the Portuguese, who gave the island its foreign name of Formosa, 'the beautiful'. Cheng attacked and drove out the foreign occupiers, and made himself lord of the whole island. Many thousands of mainland Chinese, fearing and hating the Manchu conquerors, took refuge on the island and settled there. The Western navigators soon did good business in guns and arms with the new master of Formosa, who was known to them by his title, which they rendered from the south Chinese Kok Sing Ya, as 'Koxinga'.

Soon the last Ming pretender was driven from China into Burma, where he was betrayed to the Manchus. Koxinga, safe beyond the seas, now declared himself Emperor, or King of Formosa. The Manchus could not reach him; he could not re-conquer the mainland. Two Chinas came into existence, but as ever, neither side admitted the legality of the other. Sea warfare, or plain piracy, continued along the China coast.

After a rule of two years Koxinga died, still master of Formosa. His son, Cheng Ching, held the island for twenty years, but later successors were not men of his strength and skill. They quarrelled, and the weaker party sought the help of the Manchus, acknowledging their authority. Very soon the imperial government at Peking was able to make an end of the Cheng family and their kingdom. Formosa was occupied, and placed under the governor of Fukien as an integral part of that province. Thus the independence of Formosa, the Second China of the seventeenth century, lasted for in all twenty-five years. Had the Manchu rulers been more acceptable in South China, from which China's sailors mainly come, they could have built a navy in a shorter time and invaded the island.

The story of Koxinga has so many and such close re-semblances to that of Chiang Kai-shek and his Nationalists that no Chinese can fail to remember and reflect. Koxinga, indeed, has been elevated in Formosa today to the status of a national hero and forerunner. His effigy has been placed on the stamps. But the sequel to his life, the quarrels of his grandsons and followers, the ultimate acceptance of the rule of Peking, are not a part of the story on which the Nationalist propaganda cares to dwell. In so far as it underlines the importance of the part which the inhabitants of the country must one day play in deciding its destiny, it is a valuable hint to foreign observers.

There are, of course, some vital differences between the Formosa of Koxinga and that of Chiang Kai-shek. Koxinga did some useful trade with the European voyagers who were just beginning to penetrate to the western Pacific. He had no foreign ally of any importance, Japan was entering her period of seclusion, and played no part in world politics. Chiang Kai-shek is the ally of the United States. No one can doubt that without that alliance the story of Koxinga would be followed to its same conclusion, perhaps very much before twenty-five years had passed. But with that alliance, so long as it operates to defend Formosa from mainland invasion, the parallel cannot hold.

The continued existence of Two Chinas thus depends, not on the views of the Chinese alone, but also on the power of the United States. It is no doubt possible that were the Formosan Chinese to opt for union with the People's Republic, America could prevent such a union coming into being. To do so it would be necessary to land forces in the island in addition to the air bases already operating there; the 7th Fleet would guard the seas, and unless China was prepared to engage in open war with the USA, her forces could not pass the strait. America could well expect that China would not, in fact, dare to provoke a world war for this purpose; Russia, her indispensable ally, would not wish to run the incalculable risk of nuclear warfare to establish the Communist Chinese in Formosa. The danger is incommensurate with the possible profit.

American intervention could therefore stifle a movement to end the Two China situation. The risk of complications and wider war would be severe, but there are certainly many serving officers in the US forces and administration who believe that the risk could safely be run. President Eisenhower may not be one of them, but he will not be president after 1960. If the risk were taken, and succeeded, America would find herself in a situation very repugnant to her traditions, for her position in Formosa would be indistinguishable from that of a colonial power. No doubt Chinese could be found to man a subservient and puppet government, but no one would any longer be able to claim that this regime in any sense represented the Chinese people, or existed for any other reason than because America willed its continuance.

World opinion would be hostile, and alarmed. Asia would be alienated, and it is even possible that China might gain more than she lost in the goodwill and outright alliance of key countries in the south-east of Asia. It is at least doubtful whether the United Nations would still accept the representative of such a Formosan regime as the properly accredited delegate of China. A resort to open force to maintain Two Chinas would thus be effective on the military plane, but destructive on the political level, and would in itself constitute an admission of diplomatic defeat.

American public opinion would be far from unanimous in support of such policy. Already there is a growing unease at the mounting evidence that the present policy does not command the support of many of America's best friends, and is failing to promote that co-operation among the Western allies which is essential to their success. It is now recognized that the trade embargo on Communist China has virtually collapsed except in respect of American trade. The swift disclaimers and reservations with which Western statesmen met the threat of military operations in the South China Sea when the off-shore island crisis occurred in January 1955 was a significant pointer to the attitude which would be adopted if intervention in Formosa to maintain a Nationalist regime took place. The dangers of 'going it alone' to the whole structure of the Western system were sufficiently illustrated by the Suez war, and these dangers would not be avoided if it were America rather than her Western allies who 'went alone'.

On the other hand, for America to do nothing, to watch the collapse of the Nationalist regime through quarrels, treachery, or mass desertion to the other side, would be almost equally calamitous in a different way. It is true that there would be no risk of a world war. The Liberation of Taiwan would be celebrated throughout China with delirious enthusiasm; but it is not very likely that the shrewd men who govern China would embark large forces for Formosa, to be isolated by American seapower at will. The newly converted Nationalists, forgiven and redeemed, would be left to hold the island, discreetly and silently reinforced by Communist cadres, drawn wherever possible from native Formosans. China would seek to show the world that she was content with the restoration of her national unity, and to exploit to the full her diplomatic victory throughout Asia and beyond.

It may be that in fact the strategic situation in the Far East would not be profoundly altered. America would still hold Okinawa, and her bases in Japan. Japan might find this relationship more comfortable when the Chinese Communists were in Formosa. The Philippine Republic to the south would also welcome American protection with more enthusiasm and less fretfulness. The development of long-range missiles might reduce the military value of Formosa to insignificant proportions, especially to a power able to use both Japan and the Philippines as bases for such weapons. Moreover it is obvious that the Chinese would not launch any attack upon either Japan or the Philippines unless a world war were already in progress. If that catastrophe occurred, Formosa would hardly be a significant factor in the calculations of either side. Just as America could use military force to prevent the reunion of Formosa with China, so she could refrain from using that force and suffer no real military damage.

On the political front this would not be true. It is, in fact, the political aspects that dominate American policy today, even though the policy was originally adopted for military reasons.

The collapse of the Nationalist regime, however effected, while America stood 'idly by', would be seen throughout Asia as a major defeat to American policy and a major loss of American prestige. The policy of containing Communism, of the SEATO pact and of the ANZUS pact would be discredited. It would be assumed, wrongly, that if America would not fight for Chiang Kai-shek, she would not defend her other allies either. There would be an immense uplift to the prestige and influence of China. All over South-East Asia the smaller powers would run for cover.

The consequences of this disarray might be to exclude American power from all points on the mainland of South-East Asia. South Viet-nam would be undermined, Malaya and Singapore would be profoundly affected through the influence which this event would have upon their large Chinese population. Indonesia, her eyes constantly fixed on West New Guinea, would mark the lesson. It is very doubtful whether the shaky regimes which succeed each other in Thailand would maintain their present stance of hostility to China if Peking had scored so resounding a triumph. There are those, especially in Asia, who would dispute this assessment of the political consequences of an American abandonment of the Nationalist regime. It would be claimed that the ending of this cause of tension would have a calming, not a disturbing effect in Asia. This might, perhaps, be the long-term consequences of a withdrawal of all Western political and military power from East Asia. The immediate results are naturally the concern of the American administration, and few will dispute that they would be calamitous to America's present policies.

Faced with world-wide unpopularity and loss of moral prestige if she intervenes to uphold a falling Nationalist regime, and with the ruin of her Asian policy if she refrains from such intervention, the USA has little room for manoeuvre. The acceptance of the Two China solution is the only possible escape from this dilemma. It may be quite possible, indeed easy, to get the assent of her Western allies to a permanent settlement on such lines. The off-shore islands would be abandoned to

Peking, perhaps on condition that they were demilitarized. The Nationalist regime, while continuing to be a member of the United Nations, would no longer occupy the seat labelled 'China'. A 'Chinese Republic of Taiwan' might be recognized by a wide range of foreign powers if it no longer claimed to be the 'Republic of China'. Peking would be admitted as the government of China, and take the seat reserved for that country on the Security Council. Recognition of the People's Republic by all members of the United Nations would be recommended.

There is no doubt that every people in the world except the Chinese people would be glad to see such a compromise accepted and established. But there is, unfortunately, very little chance that any section of the Chinese themselves would consider it tolerable or even possible. It runs counter to their deepest sentiment, contradicts their fundamental assumptions. At best they would treat it as a temporary expedient, illegal, not binding, to be evaded if possible and abrogated at the earliest opportunity. Cessions and separations of territory have always been so regarded in China; a necessity yielded to superior force, without moral effect, impermanent and unacceptable.

After the Sung dynasty had lost North China to the Kin Tartars the capital was established in Hangchou for over a century. During that period the Sung government continued to describe it as the 'temporary or travelling capital'—implying that the Court made but a short stay there until the real capital, now that of their rivals and foes, could be regained. Chiang Kai-shek thinks of Taipei in exactly the same terms. Some two hundred years earlier, when the Sung dynasty itself had been established in North China, but not yet conquered all the separate and transitory kingdoms into which the south had dissolved at the fall of the T'ang dynasty, an embassy came from one of these southern kingdoms asking for peace, and as we would now put it, 'recognition' from the Sung. 'What crime', asked the Sung Emperor, 'have the people of Kiangnan committed that they should be separated from the Empire?' Mao Tse-tung and Chou En-lai ask the same question of the people of Formosa.

These may be the views of Chinese leaders on either side, but it is still true that the USA, supported as she might well be by the majority of the United Nations, could force an acceptance, or at least the creation of a Two China solution. She could, by threatening to withdraw her aid, compel Chiang to accept a new designation as the 'Chinese Republic of Taiwan' and the United Nations could unseat his delegate and accept the delegate from Peking. Non-aligned Asia, led by India, which is above all anxious to maintain peace, could perhaps be brought to support such a solution and to mediate with Communist China to obtain it. It is possible that rather than no bread the Chinese Communists would take half a loaf, but it is not possible to expect that they would be satisfied with this meagre fare or cease to work for the full attainment of their aims.

They could perhaps explain to their people that the liberation of Taiwan must still wait changing fortunes, and exploit what they had gained in the meantime. Peking could well prove more tractable than Taipei. For Peking would know that the loss of face, of prestige and hope, which this solution would impose on the Nationalists would be the Communists' best ally. Their propaganda would find an ever more fertile field, for what ultimate prospect would lie before the 'Chinese Republic of Taiwan'? Independent in name it would still appear an American 'satellite' owing its existence to American pressure and its survival to American support. It might well be that the imposition of such a solution upon the Nationalist regime would be a fatal medicine which would kill, not save the patient.

The mainland officials and soldiers would now have to face the undisguised fact that never, under any circumstances, could they hope to return home. They would no longer be Chinese, and the Formosan natives would not welcome them as permanent settlers monopolizing the power and command. It would be upon these natives that the new Republic would in fact depend, and the mainland exiles would be pushed aside. Rather than lose all they might well decide to surrender and gain at least the goodwill of the Communist side.

It would indeed be almost inevitable that a struggle for

power between the natives and the mainland exiles would convulse the new state. It would be necessary to encourage the native Formosans to come forward in the defence and administration of their country, since they alone could be relied upon to provide a continuing society; they at least might be ready to maintain a separate state, since they have but slight ties with their ancestral home on the mainland. But if the new Republic was really to be governed by Formosan natives, who speak a dialect strange to northern ears, the mainlanders would soon find themselves doubly exiles: from China, and from the authority in Formosa which they formerly exercised. It can hardly be hoped that this large body of discontented and disillusioned men would not be fertile soil for the persuasive propaganda coming from Peking.

Many observers already believe that the insistence of Chiang and his followers on the adequacy of their forces, the imminence of the counter-stroke, the expectation of welcome on the mainland, are not merely a 'whistling in the dark', but an essential condition of the continuing existence of the regime. If once it were admitted that hope has gone, that the chance no longer exists, that exile must be the only alternative to surrender, the mainspring of the Nationalist Party would snap, and a scramble to be first and foremost in secret negotiations for capitulation would ensue. If it is argued that no sane and responsible man can any longer hope that the Nationalists could regain China, or stage a counter invasion that would not be a total débâcle on the beaches, the answer must be that, as their writings show, the hope now rests on the conviction that a Third World War is inevitable and imminent.

Others besides the Nationalist leadership share this opinion, but while to them it is a nightmare, to the Nationalist leaders it represents the longed-for culmination of their prayers. It is assumed that in such a war to overthrow Communism America and the West would win. At what cost, cannot be, need not be estimated. For Formosa and the Nationalist regime would be an unlikely target for the main onslaught of either Russia or China. Formosa might well survive, battered perhaps, but ready to supply the army of occupation and restoration which would land in devastated China.

It would hardly be polite or encouraging to America to voice this view too plainly. In his latest book Chiang Kai-shek★ makes a different, unreal suggestion. All that is needed from the West are arms. Not even nuclear weapons, conventional armaments, liberally supplied, will suffice. Then China— Nationalist China—in alliance with Syngman Rhee of Korea and Ngo Din Diem of South Viet-nam, with other, unspecified anti-Communist Asian states (Thailand perhaps?) will open the great offensive to free Asia from Communism. Russia will not intervene, for fear of America. It will be the Korean War over again fought on a larger, wider stage. If only America had permitted Chiang to lead his army to Korea, this could all have been accomplished six years ago.

It is not easy to believe that an experienced general and ruler can really persuade himself that this is a feasible project. It is impossible that he can ignore the development which has transformed China, and therefore to make the scheme plausible it is necessary to postulate that the Chinese people, enslaved by the tools of Russia, are longing for deliverance. The fact that if this is so, it is unlikely that Russia would stand aside while Chiang, Rhee, and Diem grabbed her prize is conveniently ignored. If the plan has any meaning, it is an attempt to induce America to give Chiang the arms with which he would start a conflict which must, and would, involve the whole world.

It can be assumed with certainty that President Eisenhower and any conceivable successor to his office will be very unlikely to fall into this simple trap. America will not give Chiang enough arms, or ships, to make an invasion even remotely possible. But as this determination becomes more and more manifest, the problem of how to implement the Two China policy becomes also more pressing. America cannot let the Nationalists go, she cannot help them to recover China, can they be maintained in Formosa when all hope of return has been for ever banished? How long, moreover, will it be possible

★ Op. cit.

to avoid a public pronouncement indicating that America will only protect Formosa but will not assist a counter-invasion?

Up to a very recent date Mr Dulles, when he has spoken of Far Eastern policy, has still talked in terms which it is only fair to believe are not a real indication of his, or his President's, intentions. No mention of China is regarded as full or complete unless it contains the suggestion that the Peking regime is tottering to its fall, has no public support, and represents the worst of all possible governments for China. No attempt is made to acquaint the public with the very real material development which has taken place under this government, and by a systematic ban on all visits to China by US citizens, including the Press, every effort has been made to prevent the American public from learning the facts. Nationalist propaganda stories are endorsed as if they were proven truths, objective reporting is condemned as Communist propaganda. Vague but menacing language is used suggesting the ultimate use of force against China in favour of the Nationalist regime.

Such speeches are no doubt made under the necessity of placating some powerful political group—the China Lobby—or merely to stem the tide flowing towards recognition and normal trading relations. But they are none the less dangerous and mischievous. To the Communist Chinese they are a gift, a confirmation from the enemy himself of all that the system of Persuasion can say against him. To the Nationalists they are a beguiling lure, raising false hopes, lulling fears, creating expectations which will never be fulfilled, and thus inhibiting any objective consideration of the problem. To America's Western allies they are a gratuitous irritation; known to be at best a very imperfect statement of real policy, emphasizing all the aspects of that policy which cause most uneasiness and evoke the least sympathy, clouding the real issue and complicating and exacerbating the conflict of opinion between the Western nations and the non-aligned peoples of Asia.

No one, and certainly not the government in Peking, expects that the United States should expel Chiang and his Nationalists by force and hand the island of Formosa over to the Communist regime. No one would suggest that the United States intervene directly in the politics of Formosa to impose this or that solution by her might and military power. To combat these propositions is to engage in a sham fight against an imaginary antagonist. What the allies of America and the people of Asia clearly would hope to see is a rational and balanced declaration of policy which contains concrete propositions for a compromise and omits ideological challenges and moral exhortations.

Two Chinas may be the only possible solution for the time being, but it should not be cast in a rigid mould which would make any future change impossible unless accomplished by a destructive war. It is unwise to talk in terms of irresistible forces and immovable obstacles, for in politics, which are the expression of the passions and beliefs of mortal men, nothing is permanent, nothing unchanging.

CHAPTER TEN

CHINA IN ASIA

TO THE GREEKS and Romans, as Gibbon* puts it, China was an 'extreme and inaccessible part of Asia' of which they had at best but scanty knowledge. The later western Europeans, the heirs of the classical civilization, tended, like their predecessors, to consider all beyond Europe as remote, probably barbarous, even though from the end of the fifteenth century onwards these regions ceased to be inaccessible. The name, 'the Far East', reveals the Europe-centred outlook, an attitude which still lingers not only in the public mind, but also in the universities, chanceries and foreign ministries of the West. To the Chinese their country was, and still is, 'the Middle Kingdom', the central core of the world, the heartland of civilization. This outlook is just as persistent among the Chinese as the European viewpoint is in the West. The basic conflict of assumptions, both unreal, underlies much of the surface tensions and strains in the international relations between China and Western countries.

But in one respect the Chinese outlook is still true, and the West has tended to ignore this fact at its peril. China is the middle kingdom of Asia, geographically she is the heartland of the vast region east of the Hindu Kush. Since the decline of the Manchu power at the end of the eighteenth century the importance of this situation became obscured. Sea power dominated the coasts of Asia, and the sea power was Western. Along the whole vast southern coast of the continent the European nations either seized the sovereignty of the seaboard countries or imposed their domination over the few which retained an impaired independence. China did not escape this fate; the 'Unequal Treaties' established not only the British colony of Hong Kong, but Treaty Ports, Concessions, leased territories,

* *The Decline and Fall of the Roman Empire*, III, 13–14.

from the Indo-Chinese frontier to the port of Dairen in Manchuria.

The old routes across Asia which had from the earliest times been the lines of communication in peace and war, 'the silk road' and the war path of nomad invaders, fell into disuse. Yet occasionally there occurred an incident which served to remind the Western intruders that the true strength of China lay inland, and that demonstrations of power along the sea coast could not always impose a desirable solution to the current problem. When, in 1901, the Boxer rebellion involved the Court of the Empress Dowager Tz'u Hsi in a foolish and obscurantist attempt to destroy the Western residents and expel their power from China, Peking was soon captured by an international Western army, the Court forced into rapid and disorderly flight to the western provinces. Victory seemed complete.

But the Court continued to fly west until it reached Sian, the ancient capital of the Han and T'ang dynasties, hundreds of miles from the sea, as yet unconnected by any railway. There the Empress Dowager stopped. Tribute and revenue was redirected to the new capital, the armies regrouped in the mountainous provinces beyond the North China plain. The foreign powers became disturbed. They wanted a tidy, swift settlement of the crisis, the resumption of trade with the interior, the Court back in Peking where the diplomatic corps could deal with it, virtually under the guns of the navies, while the legations themselves were protected by newly established Legation Guards. The Chinese chief negotiator, the suave and able Li Hung-chang, agreed to all that was proposed, but pointed out that if onerous terms were imposed the Court might prefer not to return to Peking. . . . Sian was an ancient and a fine city; the Empress was now comfortably installed, the Palace there had been repaired and enlarged, she liked the climate.

This prospect appeared bleak to the Western diplomats. They had just, with great peril, survived the hostility of Court and country in Peking, barely eighty miles from the sea. In Sian, which was more nearly three hundred miles inland, how could they be saved in another crisis? Months might pass before a Western army could fight its way across China, without communications, far from the navigable rivers. For the first time in their dealings with the West the Chinese Government had found out how to 'sell space to gain time'*—and more than time. The Western terms were modified, the Court, some two years later, deigned to return to Peking, and the nightmare of trying to occupy or penetrate into the vast west of China was dissipated for the European governments.

But the lesson had been learned; the fashionable game of carving up China into spheres of influence which should be colonies tomorrow, a game which had represented for some decades the principle motive of the China policy of all the European powers, was now tacitly abandoned. It was thought far better to have a Chinese government near the coast, which could be bullied, but still exercise authority in regions where the West would find it very hard to do so. Japan, forty years later, was to rush in where the West had wisely feared to tread, and thereby roused in the heart of China that national and universal resistance which gave the Communist Party its decisive opportunity to expand and triumph.

As a consequence of that victory and the reorganization which the Party has imposed, China is once more a power in Asia. A power based, as in earlier times, on her land mass, her central situation, her vast human resources. To these have been, or soon will be added a new industrial strength, a heavy industry which also draws its supplies and is itself established in the western inland provinces far from the sea and the frontiers. In the days of China's weakness Western statesmen often declared that they had no other aim in China than to see that the country became a strong, independent and well governed modern state. They now have their wish, but they did not, of course, expect or desire that the strength, independence and government should be provided by the Communist Party. The West has thus a double problem in dealing with the new China: a *modus vivendi* must be found which no longer ignores,

* The phrase was coined by General Pai Chung-hsi during the war with Japan.

but explicitly recognizes that China has rights and powers, a place in Asia among the greatest. These new equalities must also be conceded to a Communist regime, since there is no prospect that any other regime will come to power: and the Communist regime is the declared ally of Russia.

It is this fact that causes the doubts and hesitations among the Western nations. They would now agree that China has not hitherto had her rights, that nineteenth-century policies were often unwise and short-sighted, that a nation of China's size and potential strength should be acknowledged a great power and her views in the east of Asia be respected. If only she were not under a Communist government, and even if that must be, if she were not the friend and ally of Russia. To many Western critics it seems as if this friendship is a gratuitous pro-vocation offered by the Chinese, an unnecessary spurning of Western friendship, a turning away from true friends to seek support in a dubious and sinister quarter. This attitude of out-raged sensibility marks much American policy towards the People's Republic. It reveals hopes dashed and plans frustrated.

American policy during the Second World War, to the considerable astonishment of the good European Winston Churchill, was to treat China as one of the 'Big Four'. China must be accorded the status of a world power even though her strength was manifestly far short of such stature, her internal disorder and conflict inconsistent with such a pretension, her economy backward. But, now that Japan was the enemy, China must be given the title of Great Power so that Asia should not feel deprived of all influence and leadership in the councils of the Grand Alliance. The Americans were not disposed to recognize an India still subject to British rule as fulfilling this role in any way. They feared, with justice, that without China the Western powers would be represented in Asia as foreign colonial aggressors, and Japan might be really welcomed as a liberator and friend. There had been ominous signs of such an attitude in many countries of South East-Asia. Japan herself, by the stupidities and brutalities of her occupation policies, was the best insurance against its spread.

So America was only too willing to concede to a China which lacked the necessary attributes a status which she now denies to a China that has gained them. Nationalist China, with all its weakness and corruption, was anti-Communist. Its leadership was largely American educated, it could be relied upon to be the friend and ally of the United States, and even if in the stress of war such hopes had been cherished in respect of Soviet Russia, they had received very little encouragement from Russia herself, and were to fade entirely with the dawn of peace. China, Nationalist China, which America had supported and sustained in the long years of war, held greater promise. She had a common frontier with Russia, stretching for thousands of miles far into the depths of Asia. She was a vast market, still undeveloped. America would have been a good friend, ready to supply finance for development, arms for defence, diplomatic support. China rejected all this, wantonly and wickedly. She chose Russia and Communism. Having made this choice she must abide the consequences; no recognition, no admission to the United Nations, support for Chiang Kai-shek, trade embargo, diplomatic hostility at all points, all harm short of war.

Why then did the Chinese choose Communism and Russia, could they too not see what must be the result of this reversal of alliances? The reasons why the Chinese people finally welcomed and accepted the People's Republic have been fully examined elsewhere;* the reasons, apart from the obvious sympathy of two Communist regimes, for the close alliance with Russia are worth examination. Accustomed to our own seafaring story, and tending to think of all foreign countries as 'beyond the seas', Western peoples frequently ignore the history of the great Russian expansion into northern Asia. But this movement was for China ultimately of much greater significance than the relatively minor intrusions of the Western 'sea foreigners' along the coasts.

Since the dawn of their history the 'enemy' for the Chinese was the nomad of the Mongolian steppe and the vast unknown

---

* C. P. Fitzgerald, *Revolution in China*. Cresset Press, London, 1952.

reservoir beyond. From this bleak and inhospitable region 'where not even a hair will grow' as the Chinese saw it, came fierce hordes which swept into the civilized land of China. To keep them out the Great Wall was built. Great Emperors campaigned deep into Tartary, even into Siberia, to try to eradicate the menace at its source. It was in vain; when they had gone the nomad power reshaped, grew strong, burst forth once more.

At last an unexpected cure appeared; from the far north-west the Russians came to take the Tartars in the rear, revenging their ancient subjection by the total destruction and suppression of the nomad power, the final occupation of the great reservoir. The Manchu monarchs at the same period, the seventeenth and eighteenth centuries, dealt crushing and conclusive blows at the Mongol tribes nearer to China. Between the two Empires nomadism was crushed; modern arms and industry confirmed its fall; the 'scourge of God', a modern Tamerlane, can never again rise up to sweep across Asia and deep into Europe. All of which, although the most important long-term development in China's foreign relations, has been very nearly forgotten and ignored by the West.

The consequences of this profound change along the northern frontiers of China were not at first apparent. The Manchu Emperors had no sooner delivered China from the age-old menace of the Steppe before the new, unprecedented aggression of the sea foreigners broke along the coasts. But while the Court tried, not quite without effect, to fend off these intrusions at the ports, the new northern neighbour, Russia, consolidated her hold upon the former nomad reservoir. Already in the seventeenth century the Russians were on the Amur, the northern frontier of Manchuria. In the sixties of the last century, when China was distracted by the T'ai P'ing rebellion and its aftermath, they secured the cession of a large region over which the Manchus had claimed a vague suzerainty, and created in it the Maritime Province with the new city and port of Vladivostok as its capital. When China temporarily lost control of Sinkiang, or Chinese Turkestan, the Russians moved into the Ili valley, and remained there for many years.

These encroachments and threats did not affect the Chinese as closely as the far more limited penetration effected by the sea foreigners on the coast. The great cities of China lie along the coast and the rivers. Canton and Nanking were stormed by the British in 1842, Peking itself occupied by British and French forces in 1860. Many lesser but large cities had seen the Western soldiers in their streets. There were at that time no Chinese cities in Manchuria north of Mukden, there were no settlements except the dreary quarters of exiles in the far north, and Sinkiang was a colonial territory inhabited by alien peoples.

But there was, none the less, a significant difference between the sea and the land pressures. The Westerners had come to trade, to make money and go home; the Russians had come to stay, to settle and till the soil. Sea power depends on navies, which may decline or be defeated; land power depends on occupation of the soil; its effects are slower, but more enduring. No nation can permanently occupy the sea; but once settled and established a land-rooted population is hard to remove. The Chinese knew this from their own story. They had spread and moved south more by the power of the plough than the might of the sword. By the middle of the nineteenth century China had for the first time in her long history a powerful and civilized neighbour, with a common frontier stretching from Korea to Central Asia.

Several decades passed before the Chinese found out what this new northern power upon their frontiers implied. The Russians did not complete the great Trans-Siberian Railway until the century had turned, and before that essential link had been built, eastern Siberia was so remote, so neglected and so weakly held that it poised no threat to the Chinese Empire. But when once the link was complete the situation changed abruptly. Following the Boxer Rebellion in 1901, Russia occupied Manchuria and pushed down to the warm water ports of Lushun and Talienwan, which she obtained on lease, and renamed Port Arthur and Dalny. Russia was now established in that very territory, South Manchuria, from which the Manchu power itself had derived, and in which, in earlier centuries, the Tartar dynasties of Liao and Kin, later masters of North China, had grown to power. The threat to China from the north was once more real and urgent, and this time it did not come from nomad horsemen.

The Russians were driven out of Port Arthur and Dalny by the Japanese, in 1905, in a war fought on China's territory, but in which China herself was a neutral. But northern Manchuria remained in Russian hands; southern Manchuria was now dominated by the Japanese. The shadow still lay over Peking and it was rather the rivalry of the two invaders than the strength of China which preserved the declining Empire. Soon, with the Russian revolution and the early Leninist policy of abandoning imperial pretensions and claims, the Russian threat receded. The Chinese were able to reassert some authority in Northern Manchuria, and began covertly to compete against the Japanese in the exploitation of this hitherto virgin land.

A decisive change was a direct consequence, not of conscious Chinese resistance, but of the economic development brought about by Russian and Japanese intrusion. New cities were building up along the new railways which criss-crossed Manchuria, labour was in short supply; Russia was too far, Japanese labour too dear, the north Chinese from Hopei and Shantung poured into the land of promise and supplied the need. They soon settled down to farm the land and to develop commerce in the towns. Within thirty years of the Russian concession to build the railway from Manchuli on the frontier to Port Arthur and Mukden, more than thirty million Chinese are estimated to have come into Manchuria. Whatever the future political allegiance of the country it was now and henceforward, ethnically a Chinese region. Once more the plough had outlived the sword.

Elsewhere along the vast frontier Russia had her successes to record against this setback. Mongolia, reduced to vassalage by the Manchus, rebelled against the Republic, was briefly occupied by a White Russian Army, 'liberated' by the Red Army, and established as a People's Republic, the first satellite. China did not acknowledge this state until, as a consequence of the Yalta conference, she was pressed into doing so by the United States, which had undertaken this duty as part of the Yalta bargains. The region called Uriang Hai or Dzungaria by nineteenth-century writers, in the far north-west of Outer Mongolia, became the Republic of Tannu Tuva. Later this Russian creation was absorbed by the USSR.

Seen objectively, it was clear in the late thirties that China, weak and wracked by civil war, was not only losing territory to imperial Japan, which had detached Manchuria and now dominated North China, but was also menaced by the less clamorous, but persistent pressure of Soviet Russia upon her remote peripheral regions. The governors of Sinkiang were forced into ambivalent relations with Moscow, which seemed to portend a similar series of developments in the north-west. Meanwhile, by the late thirties, the Western powers had largely renounced their ambitions in China. They still clung to Concessions and Treaty Ports, insisted on extraterritoriality for their citizens, but no longer even mentioned spheres of influence. They were reluctant to give up what they still enjoyed, but unwilling to assume new commitments or embark on far-reaching adventures. The mistake of Nationalist foreign policy was to batter upon this half open door, and ignore the massive obstacles of Japanese and Russian ambition.

When Japan struck, in 1937, intent to conquer all China and reduce the country to subservience, Russia remained neutral. Nor did the USSR break with Japan until Germany had already been brought to surrender. So far from flying to the assistance of the Chinese Communists, who had for eight years maintained a bitter guerrilla struggle against the Japanese occupation, Russia remained in full diplomatic relations with Japan until the Atomic Bomb had already fallen upon Hiroshima. Then, in the Nine Days War, which Japan had done nothing to provoke, Russia swiftly occupied all Manchuria down to the Great Wall. The Chinese Communists were at first also denied entry into 'liberated' Manchuria. The Russians, indeed, presently negotiated with the Nationalist government, which they recognized, for the evacuation of Manchuria and the take-over by Nationalist troops flown in for the purpose. But the Russians did not, perhaps could not, prevent the infiltration of the Chinese Communists from nearby Hopei province, and allowed the Japanese arms dumps to fall into their hands.

There exists no small amount of evidence pointing to the conclusion that Russia did not wish to see the Chinese Communists gain a swift victory, and did not expect them to be able to do so. Equally, although the Nationalists did not even succeed in occupying the extreme north of Manchuria and the city of Harbin, a Russian creation with a large Russian population, the Chinese Communists did not set up their capital in this, the first major city to come under their authority. Maybe it was too close to Russia. At least the pattern of these events differed strikingly from the earlier models of Mongolia and Tannu Tuva, and from the contemporary and nearby happenings across the border in North Korea.

When the Chinese Communists had definitely won the civil war, and not before the Nationalist forces had finally been driven from the mainland, Russia withdrew her embassy to the Nationalist government and recognized Peking (3 October 1949). A few months later she negotiated with the new government a treaty which, entitled the Sino-Soviet Treaty of Friendship, Alliance and Mutual Assistance, also gave back to Russia her share in the control of the railway across Manchuria and her naval base at Port Arthur together with her commercial concessionary rights in Dairen or Dalny. It seemed as though China had had to pay a stiff price for Friendship, Alliance and Mutual Assistance (14 February 1950).

All these events can as yet only be observed from the outside. It cannot be proved that the Chinese Communists resented the revived intrusion of Russia into South Manchuria; they declared in public that acts which might be outrageous encroachments by enemy, exploiting, capitalist imperialists, were, of course, quite different when done by agreement between trusting Communist allies. They cannot, however, have ignored that fact that such agreements gave their opponents valuable ammunition for their propaganda, and showed the Communist regime in an unfavourable light to many true nationalist patriots.

At this time, wrongly no doubt, but still unquestionably sincerely, the Chinese Communists believed that their regime was in real danger of attack by the United States; they feared that, as they could not defend such places as Port Arthur effectively in such an eventuality, they might be seized by the USA and handed over to the Nationalists. The developments of the Korean War at first seemed to confirm these fears. General Macarthur advanced from Inchon upon the Yalu, beyond which lies Manchuria, which is China. Russia, it was clear, was not disposed to save her protegé, North Korea, at the risk of world war. So China intervened; China, who had little to lose, since she had already incurred the wrath and enmity of the United States, which had also already declared Formosa inviolable.

China intervened, by means of 'volunteers', armed by Russia. To the great surprise of the world, and perhaps of the Chinese people also, the intervention was at first a resounding success. Macarthur was thrown back into South Korea. Thereafter the war was harder, and stalemate gradually developed, to end in prolonged negotiations and armistice. But for China the essential, and double victory had been gained. North Korea was saved for Communism, but now depended for its preservation on a Chinese, not a Russian army. The Chinese had now a modern army, battle tested, equipped with the latest weapons; and—unspoken, secret triumph—it was this Chinese army which now occupied Manchuria in overwhelming strength. This last fact, in due time, produced its logical consequences. Late in 1954, following talks held between the Chinese and Soviet governments in Peking, it was announced that Russia had given up her naval base in Port Arthur—now once more named Lushun (12 October 1954). There is, undeniably, a concealed tension between China and Russia in the region of Manchuria and eastern Siberia. In 1937, when Russia believed herself menaced by Japanese aggression, and China was dis-

tracted by the Japanese invasion, the Russian reaction was not
to assist China to resist Japan, but to take swift and ruthless steps
to deport and eliminate the large Chinese community which
had resided in eastern Siberia and above all in Vladivostok.
In 1926, according to Soviet statistics, this population exceeded
22,000 in Vladivostok alone. Fifty per cent of the coalminers
in the Ussuri province were Chinese, thirty per cent of the timber
workers. There had already been signs of local Russian hostility
to this community, although this attitude was opposed by
Moscow. But in 1937 it was decided that the Chinese, like the
Korean community in Siberia, must be removed. It was
secretly deported to the interior of Russia, where no certain
evidence of its subsequent fate exists. The 1952 edition of the
Large Soviet Encyclopaedia makes no mention of a Chinese
minority in eastern Siberia.*

The history of Sino-Russian relations both in the time of the
two Empires and in the subsequent periods of republican, then
Communist China, and Soviet Russia shows that China can
never ignore the change that has come over the regions to the
north of her frontiers. Any Chinese government must choose
between the friendship and the hostility of the regime which is
ruling Russia; and moreover, if any Chinese government
quarrels at the same time with both Russia and Japan—or whoever exercises the strategic power deriving from control of
Japan—the result is certain to be calamitous. The Manchu
Empire failed to understand this risk, and so lost first Korea
and then Manchuria: the Nationalist Party did not profit from
the mistakes of the Manchus, and thus when Japan set out on
her programme of imperial expansion at China's expense,
Russia was not available to act as the ally of China in restraint
of Japan.

Even when, in 1939, serious border clashes occurred between
Japanese and Russian troops in the frontier region of Outer
Mongolia and Manchuria, it does not appear that the govern-
ment of Chiang Kai-shek made any attempt to exploit this

* Walter Kolarz, *The Peoples of the Soviet Far East*. George Phillip & Son. London.
1954. Pp. 44–48.

situation to China's advantage, or seek by giving Russia support to embarrass the Japanese who had already started the invasion of China. Anti-Communism was the fixed policy of the Kuomintang; Russia was the arch-Communist country, so no close relations could be contemplated. Throughout the long war with Japan Russia held aloof, and it would seem that the Nationalist government was quite content to see her maintain a neutrality so advantageous to Japanese ambitions.

When Japan had been defeated, and America occupied the strategic position which had been the source of Japan's power, the Nationalist regime did indeed seek to use American power to check Russia and oppose the Chinese Communists. But America had not the same direct and overriding interest in the preservation of China's territorial integrity as Japan had felt for the retention of her own acquisitions on the mainland of East Asia. Manchuria was not an American possession, not even a land occupied by American forces. Even in respect of Korea American policy was unsettled, vacillating, and anxious for disengagement. To conciliate Russia and obtain her alliance against Japan, America, at Yalta, had undertaken to persuade or, virtually compel the Chinese Nationalist Government to concede the complete independence of Outer Mongolia. The problem of China was only one of many which engaged the attention of the government of the USA. To Japan it had been the primary objective of her foreign policy, and by reason of geographical propinquity must ever remain her first and most urgent problem.

It must be assumed that the Chinese Communist regime, aware of this history, and in any case impelled by ideological sympathies, deliberately decided that Russia was the desirable ally for the New China. 'We lean to one side' as Mao Tse-tung put it, and justified this position on ideological grounds. He cannot have ignored the fact that there were also other reasons for this choice. The rise of Russia to the position of one of the two remaining first-class powers in the world, the unalterable fact of her common frontier with China, the elimination of Japan, and the hostility of America—the heir of Japan, all argued in favour of the Russian alliance. There was no real alternative except a dangerous isolation. Britain and the other former imperial powers influential in the Far East had either fallen in the war or withdrawn their interest and accepted America's leadership in that region. China was weak, and believed herself to be threatened with foreign intervention.

Under the shield of the Russian alliance, and with Russian economic and military aid, China has now grown relatively strong. The Peking Government has forfeited the goodwill of America, which would have been hard to obtain, and remains under the suspicion of other Western powers, America's allies. But China has regained control of her whole national territory, including those border regions where formerly Russian encroachment seemed an imminent threat. China has acquired a stature in Asia which has profoundly altered the balance of forces in that continent; and more recently there have been signs that China is beginning to exercise an influence upon Russian policy which none of the eastern European 'satellites', nor even independent Yugoslavia, can hope to emulate. Seen from the point of view of the Chinese Communists these results are ample and complete justification for their policy: nor have any Western statesmen been able to suggest how any contrary policy could have obtained commensurate advantages for China.

No longer preoccupied with hostile attitudes by powerful neighbours along her northern and north-eastern frontiers, China has been free to turn her attention southward, to those regions of Asia, which formerly dominated by the European colonial powers, are now independent, or about to become so. The nature of this Chinese interest in South-East Asia, the aims of her policy there, and the methods by which it is pursued have become issues of the first importance for all the countries of Asia and for the Western peoples who have established in the Pacific two nations of European culture and population, Australia and New Zealand.

Although the newly independent nations of Asia, India, Ceylon, Burma and Indonesia had established diplomatic relations with the Peking Government within a year of its establishment, by June 1950, the Chinese Communists for some time thereafter continued to treat these former colonial countries with aloof suspicion. It did not, at this period, fit the formulae of their propaganda to admit that nationalist movements, unsupported by, or even opposed to Communism, could win independence for the nations of Asia. It was not until 1953, when the good offices of India in the implementation of the Korean armistice were fully apparent, that any change of attitude became clear.

Early in 1954, when the dangerous Indo-China crisis had been staved off by the Geneva Conference, Chinese relations with the Asian countries grew closer. On 29 April 1954 there was signed in Peking an agreement with India relating to trade and intercourse between that country and Tibet, where the Chinese People's Republic had three years previously (May 1951) established its undisputed authority. It was in this agreement that the 'Five Principles of Co-existence' were for the first time announced as the policy of the People's Republic, and accepted by India as the basis of her relations with the new China. A few days later, on 2 May, the five 'Colombo powers', India, Pakistan, Ceylon, Burma and Indonesia, at the conclusion of their Prime Ministers' conference in Colombo, issued a statement which, in addition to calling for a cease-fire in Indo-China, asserted the right of the Peking Government to recognition and the seat of China at the United Nations. The stage was thus set for a significant change in the policy of China and a much clearer definition of the Colombo Powers' opposition to Western policy in Asia.

In June, while the Geneva Conference was recessed, Chou En-lai visited India and Burma, and in both these countries declarations were issued adopting the Five Principles of Peaceful Co-existence as the basis of relations with China. The new policy was developing rapidly, but it was not until the following year, when both Nehru and U Nu of Burma had in turn visited China, that this policy found its full and complete expression at the Bandung Conference of Asian and African countries (18–24 April 1955). The final communique* of that conference, while not naming the Five Principles as such (since this would have committed certain strongly anti-Communist states to open support of a policy sponsored by China) actually incorporated all of the Five Principles in the ten principles which it recommended and adopted as the proper basis for international relations.

In his speech to this conference, Chou En-lai, Prime Minister and chief Chinese delegate, declared:

> On the basis of strict adherence to the Five Principles we (China) are prepared now to establish normal relations with all the Asian and African countries, with all the countries of the world, and first of all with neighbouring countries.†

In view of this commitment it is interesting to examine the reaction which this declaration has produced in other countries both in Asia and elsewhere. It is clear enough that to the Colombo powers and certain others, who have adopted similar policies, the Chinese invitation is acceptable, and is indeed welcomed as a firm foundation for normal relations. Nehru has declared that the Five Principles are 'the only successful basis of peace in Asia'.‡ Nor would it seem likely that there is in these Five Principles any point which the Western Powers would find inacceptable. The difficulty lies rather in the interpretation which may be put upon their application.

The Five Principles ('Pancha Sila') which now play so large a role in the thoughts and foreign policies of the Asian countries are in themselves simple statements, taking reciprocity as their basis. They are:

1. Mutual respect for each other's territorial integrity and sovereignty.
2. Mutual non-aggression.
3. Mutual non-interference in each other's internal affairs.
4. Equality and mutual benefit.
5. Peaceful co-existence.

* Final Communique of the Asian-African Conference. Section F. Para. 3. *The Facts of the Bandung Conference.* Australia-China Society. Sydney, 1955.
† Ibid.
‡ Indian Parliamentary Debates, 15 May 1954, vol. V, No. 70.

At first sight it may be asked why any nation should find difficulty in establishing normal relations with China on the basis of strict adherence to these principles. For what reasons have not only the United States, but several other powers such as Australia, Canada, the Philippine Republic, Japan and Thailand in the Pacific region, and many of the European powers in the West, found that they cannot admit the Five Principles as an adequate basis for recognition and normal relations with the Chinese People's Republic? It immediately becomes obvious that the real difficulties are not matters of principle but almost exclusively of application and interpretation.

'Strict adherence' in Chou En-lai's phrase, to the first principle would mean to China nothing short of the cessation of all attempts to save and uphold, recognize and encourage the Nationalist regime in Formosa. China claims that that island is her territory; recognition and alliance with, or merely recognition, of the Nationalist regime is thus a violation of the first and third principles.

On the other hand certain Western powers have upheld the contention, supported by a vote in the UN, that China was guilty of aggression in the Korean War. China does not accept this condemnation as valid. The second principle is thus brought into dispute. Just what is meant by 'aggression', and is this dangerous word interpreted in Peking in the same way as in Washington, is the question which the Western objectors will at once raise. Equality and mutual benefit, rather more imprecise, offer less cause for disagreement. But in these terms China will no doubt see a prohibition of such measures as an embargo on strategic goods, exclusion from the UN and other forms of discrimination which are still part of American policy.

The seemingly innocuous 'peaceful co-existence' in fact raises the most fundamental of all the problems between the Two Worlds. Is the aim of Communist policy directed to an ultimate world revolution, or is it limited to the security and survival of the existing Communist regimes, and the establishment of the right of other peoples to choose a Communist regime if they desire to do so? Is the ultimate purpose of the opponents of Communism, and the United States Government in particular, to create conditions which will lead to an anti-Communist revolution in Russia and China, and in the meantime to prevent, by force if need be, the establishment of further Communist regimes, irrespective of the apparent wishes of the peoples concerned? These questions are rarely raised and never answered by the spokesmen of either side.

The Western opponents of China and those governments which follow their lead with more or less enthusiasm are inhibited from accepting the Five Principles as a basis for negotiation and normal relations because they see that the 'strict adherence' on which Chou En-lai insists would in fact mean a radical change of policy in respect of Formosa, trade, the United Nations, and possibly the whole approach to the Cold War. On the other hand they do not seem to give so much weight to what could be required of China if these conditions were met. On the basis of the first three principles the West could ask China to give clear and sufficient proof that she had no designs upon the independent non-Communist countries of South-East Asia. The fears of the Thais could be allayed, the uncertainties of Malaya defined. If India and other non-aligned Asian states as well as China were associated in a pact which guaranteed the liberties of these weak countries on the basis of the Five Principles, would this not be a better assurance of peace and tranquility than the uneasy equilibrium afforded by SEATO?

This, or some arrangement of a similar character, can be called the Indian solution. It starts from the assumption that China should be trusted and expected to fulfil an engagement freely and equally negotiated. It is of course, negated by the view that no Communist regime can ever under any circumstances be trusted to carry out any undertaking the moment it appears safe and profitable to break it. This latter assumption, the fundamental postulate of much American thinking, leads to the inevitable and logical conclusion that there is no permanent solution short of the destruction of the Communist regimes and their substitution by others which could be trusted.

However, under modern conditions, and with the present balance of forces and power, this conclusion means an inevitable Third World War of cataclysmic proportions, from which neither system could expect victory or even survival in recognizable form.

Whatever faults and failings the Asian peoples may have, however tactless their enthusiasm and brash their nationalism, they do at least clearly perceive the nihilistic pessimism of this point of view. They therefore reject it and base their policy upon a wary, but positive belief in the possibility of 'peaceful co-existence'.

China's acceptance of the Five Principles, her 'strict adherence' to these principles since Bandung, is thus a most potent and effective policy in Asia, which has already in three years won new friends and disarmed old opponents. Much of this new diplomatic effort was the personal achievement of Chou En-lai, who in the years 1955 to 1957 visited all the countries of South-East Asia in which the Five Principles were accepted as the basis of foreign policy. The range of his journeys took him to Kabul and Katmandu, Colombo, Karachi, Delhi, Rangoon and Pnom Penh. Only Bangkok, Tokyo and Manila, the strongholds of American influence, remained beyond the sphere of direct Chinese diplomatic activity. Already in diplomatic relations with the 'Colombo powers' China in this period succeeded in virtually detaching Cambodia and Laos from the SEATO system and bringing them into the camp of the non-aligned Asian states.

The Manila Treaty, by a new and hitherto unprecedented article, had declared that such states, not party to the Treaty, as the signatories might 'designate' as in need of protection against Communist invasion or subversion, should, if they raised no objection, receive the aid of the signatory powers. In China, and also in the non-aligned states, this provision was regarded as a breach of the Geneva agreements which had ended the Indo-China war on the condition that neither Cambodia nor Laos should enter into military alliances with either side.

Following approaches which began at the Bandung Conference nearly a year earlier Prince Sihanouk Norodom, former King and actual ruler of Cambodia, visited Peking, and on 18 February 1956 issued there a joint statement with China affirming the two countries' support of the Five Principles. Prince Sihanouk also issued a statement to the Press in which he expressed the view that Cambodia was not in need of any 'designation' by the SEATO powers. Six months later it was the turn of Laos, and on 25 August 1956 Prince Souvanna Phouma, the Prime Minister of that country, made the same declaration from Peking in acceptance of the Five Principles as his royal colleague from Cambodia. Communist principles do not appear to inhibit the Chinese leadership from establishing excellent personal relations with these royal visitors.

While Chinese policy was thus circumventing some of the aspects of the SEATO system which China found most distasteful, a wider activity was for the first time bringing the People's Republic into direct relations with the states of western Asia, the Arab world. At Bandung the cordiality which had marked the relations between Colonel Nasser and Chou En-lai, twin idols of popular acclaim at all public appearances, had already been seen as a portent of changing Egyptian policy. For at that date Egypt, alone of the Arab states, was still in formal diplomatic relations with Nationalist China. In the year following the Bandung Conference Egyptian trade and cultural delegations visited Peking; on 16 May 1956 Egypt formally withdrew her recognition of Chiang Kai-shek's regime and entered into full diplomatic relations with Peking. For China this was a double success; not only had she gained recognition from a new state, but in this case the act had involved withdrawal of recognition from the Nationalists, which gave the gesture added value.

The Arab states closely allied to Egypt soon followed her lead: Syria on 10 August 1956, Yemen on 14 September. Chinese recognition of the newly independent Sudan, and subsequently of Ghana, Morocco and Tunisia, extended the range of her diplomatic contacts into Africa, a continent with which Old China, since the sea-borne expeditions of the Ming Emperors in the early fifteenth century, had had but the sketchiest of relations.

The importance of all this activity was nevertheless only marginal to Chinese foreign policy. It is no doubt useful and valuable to build up a greater body of supporters at the United Nations, in the expectation that one day the Afro-Asian block will have sufficient votes to turn the scale in the General Assembly and unseat the delegates of Chiang Kai-shek. Western Asia, and Africa too, may become an important market for the coming Chinese export trade; goodwill will further all these ends, and anti-colonialism is a sure passport to the goodwill of the ex-colonial countries. Throughout Asia and even in Africa China was beginning to make her voice heard and her weight felt. But if these were the effects of her new policy in countries with which China had had little to do in the past, the effects were on a far more significant scale in those countries where large numbers of Chinese resided and with which China had long been intimately linked.

The self-governing city and territory of Singapore has a population of which eighty per cent is Chinese; in the Federation of Malaya the Chinese number over forty per cent, and with the Indian minority equal the proportion of Malays. In neighbouring Thailand the Chinese minority is very large, and the proportion of the population which is in part of Chinese descent is still greater. There is an influential and wealthy Chinese minority in Burma, Indonesia and South Viet-nam; in the Philippine Republic the Chinese have for centuries held the dominant position in the local economy. These are the principal communities of the 'Overseas Chinese', and they have for more than a century constituted a difficult problem for the varying regimes which have governed these countries. Estimated to number in all some twenty millions, the Overseas Chinese of South-East Asia have acquired in every one of these countries a control of retail trade, commerce and industry which renders them powerful far beyond their mere numbers.

In some cases ancient settlements, which were founded as

long ago as the sixteenth and seventeenth centuries, in others more recent migrations which were evoked in response to the development of these regions under European colonial government, the Overseas Chinese share common characteristics; they all come from South China, the province of Fukien, the Canton region, and the island of Hainan, and they retain, pertinaciously, their culture, their language, and their sense of national solidarity with the home land.

These characteristics are often used to reproach them as bad settlers; but it must be thought strange to these Overseas Chinese that those who do so are themselves loud in their praise of a display of exactly similar characteristics when the settlers concerned are of British or Anglo-Saxon stock. The Australians, New Zealanders, Canadians and others are famed for their conformity to British customs, culture and forms of government. They still call the United Kingdom 'home'. Proud of their national standing and independence, they are also proud of their origin and attached to their ancestral country. The Overseas Chinese are the same.

In quite a number of other respects the Chinese settlers of South-East Asia resemble the Anglo-Saxon settlers of the Pacific. In both cases the original settlements were made by men for whom the home community had little regard. If the Chinese could not actually export their convicts to the 'South Seas' (*Nan Yang*, the Chinese term for these regions has this meaning) the settlers were none the less men who left China for their own and China's good. They were not too welcome if they tried to return. They were, in fact, under the Manchus regarded as little better than fugitives from justice. Since they came from the disaffected south many of them, like the Irish in Australia, were hostile to the home government, and had borne arms against it. They were also for the most part poor, simple and uneducated people, who left an overcrowded countryside to work in more spacious lands, which their toil and industry developed and gave them the great wealth they now possess. These are the pioneer virtues which Australians admire and claim.

The countries to which the Chinese went were often as wild and unknown as those to which the Anglo-Saxons migrated. Borneo and the jungles of Malaya were in the early nineteenth century no more civilized and secure than New Zealand at the same period. Elsewhere, as in Java, Thailand and Sumatra, the Chinese found native kingdoms in control of the country, but peoples inept at commerce and backward in industry. The Europeans, entering similar or the same countries within a few years of the Chinese, equally profited from the opportunities which the indolence of the inhabitants afforded.

But there was one, fundamental and vital difference between the situation of the Chinese and the European settlers. The Western peoples either proclaimed their own sovereignty over savage lands whose native inhabitants were too backward to contest the claim, or overthrew the native kingdoms and established their own colonial power by force of arms. In either case the Western settler found himself under his own home government or its appointed officers. The Chinese established no political power in the lands they settled, accepting either the rule of the native kings, or that of the European colonial powers.

If it is therefore argued in the West that when European settlers established their own government in an alien land, their pioneer virtues are praiseworthy and their title to the country sound; but when very similar Chinese settlers did not do these things, but took what political system they found and worked peacefully under its authority, then the same virtues and the same industry are not praiseworthy but anti-social—if this argument is proffered, it amounts to an invitation to the Chinese of today to correct the mistake and repair the omission of their forefathers. The mistake and the omission were made by the Chinese government of that age, the Manchu Empire, which was not interested in its roving subjects beyond the seas. The governments which have succeeded it in China have each in their various ways attempted to correct the error.

The Overseas Chinese were among the first to become roused to a conscious, active patriotism in the modern manner, as opposed to a subconscious innate acceptance of the fact that Chinese were 'civilized' and others 'barbarians'. In the last days of the Manchu Empire the force of the republican revolutionary movement, and most of the money which supported it, came from the Overseas Chinese. Sun Yat-sen himself, a migrant who spent his youth in Honolulu and was educated in Hong Kong, typified this aspect of the revolution. It was no doubt the sharpened sense of nationality provoked by residence in a different country, among alien peoples and under a foreign government, which first developed among the Overseas Chinese the patriotism and revolutionary enthusiasm which for a long period distinguished them from their relatively apathetic and indifferent kinsmen at home.

The triumph of the Republic, and later of the Nationalist regime, brought them some reward. They were now treated as valued and honoured citizens, not as dubious outcasts and evaders of justice. A Ministry of Overseas Chinese was established, the Chinese Consulates abroad were instructed to care for and support the Chinese community, and also to keep its allegiance to China active, and its contributions to the Party war chest up to the mark. These activities soon aroused the distrust and then the open disapproval of the colonial and native governments under whose authority the Chinese lived. In the British Colony of the Straits Settlements and in the British protectorates of the Malay States, the Kuomintang, or Nationalist Party of China, then the government party and supreme political authority in China, was proclaimed a prohibited organization.

After the revolution of 1932 in Siam, by which the absolute monarchy was converted into a constitutional kingdom where power was held by the military oligarchs responsible for the change, an anti-Chinese policy was progressively applied. Siam refused to enter into diplomatic relations with Nationalist China. Only after having taken the Japanese side in the war, but escaping the consequences of defeat by a timely change, did the government of Siam accept a Chinese diplomatic mission. Pressures of various kinds were none the less still applied to the Chinese community, mainly for the purpose of forcing them out of certain industries and occupations. The result of these policies has been to make the Chinese take Thai partners, who draw an income, give the concern a Thai name, but leave the conduct of business as before in the hands of the Chinese.

In Malaya and Thailand the very large proportions of the Chinese minorities give real reason for anxiety to the native peoples, who are already dependent on the Chinese for the conduct of business commerce and industry, and may well fear that the day will come when they will be outnumbered as well as outclassed in their own country. In Burma, Indonesia and the Philippines the problem is not the same. Here the Chinese, although prominent in commerce, are a small minority of the total population, and almost exclusively an urban community. Their situation has a strong resemblance to that of the Jews on the continent of Europe before the Second World War. They also experience the same ill will, though usually without the religious background which had originally embittered the relations of Jews and Gentiles.

From the point of view of the Chinese themselves the Overseas Communities can thus be divided into two categories. Malaya and, above all, Singapore, where the Chinese are almost an equal or actually a predominant proportion of the whole population, constitute what an American scholar* has felicitously named the 'Third China'. In Burma, Indonesia, the Philippines and South Viet-nam, the Chinese are a powerful commercial minority, but are not and never likely to be a majority of the population. Intermediate between these two groups stand the Chinese in Thailand who are a very large minority, have permeated the Thai race to a marked degree but are still treated and regarded as an alien people.

Now that all these countries are either independent or fully self-governing members of the British Commonwealth the problem of the Chinese communities has taken on a new urgency. This would have occurred whatever government

* Professor Paul Linebarger, of Johns Hopkins University, Baltimore.

ruled in China, yet it must be recognized that for the nations of South-East Asia, whether members of SEATO, supporters of the Five Principles, or uncommitted to either camp, the advent of the People's Republic has given the problem a new twist and enhanced importance. It is now not only the aspirations of the Overseas Chinese themselves which must be taken into account, but also the policy of a new, powerful China which is, or soon will be, able to back such policy with massive military strength.

The Nationalist regime in China had incurred considerable unpopularity with the colonial and independent South-East Asian governments by its open and sustained policy of encouraging the Overseas Chinese to think of themselves primarily as Chinese, retain Chinese nationality, and give financial and other support to the Nationalist Party in China. But though unpopular, the Nationalist government was also weak, ineffective and remote. It could not in practice influence the policy of the South-East Asian governments in favour of the Overseas Chinese. Thailand continued to pursue her restrictive policy; Malaya and Singapore prohibited further immigration. Indonesia did the same. In the Philippines restrictive laws, immigration bars and other practices inimical to the Chinese were freely adopted. Burma, which alone of these countries has a common frontier with China, was more careful.

The fall of the Nationalists was not in itself unwelcome to these governments; but the triumph of Communism in China, and the rapid progress towards modernization, economic power and above all the political prestige of the New China was a still more unwelcome and unexpected development. It became obvious that whatever their standpoint on the colonial issue, or the Cold War, these countries might come together in common fear of the People's Republic and the Overseas Chinese who might become its instruments. Thailand and the Philippines, the most active in anti-Chinese legislation, are stimulated in their enthusiasm for SEATO and anti-Communism as much by concern for the power of their Chinese minorities and the support which these may seek from China as by any ideological dislike of Communism as such. In Malaya and Singapore, apart from the long-standing Communist insurrection, largely, though not exclusively recruited from the Chinese community, there has been a strong tide of sympathy and admiration for the New China among the Chinese youth in both countries.

At Bandung Chou En-lai announced a new policy clearly designed to allay these fears and disrupt any potential coalition of anti-Chinese South-East Asian states. In the middle of the conference it was announced that China and Indonesia had negotiated a Treaty on Dual Nationality, which represented a reversal of the policy hitherto followed by the former Nationalist government of China. By the terms of this Treaty all Chinese resident in Indonesia were given a year to choose whether they wished to retain Chinese citizenship or to become naturalized Indonesians. If they chose to remain Chinese, they would be subject to any immigration or residential restriction laws which Indonesia might adopt; they would also be free to return to China, where work and employment were promised to all. If they chose to become Indonesian citizens they must renounce their connections with China, and endeavour to fulfil their duties as citizens of their new country, and to assimilate with the inhabitants. China, for her part, would take no further interest in these new Indonesians.

Speaking on this subject in Bandung Chou En-lai declared that China had room for all her citizens at home, would welcome the return of technically and professionally trained men and women, and had no desire to maintain colonies of Chinese citizens abroad in the manner of the Nationalist regime. He also offered to negotiate similar treaties with every other state in which there was a Chinese minority, provided that such states entered into diplomatic relations with the People's Republic. This offer has not been taken up by any other nation, and the Indonesian government itself, partly on account of internal political reasons, has not yet ratified the Treaty on Dual Nationality; but the new Chinese policy has none the less produced significant effects.

It is not now possible to use the former Nationalist policy in respect of the Overseas Chinese as a weapon of propaganda against the Peking regime. Peking can disclaim, with proofs, that this is in fact her policy. The blame, if blame there is for the problem of the Chinese minorities, must now be borne, so runs the argument, by those governments which wilfully refuse to recognize and negotiate with the real government of China. These governments in turn protest that by means of local Communist Parties China can and does pursue a policy even more dangerous than the nationalism of the Kuomintang. But this can be more easily alleged than proved; Communist parties are not exclusively manned by Chinese, in Indonesia and in the Philippines they are on the contrary overwhelmingly recruited from the native inhabitants.

The question of what is the true aim of the People's Republic in respect of the 'Third China' or of the smaller overseas communities remains obscured by clouds of propaganda, emanating from both sides. China has recognized the newly independent Federation of Malaya, but has not yet received a reciprocal recognition from Kuala Lumpur. In Singapore the steady progress of the People's Action Party, which is often seen as a 'fellow travelling', or even as a concealed Communist Party, portends developments in that overwhelmingly Chinese inhabited city which would make it a Chinese dependency in all but name. It has already been shown that the Second China in Formosa is an unstable organism, at variance with a strong and enduring Chinese tradition; there seems no real reason to expect that a Third China in Malaya and Singapore will prove more resistant to the ancestral pull of the great homeland. The New China does not need the open nationalist policy of the weak Kuomintang; it leans upon South-East Asia with the growing weight of its achievement and its power; already under this stress the local regimes creak and give.

Observers who have watched the trend of opinion in Singapore can find very little determination to resist the influence of China among the people of that city. There are many wealthy Chinese families who would, it must appear, suffer personally and in their fortunes if the government of their country became dominated by Communists and followed the internal policies of China. Yet even among such families it is difficult to discover any positive standpoint in opposition to the New China.

The Chinese gift for compromise, the age-old tendency to accept the government and then make the best of it, the sense of inevitability, and the tradition of a cyclic movement in human affairs, prosperity followed by adversity, then renewed fortune, all these characteristics which the long history of the Chinese people has woven into their culture, work in favour of the passive acceptance of change. The younger generation is deeply impressed by the prestige of the People's Republic, idealism is enlisted in the sweep and surge of the great Chinese revival; older men may wonder and doubt, but if their sons and daughters are already converted, why struggle against the tide?

Although the Chinese of Malaya and Singapore have not had the disillusioning experiences which their kin in China encountered in the last years of the Nationalist regime, the state of public opinion is reminiscent of that which then prevailed in China. Many will regret that these things are coming to pass, few will attempt to withstand them and strive for an alternative. One component in this attitude is, no doubt, the growing feeling that now that the British, who held the ring, have gone, the Chinese must stand up for themselves in an internal struggle for power against Malay nationalism. The example of Thailand, where they are under severe pressure and denied all political power is before them, even if the government of the Federation gives no sign of wishing to follow such policies. Yet how is it possible to forget that China, the new great China, is close at hand, would, at her price, be willing to help, at least to mediate? Accustomed to living under the shelter of the British power the Malayan Chinese are prone to seek a new protector, and for that role China is the obvious candidate.

If the Second China, Formosa, really offered an alternative allegiance, as American opinion would fain believe, it might be expected that there would be found among the Overseas Chinese some overt signs of enthusiasm for that regime, some

269

move to associate the new governments in Singapore and Kuala Lumpur with Taipei. Few such evidences exist. There is, on the contrary, even in the most unlikely quarters, an immediate recognition of the fact—accepted as beyond dispute— that American support, American financial backing, or open reliance upon American aid is political suicide in Singapore. It is far from apparent that the converse is true—that leaning to the side of Communist China does any one any harm.

Thus, as Chou En-lai remarked to a recent Western visitor, 'China exists, and China can wait.'* Wait to regain, with very little further effort, by 'peaceful co-existence' that rightful place in Asia which the Manchu Empire forfeited by weakness, obscurantism and lack of flexibility. If that were all that China existed for and expected, the rest of the world would soon accommodate itself to an inconvenient but inevitable development. There remains the doubt whether this resurgence in Asia is in fact all that the new China seeks to obtain, whether it is not rather a first step, the establishment of a position of local supremacy which will facilitate other, more ambitious moves.

It is already plain that China has played in the circle of Communist powers a part of increasing, if obscure significance. It is not only in Asia that Chou En-lai has paid his calls, but in Warsaw, Prague and Budapest, as well as Moscow. It has been suggested that the policy of Peking has become a factor of importance in the affairs of Poland. If this is indeed the truth it is the first time for seven centuries, since the age of Ghengiz Khan (not himself a Chinese), that the ruler of the Middle Kingdom has exercised direct influence upon the politics of Europe.

Southward of China, beyond the sea, but yet linked to Asia by the long chain of the Indonesian archipelago, lies Australia, haunted by a traditional fear of 'Asian hordes' ready to swarm into that empty land. The fear is probably largely imaginary and in the popular form unreal. Most of Australia is a land singularly ill-adapted to the farming techniques of the Asian peasant. In South-East Asia the Chinese migrant, though a

* Mr James Bertram, *Return to China*, p. 89.

hardy pioneer, much prefers to open a shop, trade with the local inhabitants, lend them money, start an industry, than work the soil in direct competition with an established land-owning population. But in a new form the old anxiety is more justified. A powerful, industrialized China, exporting consumer goods at low cost to South-East Asia and beyond might be a good customer for Australian raw materials and primary produce, but would in a relatively short time dominate the economy of the Far East.

Economic power cannot long be separated from political influence; it would be increasingly difficult for Australia to pursue policies in Asia, such as SEATO, which China deems to be inimical to herself. The real prospect before Australia is not the invasion of cheap Asian labour which has been the traditional fear, but a pressure to conform in matters of trade and foreign policy with the desires of China rather than to provoke the hostility of a most powerful neighbour. Only a few years ago such a situation would have seemed fanciful and wildly improbable; it was Japan, the naval power, perhaps once more militant, that roused Australian alarm. There was as yet no realization that China was a possible competitor for the dominance of East Asia left vacant by the fall of the Japanese Empire, nor is it yet certain that the full significance of China's revival has been measured and a policy designed to meet the new age. What is certain is that the pace of Chinese development and reorganization leaves little scope for procrastination.

China resurges: at home a vast transformation of the social system, the economy and the morale of this enormous nation has unleashed energies and enthusiasms which the Communist Party seeks to guide towards the realization of its own programme, but which are themselves so dynamic that their ultimate consequences cannot yet be foreseen. Today the Party and the nation are led by men of outstanding and unusual ability who are themselves fully aware both of what they have pulled down and what they seek to build in its place; but they must be succeeded by men who never knew the old order and have lived and grown to manhood in the swiftly changing turbulent revolutionary process. They cannot share the experiences even if they have the ability of the men of the first great revolutionary generation; they will be the men of faith, the children of persuasion, and their outlook, like their background, will be profoundly different from that of the founders of the People's Republic.

Abroad China also demands her ancient place as the leader of eastern Asia, the font of Far Eastern civilization. But the new civilization which she fosters is a Chinese interpretation of Marxism, the latest and the most far-reaching attempt to achieve that synthesis of the science of the West, which means modernization, and the worldly wisdom of the East which taught that 'as the wind blows, so the grass bends'; the ancient authoritarian Asia which never accepted the idea that individual liberty should take precedence over the welfare of the group.

INDEX

273